Kitchen Capitalism

SUNY series in Urban Public Policy
C. Theodore Koebel and Diane L. Zahm, editors

Kitchen Capitalism

Microenterprise in Low-Income Households

Margaret Sherrard Sherraden,
Cynthia K. Sanders,
and
Michael Sherraden

STATE UNIVERSITY OF NEW YORK PRESS

Published by
State University of New York Press, Albany

For information, contact State University of New York Press, Albany, NY
www.sunypress.edu

Production by Diane Ganeles
Marketing by Michael Campochiaro

Library of Congress Cataloguing-in-Publication Data

Sherraden, Margaret S.
    Kitchen capitalism : microenterprise in low-income households / Margaret Sherrard
    Sherraden, Cynthia K. Sanders, and Michael Sherraden.
        p. cm. — (SUNY series in urban public policy)
    Includes bibliographical references and index.
    ISBN 978-0-7914-6171-6 (alk. paper)
    ISBN 978-0-7914-6172-3 (pbk.: alk. paper)
    1. Self-employed—United States.   2. Poor—Employment—United States.
3. Entrepreneurship—United States.   4. Small business—United States.   I. Sanders,
Cynthia K., 1964–   II. Sherraden, Michael W. (Michael Wayne), 1948–   III. Title.
IV. SUNY series on urban public policy.

HD8037.U5S47 2004
338.6'42'0973—dc22
                                                                                    2003065730

10   9   8   7   6   5   4   3   2   1

To our parents Connie, Tom, Madeline, and Bob,
and to our children, Catherine and Sam.

–Margaret Sherrard Sherraden and Michael Sherraden

To my mother, Fae Sanders. Thanks to Ann Agnew and my dear
friend, Ed Scanlon. Ed has always had a supportive ear and
has never failed to offer a humorous perspective on the trials,
tribulations, and triumphs of my work.

–Cynthia K. Sanders

I really want to be a hair doctor–that's my nickname in the field. I would fix people's hair in my kitchen.

–Lessie, hairstylist

Contents

Tables

Acknowledgments

We thank many people for their help and encouragement as we conducted this study. Our deepest appreciation goes to the microentrepreneurs we interviewed for this study. They gave us their time and answered our questions with insight and patience and did their best to help us understand what it was like to be a microentrepreneur and we hope we have depicted their experiences accurately.

Without leadership from the Charles Stewart Mott and Ford foundations, we would have little understanding of microenterprise in the United States. We thank them for support for this research through the Aspen Institute's Self-Employment Learning Program (SELP) and through the Center for Social Development at Washington University, St. Louis.

When Amy Kays Blair and Peggy Clark of SELP came to us with the idea for this research, we were excited about the opportunity to speak at length with the microentrepreneurs in the SELP study. After several years of surveying the entrepreneurs, Blair, Clark, and others working with SELP had concluded that it would be helpful to interview business owners in a more candid and informal manner. Working closely with SELP, we designed an interview guide that could begin to reveal the entrepreneurs' motivations and experiences in business ownership. SELP staff also provided access to prior waves of surveys. We are grateful for Blair and Clark's assistance, as well as that of their SELP colleagues, including Lily Zandniapour and Enrique Soto.

Directors of the Microenterprise Development Programs who participated in SELP provided orientation to their programs and to service delivery issues. We are especially grateful to the late Penny Penrose of the Good Faith Fund, for her insightful comments and suggestions.

Inspiration for this study came from several sources. Our work with the Community Economic Development (CED) Committee of the Missouri Association for Social Welfare (MASW) suggested that microenterprise was a strategy that deserved further attention. MASW and CED committee colleagues, including Betsy Slosar, Peter De Simone, Vanessa Finley, and Dianna Moore, encouraged us to understand the motivations and experiences of microentre-preneurs. Insight also came from reading the works of Ivan Light, Steve Balkin, Salome Raheim, Catherine Alter, Mark Schreiner, Lisa Servon, Timothy Bates, and others who are responsible for launching the study of microenterprise in the United States.

To aid in interview design, we conducted two focus groups with microen-trepreneurs in St. Louis (who were not part of SELP). Our appreciation goes to LaDoris Payne, director of the Imani Center and to Richard Neitzel, formerly of Mustard Seed Partnerships, for helping us contact the entrepreneurs. We ex-tend our appreciation to these St. Louis microentrepreneurs for describing some of the ins and outs of operating a small business.

We owe a debt of gratitude to the staff, students, and faculty at the Center for Social Development (CSD) at Washington University in St. Louis. Karen Edwards coordinated and monitored data collection. Prof. Letha Chadiha pro-vided guidance to the project and conducted interviewer training. Freda Bady, Carla Gay, Leslie Enright, Rosio Gonzalez, Kathryn Lane, Aida Rodriguez Parna, and Will Rainford, graduate students at the George Warren Brown School of Social Work at Washington University were skilled and dedicated in-terviewers. Suzanne Callahan, a SELP colleague, also conducted interviews and offered insightful comments about each participant. Fred Ssewamala pa-tiently extracted findings from prior SELP waves of surveys and also con-tributed to the chapter on motivations for self-employment. Jamie Curley, Carla Gay, and Leslie Enright helped to transcribe, create respondent profiles, and code the interviews. Mark Schreiner, Senior Scholar at CSD, provided numer-ous suggestions. Our thanks to Diane Ganeles, our editor at SUNY Press, for her guidance and careful editing. Although this was truly a team effort and is the result of many people's work, we take full responsibility for shortcomings and errors.

M.S.S.
C.K.S.
M.S.

CHAPTER 1

Little Businesses, Large Hopes

*I wouldn't work for someone else if they offered me $100,000, an-
other house and a car. No way, no how. I like being self-employed.
I like the meaning of it, the whole connotation. Being independent. Not having someone else tell me what do to do. . . . I love
having my own business, and I know that one day . . . all the
dreams that I had for it are gonna manifest, sooner than later.*

–Lessie, hairstylist

*Working for someone else, you don't have to worry as much.
[You] still have to worry about the bills, but you don't have to
worry as much because you know you are going to have a check
to spend. Working for yourself, you have to worry about the bills
and whether you are going to have any income.*

–Diane, homemade crafts

Lessie was trained as a beautician and had been working in other people's
hair salons for many years. When she finally opened her own business, she had
trouble managing it on a day-to-day basis. But she did make some profits,
which she was able to reinvest in the business. Despite two family crises that set
back her business, she believed that it had a promising future. Highly committed, she drew enormous satisfaction from doing people's hair and making them
feel good about themselves.

Diane, a single mother with one child, was also excited about opening her
crafts business. Unhappy with her job, she looked forward to working full-time
designing and creating the small figurines that had earned praise among friends
and acquaintances. Unfortunately, her plan, to sell at craft fairs and later
through magazines and catalogs, never materialized. She found the production
work, marketing, and business accounting more draining than she imagined.

1

Even with support and loans from the microenterprise development program, she lost her motivation to continue, closed her business, and took a low-wage job. Even though her job paid only a little over $12,000 a year, she felt more secure financially and emotionally than she had in business.

This book is about Lessie and Diane and other low-income microentrepreneurs who took part in a new approach to fighting poverty. Microenterprise development programs (MDPs) around the United States assisted these microentrepreneurs in building businesses that hopefully over time would generate enough income to support them and their families. Microenterprise is a sharp departure from traditional approaches to poverty alleviation. Since President Roosevelt's New Deal, the principal approach to supporting the poor has been through providing income subsidies to help families make ends meet, month-to-month, through a variety of support, such as monthly income, food and housing subsidies, health coverage, and jobs programs. A turn to microenterprise represents a major change toward "capitalism for the poor" (Peirce & Steinbach, 1987; Stoesz & Saunders, 1999). Does it work?

Estimates suggest that there are upward of two million very small businesses, known as microenterprises, in the United States (FIELD, 2000). Hundreds of microenterprise development programs spend between $70 and $100 million a year to provide loans, technical assistance, and other support services to new and expanding microenterprises (AEO 2002b; Walker & Blair, 2002). Still, relatively little is known about how well microenterprise works, for whom, and under what circumstances.

Only recently has policy promoted microenterprise as a way to build the economic foundations of poor families in the United States. Policy has traditionally focused on entrepreneurs with more resources, leaving low-income microentrepreneurs to cope on their own (Balkin, 1989). Moreover, historically, people of color, especially African-Americans, have faced discrimination and other enduring barriers in developing businesses (Butler 1991; Oliver & Shapiro, 2001). Several changes in the 1980s and 1990s encouraged community development analysts and practitioners to wonder whether microenterprise might be an effective method to combat poverty in the United States. Successful microenterprise efforts abroad and rapid growth of new small U.S. firms in the 1980s and 1990s, further encouraged microenterprise development (Devine, 1994; Dennis, 1998; Manser & Picot, 1999). Would it be possible for public policy to generate and support growth of successful businesses among the poor?

Advocates proposed that microenterprise could build on the strengths of the poor while bringing them into the economic mainstream. This book analyzes the results of these efforts through the eyes and experiences of low-income microentrepreneurs who participated in one of several microenterprise programs across the United States. With data from in-depth interviews and with data from surveys conducted over a five-year period, this book addresses the potential of microenterprise as an anti-poverty strategy. Who are they and what motivates them to open businesses? Where do they get help? How do their businesses fare? How do they evaluate their experiences as microenterprise owners? What role do the microenterprise development programs play in helping them? What are the implications for the expansion of microenterprise as anti-poverty policy?

Development of the Microenterprise Strategy

Community development advocates, intrigued by the idea of promoting microenterprise as an anti-poverty strategy, began to look overseas at apparently successful microenterprise programs like the Grameen Bank in Bangladesh, Bank Rakyat Indonesia, and BancoSol in Latin America that assisted the very poor in opening microbusinesses (Balkin, 1992).[1] Arguing that poor people in the United States are faced by many of the same problems as the poor in developing nations, they borrowed principles and design ideas from these international programs (McKee, et al., 1993). This model resonated among Americans. Building on the ingenuity and resilience of the poor, and perhaps reminiscent of "rags to riches" legends that are part of the fabric of the American Dream, microenterprise captured the imaginations of growing numbers of policymakers, practitioners, and potential microentrepreneurs.

Microenterprise also emerged at a time when U.S. policymakers were searching for alternatives to welfare and other poverty programs. A model of self-reliance, local government control, and private sector responsibility gained momentum and throughout the 1980s, policymakers chipped away at the welfare state, citing high costs and "dependency."

In the face of budget cuts, policy analysts, social service beneficiaries, and social welfare practitioners defended income supports and social services, but they also recognized that the rules of some social welfare programs actually prevented or discouraged full and equal participation in the economic mainstream (Friedman, 1988). For example, public assistance programs for the poor reduced assistance based on take-home pay, thus creating disincentives to work.

For some, the challenge in this new era was to make sure that less-politically powerful groups could capture a fair share of resources and access to economic rewards in the new global economy. The "New Democrat" President, Bill Clinton, "ended welfare as we know it," giving further momentum to welfare-to-work initiatives that had begun in 1988 with passage of the Family Support Act. But the focus on "self-sufficiency" made it imperative to create more progressive models for assisting the poor. Some policy analysts suggested that microenterprise might be a way to lend a hand to the poor in this new era, assisting them in entering the economic mainstream and increasing the numbers of jobs in low-income communities (Friedman, 1988; Boshara, et al., 1997).

On the scholarly front, asset theory and social capital theory contributed to the debate about microenterprise. Asset theory proposes that accumulation of assets in low-income and low-wealth households would yield an array of positive social and economic effects, especially over the long term (Sherraden, 1991). Underlying this approach is the idea that asset accumulation builds opportunities and changes perceptions about the future in ways that income does not. As Michael Sherraden writes, assets are "hope in concrete form" (1991, 156). Sherraden proposes that asset accumulation, in addition to income support, should be a cornerstone to anti-poverty and community development efforts. One of the ways to increase asset ownership among the poor is through business development (Friedman, et al., 1995; Boshara, et al., 1997).

Until recently, however, social policy excluded the poor from systems of asset accumulation, while subsidizing middle and upper classes (Sherraden, 1991; Howard, 1997; Seidman, 2001). A middle-class person, for example, can save for retirement through an employment-based 401(k) plan or can buy a home with a generous subsidy from government in the form of a mortgage-interest tax deduction. In contrast, the welfare poor cannot save without risking the loss of welfare benefits, including cash, health care, or housing assistance. Therefore, welfare policy guarantees a month-to-month financial existence.[2] Moreover, the working poor rarely have jobs that include asset accumulation features, such as retirement savings plans (Orszag, 2001).

For minorities, especially African Americans, asset accumulation has been systematically restricted (Oliver & Shapiro, 1995; Conley, 1999). Striking findings show that over two-thirds of Blacks own no net financial wealth, compared to less than one-third of Whites who own no net financial wealth (Oliver & Shapiro, 2001, 225). Furthermore, home ownership rates among Blacks are 20 percentage points less than among Whites (Oliver & Shapiro, 2001, 225). Lack of assets has been demonstrated to have an impact on African American entry into self-employment (Fairlie, 1999). Net worth in Hispanic households is also very low in comparison to White households (NCLR, 2001), although the effects on the Black community are the most persistent (Oliver & Shapiro, 2001, 227).

Accumulating wealth in businesses has been particularly challenging for African Americans for historical reasons (Butler, 1991). Systematic and enduring discrimination—from slavery to lynchings of black business owners, to the bombing of Tulsa, Oklahoma's Greenwood business community, to lack of access to business loans—has resulted in lower rates of business ownership among African Americans. Constrained by racism to operate only within the African American community, while other businesses could operate virtually anywhere, Black businesses have suffered (Bates, 1989; Butler, 1991).[3]

In addition to recognition of the importance of asset accumulation and the structural barriers to business ownership among the poor, the other theoretical development that contributed to microenterprise was social capital theory (Putnam, 1993). As a resource that has "economic and noneconomic" value, Coleman and others make the case that social capital, like financial and human capital, "is productive, making possible the achievement of certain ends that in its absence would not be possible" (S98). In other words, business success cannot be viewed only as a result of the presence of financial capital and human capital, but has to take into account the structure of social relations that facilitate productivity. Social capital theory provides a theoretical rationale for linking social and economic development that lead to different ways of thinking about poverty, including the microenterprise approach.

For development to occur, therefore, analysts emphasized the importance of integrating economic and social approaches and increasing individual, family, and community capacity and capabilities (Midgley, 1995; Sherraden & Ninacs, 1998; Sen, 1999; Rubin & Sherraden, forthcoming). Potential strategies include home ownership, microenterprise and business incubators, savings and investment opportunities, financial education and services, training and technical assistance, along with support services. This book addresses only one of these strategies—microenterprise.

Promoting microenterprise among the poor appeals to groups across the political spectrum (Taub, 1998). Consistent with values of self-reliance and personal responsibility, it provides economic opportunity for poor families and encourages development "from below." Microenterprise is attractive because it is an "American solution" that balances individualism and community (Peirce & Steinbach, 1987; Stoesz & Saunders, 1999). Viewing the poor as fundamentally resourceful and motivated (Solomon, 1992), advocates suggest that, with adequate access to resources and training, a significant number of poor people should be able to be successful in business (Balkin, 1992). Moreover, because a large share of new jobs are in full- and part-time small businesses (SBA, 1999), microenterprise might be able to create new jobs in poor communities. Successful microentrepreneurs, the thinking goes, might not only move themselves and their families out of poverty, but also eventually build a platform for community-building (Servon, 1998). Finally, some also argue that microenterprise helps poor families build financial assets, human capital, and social capital (Clark & Kays, et al., 1999).

Microenterprise is also viewed as a viable economic strategy for women. Microenterprise could be a viable alternative to traditional employment (Raheim & Alter, 1998) for women who experience disadvantage in the labor market, such as unequal pay, occupational segregation, and limited future opportunity (Abramovitz, 1996; Bernstein & Hartmann, 1999). Assistance and support from an MDP might also help overcome disadvantages experienced by women in self-employment. Furthermore, self-employment could offer a flexible work option that could meet more of women's daily needs and accommodate multiple family and community roles (Stoner, Hartman, & Aurora, 1990; Novogratz, 1992).

During the 1990s, microenterprise took on characteristics of a social movement (Bhatt, 2001). First Lady Hillary Rodham Clinton, an unabashed supporter of microenterprise, initiated annual White House awards for the best microenterprise development programs in the United States and authored the foreword to the *1996 Directory of U.S. Microenterprise Programs* published by the Aspen Institute. She wrote,

> Over the past decade, President Clinton and I have watched with pleasure as the microenterprise movement has grown and developed in this country. At home in Arkansas, and in our travels around our nation and the world, we have heard the dramatic and inspiring stories of low-income women and men who have used small amounts of credit and business training to build businesses that provide needed income and assets for their families. We have tried, through our efforts to publicize the effects of microenterprise development, to recognize the leading programs in the nation, and to call for improved federal support of microenterprise programs, to support the growth of this important movement. (Severens & Kays, 1997, ix)

A "Microcredit Summit" promoted microenterprise in a global initiative designed to reach one hundred million of the world's poorest families by the year 2005 (Microcredit Summit Secretariat, 2001). Since the 1980s, influential foundations, such as the Ford and Charles Stewart Mott foundations, actively promoted microenterprise development. Federal budget increases for microenterprise demonstrated a growing public policy commitment to microenterprise (Else with Gallagher, 2000).

Some, however, raise a note of caution about the promise of microenterprise. Suggesting that targeting the poor for microenterprise assists political movements in shredding social safety nets and makes the poor responsible for generating their own resources (Balkin, 1989), they worry that a "neoconservative" model of self-reliance and self-sufficiency will replace New Deal and War on Poverty programs. Other skeptics argue that providing business loans to the poor cannot reduce poverty substantially. In fact, easier access to credit could contribute to already large debt among people with low incomes. Low self-esteem, lack of skills and education, social isolation, and discrimination and racism may contribute to problems of the poor who choose or are forced to turn to self-employment (Neff, 1996). Others have suggested that seldom does microenterprise alone support a household (Spalter-Roth, et al., 1994), or, worse, microbusinesses support low-paying jobs that further ensnare individuals in poverty (Bates & Servon, 1996; Bates, 1997; Ehlers & Main, 1998), in part because of lack of benefits (Devine, 1994).

Public enthusiasm for microenterprise may exceed its potential to do good, according to others (Buntin, 1997; Taub, 1998). Based on a case study of one of the nation's oldest microenterprise programs, Richard Taub (1998) suggests that programs modeled after the Grameen Bank will not alleviate poverty in the United States. The requirements for capital and skills are much greater in this country than in less developed countries and may be beyond the capacity of MDPs (Schreiner & Morduch, 2002). Furthermore, Taub argues that microlending will not help those who rely heavily on social safety nets and is more likely to help those who are already in a position to take some risks—such as households with at least one secure income. Mark Schreiner (1999a) concludes that microenterprise programs may work well for a few, but are unlikely to help a large number of people in the United States, perhaps especially those transitioning off welfare.

Microenterprise Policies and Programs

Microenterprises are sole proprietorships, partnerships, or family businesses with fewer than five employees (Severens & Kays, 1997; see Appendix A). They are typically launched as part-time, self-financed operations, although some receive small loans, ranging from several hundred to a few thousand dollars, for start-up or expansion. Sometimes loans are secured from banks; however, entrepreneurs often turn to microenterprise development programs because their businesses are too small and/or lack collateral for traditional loans. Microenterprises typically start out in homes, garages, or open air or street markets.

Because microenterprises are often opened by people with little or no business experience, low levels of resources, and other barriers, "the structure of a microenterprise program must account for the attendant problems facing its borrowers" (Solomon 1992, 216). For this reason, many microenterprise development programs combine *economic development components* (pre-loan education and training, business training, financial education, and loan pools and guarantees) with *social development components* (peer support, mentoring, personal effectiveness training, and counseling). The full range of services is difficult for one agency to deliver; therefore, MDPs typically partner with a variety of public and private organizations.

Microenterprise development programs commonly target people with low-incomes but they also serve people with more economic resources (Langer, et al., 1999). Those targeting low-income entrepreneurs, in particular, have been influenced by policy and program innovations in other countries.

Policy Development in Microenterprise

In the 1960s, the International Labor Organization (ILO) suggested that the informal sector, which employed half or more of the population of poor countries, should be examined for its potential to provide better jobs for the poor. Access to credit for microenterprise was viewed as a way to mobilize indigenous resources and to create development from below, especially in areas where there were not enough jobs to support large sectors of the population. Drawing inspiration from Mahatma Gandhi's movement for self-sufficiency through cottage industry, Mohamed Yunus, economics professor and founder of the Grameen Bank, maintains, "microcredit views each person as a potential entrepreneur and turns on the tiny economic engines of a rejected portion of society. Once a large number of these engines start working, the stage can be set for enormous socioeconomic change" (1999, 119).

In 1976, Yunus and his students initiated a groundbreaking project to provide credit to poor women. It was based on the philosophy that if poor people receive small amounts of credit, they could become self-employed by starting and/or enlarging small businesses.[4] The Grameen Bank, or "Village" Bank, is now among the world's largest rural credit institutions with 3.1 million mostly women borrowers in 43,681 villages served through more than 1,100 branches (Grameen Bank, 2004). Participating women repay their loans, increase their household income, develop assets, and are more likely to use family planning, in addition to other positive indicators (Balkin, 1989, 102–3; Hashemi, 1997; Grameen Bank, 2002). Microcredit programs have proliferated in the last twenty years, including the well-known ACCIÓN International and FINCA International (Ashe, 1985; Balkin, 1989).[5] Even organizations like U.S. Agency for International Development (U.S. AID), the World Bank, and the Inter-American Development Bank promote and study microenterprise.

While microenterprise was promoted in poor countries as "development from below," wealthier European nations began to examine microenterprise as a way to handle unprecedented high rates of unemployment in the 1970s. Viewed as a way to put people back to work, policymakers made it possible to use transfer payments to fund microenterprise. In France, Chômeurs Createurs (Unemployed Entrepreneurs) enabled any citizen who became eligible for unemployment compensation or welfare to collect the cash benefit in one lump sum to help start a business (Bendick & Egan, 1987). The one-year survival rate for the businesses was 84 percent. In 1982, Britain introduced the Enterprise Allowance Scheme (EAS) which also allowed individuals to claim unemployment compensation during the time of their business start-up. The program created jobs at a rate of 68 full- and part-time jobs for every one hundred businesses created (Balkin, 1989, 105; Parker, 1996). Start-up firms generally were small, drew on small amounts of start-up capital, and had low earnings. Marc Bendick and Mary Lou Egan (1987) conclude that the British and French experiences tended to generate small incomes and unstable employment, and the most disadvantaged entrepreneurs were least likely to succeed.

In the United States, as early as 1964, the Small Business Administration (SBA) had created a business development program called the "Equal Opportunity Loan Program" (EOL) as part of the War on Poverty (Balkin, 1989). Loans of up to $25,000 for fifteen years at low interest and with no required collateral were directed to the disadvantaged. Timothy Bates and William Bradford (1979) argue that high-loan default rates (50 percent of all loans and 70 percent of new business loans) resulted from investing in too many poor credit risks, including small retail operations in inner-city minority communities. Support for microenterprise, according to Balkin, "was quickly abandoned in favor of those who operated larger, more sophisticated businesses" (1989, 82). In the years that followed, small business development for the poor was attempted through a variety of programs in the Economic Development Administration, through Community Development Block Grants, and through a small program within the Comprehensive Employment and Training Act (CETA) (1989).

Meanwhile, borrowing from Western European examples, government officials proposed microenterprise as a possible solution to unemployment (Balkin, 1989; Meyerhoff, 1997). The States of Washington and Massachusetts were sites of the first two federally sponsored self-employment pilots, known as the Unemployment Insurance Self-Employment Demonstrations (U.S. Department of Labor, 1994, 1995). Results were mixed. Some researchers suggested that these programs were cost-effective reemployment programs (Benus, et al., 1995), while other researchers contended that overall impacts were small (Schreiner, 1999b). In 1991, the Economic Dislocation and Worker Adjustment Assistance Act (EDWAA) Job Creation Demonstration explored the effectiveness of self-employment programs in community development for dislocated workers (Drury, et al., 1994). In 1993, states began to offer self-employment assistance (SEA) to the unemployed (U.S. Department of Labor, 1994, ix; U.S. Department of Treasury, 2001). And by the mid-1990s, five states had passed enabling legislation permitting use of SEA funds for the unemployed (Benus, et al., 1995; U.S. Department of Labor, 1995), although actual use was limited (Vroman, 1997).

In the 1980s, as word of microenterprise successes in poor countries began to reach across the globe, demonstration microenterprise programs were initiated. Borrowing heavily from international examples, programs tended to emphasize anti-poverty objectives and were aimed especially at women of color. Most were funded by private foundations (Meyerhoff, 1997).

The first national microenterprise demonstration project implemented in 1986, the Self-Employment Investment Demonstration (SEID), was designed to help poor single women with children on welfare (Doolittle, et al., 1991; Raheim & Alter, 1995; Boshara, et al., 1997). Local SEID projects provided direct loans (or assistance in obtaining a loan), business training and technical assistance, and counseling. Welfare regulations were temporarily waived for participants, enabling them to retain benefits through the first year of business start-up.

By the late 1990s, funding for microenterprise came from several sources (Table 1.1). The Small Business Administration administered the largest programs, including The Microloan Program, which currently provides up to $35,000 loans to microentrepreneurs (U.S. Department of Treasury, 2001, footnote 64). The SBA also operated Women's Business Centers and an Online Women's Business Center that provided assistance with loan packaging, business training, marketing, government procurement, mentoring, and networking (Meyerhoff, 1997). The Program for Investment in Microentrepreneurs (PRIME) Act, passed in 1999, supported training, technical assistance, and capacity-building for low-income entrepreneurs (U.S. Department of Treasury, 2001). Although funding for Women's Business Centers were fully refunded in 2002, other SBA microenterprise programs suffered substantial cuts in the aftermath of September 11, and are threatened in the 2005 budget (AEO, 2004). The Department of Treasury also funds Community Development Finance Institutions (CFDI's) to expand and leverage the availability of credit in distressed communities (CDFI Fund, 2003).

Within the U.S. Department of Health and Human Services a few microenterprise programs provided support to the poor. One of the more promising, the Office of Refugee Resettlement (ORR) microenterprise program, provided over $3 million for business loans between 1992 and 2002, along with support for training and technical assistance, to over 800 microbusinesses with business survival rates of 89 percent (ORR, 2002). Between 1991 and 2001, ORR spent almost $20 million helping refugees start, expand or strengthen a business (Else, et al., 2003).

The U.S. Department of Housing and Urban Development (HUD) also funded a number of microenterprise initiatives. The Self-Employment Demonstrations for Public Housing Residents provided $2 million in Community Development Block Grant funds to support thirteen demonstrations in 1991 (Drury, et al., 1994). Additional funding from HUD for microenterprise development included the Comprehensive Grant Program (CGP) and the Comprehensive Improvement Assistance Program (CIAP), which were used by various housing authorities to support self-employment through lending and technical assistance among public housing residents (Raheim, et al., 1996). HUD Community Development Block Grants directly funded microenterprises in federal entitlement communities and through state grants (U.S. Department of Treasury, 2001).

Microenterprise opportunities for people with low incomes received a modest boost with passage of the 1996 Personal Responsibility and Work Opportunity Reconciliation Act (PRWORA). With this legislation, states were permitted to regard training for and operating a microenterprise as an allowable "work" activity under the new requirements. Some states responded by providing funding for microenterprise programs, permitting self-employment as an allowable training and work activity, providing more generous income disregards, exempting loans from income calculations, and providing child care,

Table 1.1
Funding for Microenterprise in the United States (1983–1999),
in millions of dollars[1]

	Period	Yearly Average	Total Dollars
PRIVATE FOUNDATIONS			
Ford Foundation	1983–1999	$ 1.7	$ 28.9
Charles Stewart Mott	1985–1999	0.8	12.1
FEDERAL GOVERNMENT			
Small Business Administration	1992–1999	26.2	209.2
U.S. Department of Health & Human Services			
Job Opportunities for Low Income Individuals	1990–1998	4.0	23.8
Demonstration Partnership Program	1987–1992	0.8	3.3
Office of Refugee Resettlement	1991–1996	1.2	5.9
U.S. Treasury			
Community Development Finance Institutions	1996–1999	6.5	25.8
U.S. Housing and Urban Development	1996–1998	8.1	20.1
U.S. Department of Agriculture	1997–1999	5.3	15.8
U.S. Department of Labor	1994–1997	2.6	5.1
TOTAL FUNDING		$57.0	$350.1

Source: Adapted from Else, J., with Gallagher, J. (2001). An overview of the microenterprise development field in the U.S. In Else, J., Doyle, K., Servon, L., & Messenger, J., *The Role of Microenterprise Development in the United States* (1–42). A Research Report. Arlington, VA: Association for Enterprise Opportunity, March, p. 13.

[1]Includes all funding (program operations, loan pool funds, grants, and loans to programs).

health care, and transportation (Plimpton & Greenberg, 2000). The opportunity to choose self-employment may be more illusory than real, however, as some states hesitated to include microenterprise as a work activity because of an emphasis on getting people into jobs quickly in order to reduce welfare caseloads (Greenberg, 1999). Furthermore, William Dennis argues that the new rules put up barriers to self-employment because it did not allow for *unsupervised* work activity "inherent in the process of forming a business" (1998, 267).

Most microenterprise programs are non-profits, according to John Else, who estimates that a total of $70 to $100 million a year is available for microenterprise (2001, 9). This is comprised of approximately two-thirds federal funds, with the rest from local and state governments and private foundations.

Microenterprise Development Programs in the United States

The *2002 Directory of U.S. Microenterprise Programs* lists 650 microenterprise programs in the United States, including 554 "practitioner" programs, or MDPs that provide loans, training, and technical assistance, and 119 support organizations, which provide funding, advocacy, networking, program planning, design assistance, training, research, and evaluation (Walker & Blair, 2002). Most programs target low-income individuals, women, and/or minorities (Walker & Blair, 2002). Other programs focus on other population groups, including refugees, immigrants, veterans, and people with disabilities (Else, 2000). In the most recent survey of microenterprise, a total of 31,268 businesses were assisted in 2000. Of these, half were start-ups and half were existing businesses (Walker & Blair, 2002).

Core MDP elements are outreach and recruitment, training, technical assistance, and microloans. But because of the complexities of operating a business in the United States programs have also added other components, such as saving, case management, technology services, insurance, tax preparation, legal and accounting services, business incubators, and market support (Mustafa, 1998; AEO, 2000; Walker & Blair, 2002). Currently, the majority of MDPs (63 percent) offer lending and training, 33 percent offer training and technical assistance only, and four percent offer lending only (Walker & Blair, 2002), although optimal levels are debated.

Among MDPs that offer loans, approximately 18 percent offer *peer group lending* (Walker & Blair, 2002). In peer group lending, an approach made famous by the Grameen Bank, all of the members of the group assume liability for loans. In other words, each member is responsible for payment of all members' loans and additional loans are not disbursed until payments are made (Balkin, 1992). Moreover, proponents of peer group lending argue that while providing access to needed capital, peer lending also builds social capital (Light & Pham, 1998). Group members play tangible and emotional support roles for each other. Many programs also use peer group meetings to teach business skills. When capital requirements increase, business owners are assumed to be eligible for conventional lending. Although peer group lending is credited with high loan repayment in poor countries (McGuire & Conroy, 1997), Richard Taub (1998) argues that this approach is not well-suited to the U.S. context. Group members, who may not know each other well, do not consistently monitor each others' loans (Hung, 2002), and may not have much reason to view the peer group as important (Schreiner, 2002).

In the 1990s, programs moved toward *individual lending*.[6] By the end of the decade, 92 percent of the programs offered individual lending (Walker & Blair, 2002), using subjective and objective factors such as history of employment and steady payment of rent and utilities to determine credit risk (Schreiner, 2003). Average loan size in individual lending programs tends to be larger than in peer group lending programs. The average size of individual loans in 1997, for example, was $10,631 (Langer, et al., 1999).

The challenges of operating a successful microenterprise in the United States have led some MDPs to emphasize *training and technical assistance*. Many programs offer a standard set of business classes in such areas as business planning, financial statements, cash flow, marketing, credit management, and personal goal setting. Some offer more individualized training, counseling, or mentoring programs. These are the most expensive types of services offered by microenterprise programs.[7]

Many programs target women entrepreneurs, building in certain features and specialized support. By providing training services that include empowerment principles, programs aim to reduce barriers to microentrepreneurship, increase the potential for success as business owners, and facilitate economic self-sufficiency (Johnson, 1998). While Tracy Ehlers and Karen Main (1998) argue that typical microenterprises provide poorly paid jobs with little chance of success, Salome Raheim and Jacquelyn Bolden (1995, 149) argue that women are empowered as a result of increased access to credit and capital, flexibility to care for family, and increase in self-esteem.

Microenterprise from the Eyes of Entrepreneurs

This book asks several key questions of microentrepreneurs. What are their goals? What facilitates or hinders business performance? What kinds of support do they receive? How do businesses contribute (or not contribute) to the household, both economically and otherwise? Finally, how do entrepreneurs assess their microenterprise experience?

This study of low-income entrepreneurs is part of a larger study conducted by the Aspen Institute's Self-Employment Learning Project (SELP). SELP, a five-year study of microenterprise funded by the Charles Stewart Mott and Ford foundations (Appendix B), included a longitudinal assessment of 405 randomly selected microentrepreneurs, including 133 with low incomes (Clark & Huston, 1993; Clark & Kays, 1995, 1999). In years one, two, three, and five of the study, SELP evaluators conducted telephone surveys with the entrepreneurs.[8] A separate analysis of the 133 low-income entrepreneurs (33 percent of the total group) was also conducted by SELP (Clark, & Kays, et al, 1999). The focus of annual surveys was on participants' businesses, households, earnings, and experiences with the microenterprise program. The central research questions concerned changes in business and household economic well being-over time. Annual surveys also included some open-ended questions, although they had not been analyzed.

This book focuses on data collected in the fourth year of SELP. We designed and conducted in-depth interviews that would capture the experience of creating and operating a microenterprise from the participants' perspectives (see Appendix A for a complete description of the research approach). The in-depth interviews encouraged the entrepreneurs to discuss their motivations for business ownership, earlier entrepreneurial activities, how they interpreted their business successes and challenges, how they handled business and household finances, and what they believed were the outcomes of owning a business. In these ways, the interviews provided description, explanation, and help in interpreting data collected in other years of the project. Of the 133 low-income entrepreneurs in SELP, we conducted in-depth interviews with 86.[9] Information for this book is also drawn from published and unpublished data from the four years of surveys and program case studies conducted at the Aspen Institute (Clark & Huston, 1993; Edgcomb, et al., 1996; Clark, et al., 1999).

The entrepreneurs interviewed for this study were participants in seven MDPs; most were among the very first established in the United States (Table 1.2). Although not representative of the field of microenterprise, these programs vary in size, approach, target population, and geographic location:

- WomenVenture, created in 1983 as Women's Economic Development Corporation (WEDCO), was established to assist unemployed and underemployed women to transition into self-employment. Later, WomenVenture expanded to work with women on welfare and some men on business development and career planning (Balkin, 1989; McKee, et al., 1993; Edgcomb, et al., 1996).

- The Women's Self-Employment Program (WSEP) provided financing and training for low-income women for microenterprise (Bailey, 1993; WSEP, 1996). The Full Circle Fund of WSEP was based on the Grameen Bank model (Balkin, 1992; Solomon, 1992; Rodriguez, 1995). WSEP employed peer and individual lending, along with training and technical assistance (Edgcomb, et al., 1996).

- The Portable Practical Education Program/Micro Industry Rural Credit Organization (PPEP/MICRO) was formed to serve primarily Latino/a entrepreneurs along the U.S.-Mexico border. Using a slightly different model from other US programs, PPEP/MICRO

Table 1.2
Characteristics of Microenterprise Programs and Participants in SELP*

	CWED	GFF	ISED	PPEP-MICRO	REDC	WSEP	WV
Location	Los Angeles, California	Pine Bluff, Arkansas	Iowa City, Iowa	Tucson, Arizona	Raleigh, North Carolina	Chicago, Illinois	Minneapolis, Minnesota
Year created	1989 (now closed)	1988	1988	1987	1989	1986	1983
Program strategies	Peer-group lending / Individual lending / Training and TA	Peer-group lending / Individual lending / Training and TA	Training and TA / Optional credit	Individual lending / Training and TA (optional)	Peer lending / Individual lending / Training and TA (optional)	Peer lending / Individual lending / Training and TA	Individual lending / Training and TA
Mandatory training	51 hours	18 hours (72 hours for welfare program)	90 hours	TA optional	Classes optional	30 hours (222 hours for welfare program)	1 hour (80 hours for welfare program)
Number of participants[1]	213	206	721	313	312	349	113
Women served (%)[1]	81	67	65	51	53	100	96
Minorities served (%)[1]	84	83	19	85	38	86	29
Participants under poverty (%)[1]	26	31	64	36	19	49	32
Recipients of welfare (%)[1]	6	9	51	9	3	38	21
Number in SELP study	38	39	54	51	83	86	54
Number in SELP poverty sample	14	12	40	24	23	16	9
Number in in-depth interview study	4	8	29	11	17	9	7

*Adapted from Edgcomb, et al., 1996, 7, 13, 15–18.

[1] Six-month period ending 12/31/96.

formed large business associations of twenty to thirty entrepreneurs that operated as peer lending and training groups for businesses that had been operating for at least one year (Edgcomb, et al., 1996).

- The Institute for Social and Economic Development (ISED) offered counseling, training, and technical assistance, and provided assistance in obtaining (and in some cases guaranteeing) loans through its partnerships with banks (Raheim & Friedman, 1999). ISED focused on promoting self-sufficiency through self-employment for people with very low incomes, especially women moving from welfare to work (Edgcomb, et al., 1996; Kantor, 2000).

- The Coalition for Women's Economic Development (CWED), incorporated in 1988, offered training, technical assistance, and credit to low-income women with diverse levels of business experience (NEDLC/CWED, 1999). Although for a short time the CWED expanded to include an SBA microloan program, it drew back to its original focus on training and lending for the poor, and finally closed its doors in 1996 (NEDLC/CWED, 1999).

- The Good Faith Fund (GFF) was established in 1988 with the help of then-Governor Bill Clinton and Hillary Clinton as a subsidiary of the Southern Development Bancorporation. Originally proposed as a replication of the Grameen Bank model, it served mostly low-income women and minority entrepreneurs (Mondal & Tune, 1993; Buntin, 1997; Surgeon, 1997; Taub, 1998).

- Finally, using a more decentralized form of service delivery, the Rural Economic Development Center (REDC) of North Carolina, created in 1989, was comprised of a network of agencies that offered group and individual lending and training services funded by the state legislature (Edgcomb, et al., 1996).

The seven programs varied in their approach to assisting entrepreneurs. Tables 1.2 and 1.3 provide descriptions of the programs in the second half of 1996 and indicators of program performance in 1994 (Edgcomb, et al., 1996). Regarding type of service, ISED provided only training and technical assistance and assisted entrepreneurs in obtaining loans for other sources, while the others also directly provided loans. ISED and WSEP served high proportions of the poor, while REDC and CWED served the lowest proportion of poor participants. GFF served the fewest participants, while ISED served the most in 1994. The majority of participants in WSEP, Women Venture, and CWED were women, and the majority of participants in WSEP, MICRO, CWED, and GFF were minorities. In 1994, costs per participant ranged from $841 at ISED,

Table 1.3
Program Performance in Seven Microenterprise Programs (1994)*

	CWED	GFF	ISED	PPEP/MICRO	REDC	WSEP	WV
Number of participants	508	206	978	340	312	349	1,274
Cost per participant[1]	$1,300	$2,691	$ 841	$1,437	$1,511	$2,257	$1,913[2]
Cost per business	$2,110	$4,698	$2,716	$1,437	$1,904	$3,355	$4,903
Loans made	27	43	41[3]	200	98	103	36
Average loan size	$3,474	$4,879	$7,404[3]	$2,161	$4,772	$2,173	$8,059
Number of business starts	52	55	66	50	74	76	70
Number of business expansions	94	63	237	290	148	148	23

*Adapted from Edgcomb, et al., 1996, 34–36, 38–41, 57. (For number of business starts and expansions, where data for graphs are different from those in the tables, we report data from the tables).

[1]Although not reported, costs per participant may be lower than cost per business because some participants do not open businesses.

[2]Intensive services only.

[3]ISED helps participants prepare loan applications and it monitors payments, but does not directly disburse loans.

which offered only training and technical assistance, to $2,691 at the Good Faith Fund, which offered extensive services. Average loan sizes ranged from a low of $2,161 at MICRO to a high of $8,059 at WomenVenture. There was relatively little variation in number of business start-ups, but expansions were emphasized at ISED and MICRO.

Summary of the Book

In chapter 2, we review the theoretical work on microenterprise that suggests reasons why people choose microenterprise and explanations of business outcomes. We also summarize key findings of existing studies on microenterprise.

Chapter 3 is an introduction to the microentrepreneurs, their businesses, their motivation for starting a business, and their business goals. The chapter describes the ways in which many microentrepreneurs occupy a disadvantaged space in the work world and why they decided to open a business. Chapter 4 discusses resources that the microentrepreneurs brought to their businesses. Their accounts underscore relatively low levels of financial, human, and social capital. This chapter also addresses the role of MDPs in supporting business start-up, including lending, training, technical assistance, and other support.

In chapter 5 we focus on how well the businesses performed economically by presenting data on business earnings and business assets. Although the range is wide, microentrepreneurs in this study earned modest financial income from their business on average. The analysis also shows that boundaries between business and household are often blurred, compounding the challenges of sorting out financial success of business and other income-generating strategies. We detail the strategic importance of microenterprise as entrepreneurs and their families patch together income from several sources, including self-employment, wage and salaried work, and public assistance.

In chapter 6 we examine factors that influenced business performance. According to the entrepreneurs, the most important factors contributing to business profits were business skills and experience, family support, and availability of business infrastructure and capital. Except for family support, these were also important factors contributing to business losses. In addition, the economy and various life events and personal factors, such as illness in the family, also contributed to losses. MDPs helped with some of these problems, but typically were unable to offer enough support over the long term to provide an effective counterweight.

Chapter 7, where we examine the multiple outcomes of microenterprise, may be the most important chapter. Low-income people go into business for a variety of economic and non-economic reasons, and the rewards of self-employment vary. The breadth of these factors suggests the potential of microenterprise for development of poor households. We also examine outcomes identified by participants in relation to financial outcomes addressed in chapter 5.

Chapter 8 revisits the question of microenterprise as an anti-poverty strategy. Our analysis suggests that microenterprise provides some income for economic survival, although in relatively few cases does it elevate families much above poverty. It is the lion's share of household income for a few, but for most microentrepreneurs the business provides only one source of income among others. Nonetheless, entrepreneurs say they reap substantial rewards over and above income. These include opportunities for personal growth and learning, autonomy and control, and various benefits to their family. These benefits help to explain high levels of enthusiasm for self-employment. Theoretically and practically, these results suggest that microenterprise can best be advanced from a human and household development perspective.

Notes

1. Balkin (1989, 13–14) points out that there is a difference between being an entrepreneur (a risk taker, "bold and imaginative," who wants to make money) and being self-employed (a simple description of employment type). All the participants in this study were self-employed (they had opened a business on their own), but many were also "entrepreneurial," striking out against the odds and on their own, to build a business. In the end, we acknowledge the difference, but use both to describe the individuals in this study.

2. To continue receiving public assistance benefits, the Aid to Families with Dependent Children (AFDC) program disallowed accumulation of family assets beyond $1,000 and a vehicle worth more than $1,500.

3. Butler adopts the term *economic detour*, coined in the 1930s, to describe a situation where hostility and government policy has historically forced African American-owned businesses to operate in very restricted circumstances. Black businesses could not compete with businesses that could operate, relatively unconstrained, in the larger market (1991, 75, 323).

4. A great deal has been written on the Grameen Bank (see *www.grameen-info.org/bank/biblio.html* for a bibliography on Grameen), although few publications are based on independent empirical research.

5. For more information see the ACCIÓN International website (*http://www.accion.org/about/*) and the FINCA International website (*http://www.villagebanking.org/about/index.htm*).

6. Several programs offer more than one kind of loan. Moreover, very few programs deviate from the credit idea by providing outright grants to businesses. Trickle

Up, a New York-based organization, grants $100 to $700, along with training and support, to start businesses (Foderaro, 1997; *http://www.trickleup.org/*). The seed money reportedly helps businesspeople get their small business off the ground and then they can turn to other microenterprise programs or to conventional lenders for more capital.

7. Costs of providing microenterprise services vary widely depending on the intensity of training, technical support and support services, and the experience, age, and size of the program itself. Some estimates, however, have been attempted. A Mott Foundation study of 31 microenterprise programs (1985) estimated costs ranging from $500 to $39,000, with an average cost per business start-up or expansion of $10,521 (Klein, 1994). SELP estimated costs ranging from $1,437 to $4,698 per business for all types of assistance (Edgcomb, et al., 1996, 37). The cost-per-business-start-up ranged from $7,400 to $8,000 in two of the SELP agencies that tracked these data (Edgcomb, et al., 1996, 43-44). The Office of Refugee Relief spent an average of $11,836 per business (Else & Clay-Thompson, 1998). The Association for Enterprise Opportunity (AEO) estimated that the rising costs of training and technical assistance range from $630 to $12,000 per participant, and the median cost per loan, including training and technical assistance is $7,300 (AEO, 2000). According to Edgcomb and her colleagues (1996), the costs per job created in a microenterprise ranged from $4,114 in one program to $6,155 in another. This compares to costs per new job ranging from $3,469 to $7,000 in job training and placement programs working with similar populations (Edgcomb, et al., 1996, 43). In recalculations of published data, Schreiner (2002) estimates costs of about $2,000 per participant, and asks if benefits per participant are likely to exceed the costs.

8. SELP evaluators made these data available to the authors allowing a longitudinal perspective on many of the research questions. SELP evaluators had not previously analyzed open-ended questions.

9. Of the original 133 (out of 450) low-income participants, 89 had been resurveyed the year before (Wave Three) of SELP.

CHAPTER 2

Theory and Evidence

It is not immediately clear why someone would choose to become self-employed by opening a microbusiness. Operating a business takes considerable time and energy and failure rates are high. Nevertheless, a number of theories suggest why self-employment might be a desirable option for some people. Some theories emphasize "push" factors. That is, in the absence of quality, well-paying jobs, or because of discrimination in the labor market, individuals default into self-employment. Whereas other theories emphasize "pull" factors suggesting that individuals choose self-employment because of the financial and non-financial payoffs (Messenger & Stettner, 2000). Some theories focus less on the reasons for entering self-employment and more on what may help account for whether an individual is successful in self-employment.

Human Capital Theory

Economic perspectives emphasize utility maximization and human capital reward. Employment options are closely tied to human capital. Human capital as conceptualized by Gary Becker (1993) includes skills, knowledge, experience, motivation, creativity, and health. In addition to education and experience, individuals who pursue self-employment may possess psychological traits that predispose them to a need for personal achievement and control and that assist in creating a successful enterprise. Characteristics may include a moderate propensity for risk taking, a high need for autonomy and self-esteem, and a low need for conformity (Balkin, 1989).

Neoclassical economic theory rests on the assumption that people rationally choose among alternative options in order to maximize their satisfaction or utility. A greater expected payoff from self-employment would cause individuals to shift from wage labor to self-employment or vice versa (Hamilton,

21

2000). In order to take full advantage of one's skills, it is necessary to find the appropriate job. On one hand, according to Eric Fredland and Roger Little, "self-employment is an alternative for those who have or believe they have human capital which employers discount" (1985, 121). That is, a worker may decide to apply their human capital skills to self-employment, believing a higher financial reward will result than that provided by an alternative employer. On the other hand, owning a business also requires an entrepreneur to undertake many different kinds of tasks, at which the entrepreneur may not have comparative advantage. Human capital constraints may limit business pursuits and affect economic outcomes.

How do people decide where they will maximize their earnings? In some cases people will try to match their skills to the sector in which they have relative advantage (Willis, 1986; Hamilton, 2000). This has been called the "matching model" (Roy, 1951). Individuals who are equally qualified for more than one sector will choose the sector in which the variance of earnings is higher because this will potentially lead to greater pay. Alternatively, for those who are uncertain of their relative advantage, the learning model suggests that workers must learn by trial and error. The learning model may be particularly relevant for entrepreneurs who are low income and have low educational attainment. Over time low-ability entrepreneurs who lack enough relative advantage may recognize that self-employment is not a good match for their skills and drop out of self-employment (Hamilton, 2000).

Differential earnings between self-employment and wage employment are predicted in opposite directions according to investment and agency models. Barton Hamilton writes that the "investment model" suggests a steeper earning profile in self-employment compared to paid employment because human and physical capital investments, that is, equipment, are not shared with an employer in self-employment (2000, 607). Because self-employment requires greater investment in enterprise specific capital, entrepreneurs will have lower initial earnings than paid employees, but they hope to experience greater earnings growth over time. Alternatively, an "agency model" (Lazear, 1981) suggests that firms may initially pay less than an alternative work arrangement but later wages rise above alternative wages to encourage employees to remain in their job. Thus, while the investment model predicts that earnings from self-employment will surpass the earnings from paid employment, the agency model predicts the opposite (Hamilton, 2000).

Choosing self-employment results not only from financial considerations and job options, but may be pursued for non-pecuniary reasons as well. This may be especially true for women. Self-employment offers an advantage to women that traditional wage employment may not; the choice to operate a small business may be influenced by a need or desire for flexibility in work and family responsibilities (Birley, 1989; Holmquist & Sundin, 1990).

Compensating Differential Theory

Components of utility or satisfaction include not only monetary reward, but also other factors such as personal control, time spent with family, flexible hours, and enjoyable work (Carr, 1996; Blau, et al., 1998). Compared to wage employment, microenterprise may offer greater non-pecuniary rewards. Compensating differential theory speaks to workers' decisions about the industry, occupation, or firm in which they will choose to work (Duncan, 1976). Non-monetary factors, such as work environment, coworkers, managers, fair treatment, and flexibility of work hours, influence the decision to choose entrepreneurship. If all jobs were alike, the decision about where to seek work would be a simple one based on the highest wages (Ehrenberg & Smith, 1997). But the idea of compensating differential theory suggests that in some cases non-monetary rewards may compensate for lower wages. As we shall demonstrate in detail, this general idea is a useful foundation for thinking about motivations for microenterprise.

Feminist Theory

Human capital and rational choice are also impacted by factors beyond individual factors. According to feminist theory, for example, women may be as skilled and are as capable of rationality as men, but are deprived of opportunities when compared to men. Moreover, women's socialization may discourage them from developing their full capacity (Fischer, et al., 1993; Abramovitz, 1996). Gender stereotyping, discrimination against women, and the general perception of women business owners as having hobbies rather than serious business pursuits, promotes external barriers to business growth and success (Hisrich & Brush, 1987; Keeley, 1990). Such barriers may be intensified by women's education and occupational backgrounds, income, and race (Brush, 1990). Additionally, women's employment—especially for poor women and women of color—is characterized by pay inequality, occupational segregation, lower occupational status, and limited potential for economic growth and opportunity (Tomaskovic-Devey, 1993). Welfare-to-work and job-training programs frequently channel women into jobs that reinforce existing societal patterns of women's employment rather than promote economic self-sufficiency that brings women out of poverty (Miller, 1990; Bernstein & Hartmann, 1999).

Disadvantaged Worker Theory

As suggested by the differential impact of human capital on gender, a limitation to understanding microenterprise from a human capital and rational choice perspective is that individuals may be prevented from exercising their potential or comparative advantage in the labor market, due to issues of race, class, and gender discrimination (Tomaskovic-Devey, 1993; Abramovitz, 1996). Nor does everyone have equal access to human capital development. Theories of disadvantage suggest that a number of labor market factors, including unemployment and discrimination, encourage self-employment. The theory holds that individuals who possess limited wage-labor skills or face discrimination are apt to earn higher incomes being self-employed than working for wages. Disadvantaged workers, therefore, may choose business because it offers an alternative to low-wage jobs or underemployment.

Sociologists observe that disadvantage comes in different forms. Ivan Light and Carolyn Rosenstein differentiate between "disadvantaged entrepreneurs" and "value entrepreneurs." Disadvantaged entrepreneurs choose self-employment because they can earn higher wages in self-employment than in wage employment due to factors such as discrimination, physical disability, age, unrecognized education certification, or exclusion from referral or "old boys" networks (1995, 213–214; see also Keeley, 1990; Raheim & Bolden, 1995). In accordance with compensating differential theory, value entrepreneurs choose small low-profit businesses at least in part because they allow more flexibility to care for children, and greater autonomy, social status, independence, and choice of lifestyle (Light & Rosenstein, 1995).

According to Timothy Bates (1993), however, the idea of "disadvantaged entrepreneurs" pursuing self-employment for higher earnings does not account for large differential rates of self-employment by racial and gender subgroups. Sexist and racist employment practices in the labor market facing women and African Americans, for example, would suggest an overrepresentation of these groups in self-employment, which does not occur. It is, however, quite likely that sexist and racist attitudes carry over to self-employment, including discrimination in access to capital, suppliers, and markets (Borjas & Bronars, 1989). Light and Rosenstein (1995) suggest that resource-constraints help explain low rates of self-employment among disadvantaged groups. This may help account for Bates's observation that disadvantaged groups are not overrepresented in self-employment. Disadvantage not only helps explain why people might choose self-employment, but it also suggests that they might face disadvantage in self-employment as well (Loscocco & Robinson, 1991; Loscocco, et al., 1991).

Resource Theory

Bates (1989) underscores the importance of capital for business success, especially among low-income and minority entrepreneurs. Liquidity constraints, or a lack of access to capital, delays start-up (Evans & Jovanovic, 1989) and increases the likelihood of business failure (Holtz-Eakin, et al., 1994). If microentrepreneurs cannot borrow sufficiently and attain a profit-maximizing level, then those who have personal financial resources will be more successful than those who do not. From a sociological perspective, social structures define and limit the resources available. Light and Rosenstein (1995) argue that a range of resources—including social, human, and financial capital—are defined by social class and ethnic group membership (1995). The level and type of resources shapes business development and helps explain business success. The importance of resources suggests that microenterprise development programs may play an important role in facilitating business if they can offer sufficient resources to the poor for business development.

For women, management experience, access to capital, information, and networking opportunities may be particularly salient barriers to microbusiness success. Sociocultural, economic, and regulating traditions also result in barriers to women obtaining information and financing. Access to credit is a major obstacle to female entrepreneurship. The unequal economic status of women makes them less likely to have assets or to have sufficient credit to obtain adequate business loans (Haswell & Holmes, 1989; Keeley, 1990; Sanders & Scanlon, 2000).

Social Network Theory

Sociologists also address how the range of class and ethnic resources are distributed and reach entrepreneurs, suggesting that social networks define the context for entry and success in business (Aldrich & Zimmer, 1986). For example, the large numbers of Asian immigrants who pursue self-employment frequently rely on social resources from group cultural and kinship support networks. Victor Nee and his colleagues (1994) show that, despite segmentation in the labor market and the difficulties that ethnic groups face in entering the mainstream economy, (1) ethnic communities offer alternative opportunity structures even though wages and working conditions tend to be lower than mainstream labor market, and (2) self-employment options in the ethnic community are better than the wage jobs in the ethnic market and, along with jobs in the mainstream economy, are means to mobility. Suggesting that social and cultural capital resources make key contributions to entrepreneurial success, Ivan Light and Steven Gold argue that a human capital approach to understanding entrepreneurship is not adequate: "Prepared to acknowledge that economic mobility through entrepreneurship is difficult for poor people, and always has been, we deny that it is *impossible*, especially if they have supportive ethnic resources" (emphasis in original, 2000, 101). Social networks may include access to such resources as financial support (Vélez-Ibañez, 1983); customers (Light, 1972); information (Lieberson, 1980; Balkin, 1989); and labor (Waldinger, 1986). Some factors encourage or discourage entry; others block or facilitate mobility. Alistair Anderson and Claire Miller (2003) find that it is the combination of both social and human capital resources that affect growth and profitability of new enterprise.

Diversification or Portfolio Theory

The theories discussed thus far focus on comparing self-employment and wage employment. Economic diversification, or portfolio theory, suggests that efficient diversification results in higher financial returns at a given level of risk (Markowitz, 1952) and may help to explain why entrepreneurs might begin a small business and pursue wage employment at the same time. While the concept of diversification has traditionally been applied to investment portfolios, it may be useful for thinking about income streams as well (Chen & Dunn, 1996).

Diversification of income sources could provide some protection against the negative consequences of losing a source of income, perhaps due to job loss, by increasing financial stability, or by smoothing income flows (Chen & Dunn, 1996). Having more than one source of income may also allow freedom to take risks in the search for larger income gains, including starting a business. Numerous studies note that income generated from self-employment may play an important role in the income "package" of households (Spalter-Roth, et al., 1994; Edin & Lein, 1997; Clark, et al., 1999). Some have suggested that the amount of income generated from the business results in a larger overall household income than if an individual was to work in wage labor alone (Clark & Huston, 1993).

It is not clear, however, that diversification is a conscious strategy. Diversifying income and economic supports also has a social and cultural component likely beyond any conscious decision to diversify income. Studies that examine how poor households and communities survive with limited resources have documented, for example, the trading and mutual sharing of resources, income, and child care (Stack, 1974; Edin & Lein, 1997).

The question is to what extent diversification is social and cultural, simply a means of coping with poverty—adding income streams as they become available—or whether it is a deliberate strategy to diversify income sources, building a portfolio of income streams in the face of economic constraints. If households consciously diversify, what is the optimal number (and possibly type) of income sources? On one hand, too few income sources may make the household and the microenterprise vulnerable to income shocks. If low-income entrepreneurs rely on one source of income (the business), they risk the loss of all income support in the event of business failure. Likewise, people who work in the low-wage labor market and experience unstable jobs, temporary positions, and layoffs risk loss of all support by relying on one income source. It is also not very likely that self-employment opportunities are highly correlated with wage employment opportunities. It is more likely that when wage employment options are not encouraging, individuals turn to self-employment and vice versa. On the other hand, too much diversification may result in high transaction costs (Sherraden, 1989). That is, the more income sources, the more time, money, and resources it may require. For example, transportation costs and time spent commuting are likely to increase going to and from multiple jobs. This may be especially problematic for microentrepreneurs responsible for the multiple tasks of running a microbusiness. Engaging in outside employment could take away from the efficiency of the business and result in lower overall economic returns.

Another outcome of diversifying the household income portfolio may be to increase risk-taking (Dunn, et al., 1996). In other words, households with more than one source of income (provided that the variance in income sources is not highly correlated)[1] may have an increased ability to take risks for improving future outcomes with some assurance of a safety net in the present. This suggests that having multiple sources of income may enable microentrepreneurs to keep their businesses going and take risks that may pay off in the future.

According to Martha Chen and Elizabeth Dunn, "The degree to which a household would choose a smaller, but certain outcome over a larger, but uncertain outcome reflects the household's level of risk aversion" (1996, 19). Households living on the edge of survival are likely to exhibit high-risk aversion, because the outcome of risk-taking may be failure to survive. Greater economic security in a household results in more willingness to take financial risks, based on the premise that a larger payoff may occur (Chen & Dunn, 1996).

Based on their work with microenterprise and poor households in developing countries, Chen and Dunn have created a framework that is useful for thinking about poor microentrepreneurs in the United States. Risk is both temporal and spatial. Temporal and spatial factors take into account whether a crisis (and associated period of risk) may be short-term or prolonged and have a short-term or prolonged impact on household welfare. Additionally, a crisis may be localized or widespread thereby affecting the ability of communities to offer support to vulnerable households, or the ability of vulnerable households to seek support. They argue that "diversification, a strategy of engaging in multiple activities, is an important way of promoting flexibility and countering risk and uncertainty" (1996, 20).

Assessment of risk leads households to adopt precautionary or insurance strategies. When risk is more likely, precautionary strategies are adopted. When risk is less likely, greater risks can be taken. Diversification of sources of livelihood and income is both precautionary against possible fluctuations or shortfalls and responsive to actual fluctuations or shortfalls (Chen & Dunn, 1996).

Within this framework, Chen and Dunn hypothesize that the portfolio of any given household will fall within a broad continuum. The poorest households, falling at one end of the spectrum, are likely to pursue short-term survival objectives. This typically includes intensification and diversification of labor activities. Thus, the poorest and most disadvantaged microentrepreneurs, who lack social support systems and have less stable income sources, will be most risk averse. This in turn suggests that these individuals may view their business as a survival tool rather than a long-term investment. Wealthier households with stable income and resource bases would pursue long-term mobility objectives by diversifying their assets and investing their resources. Households in the middle level of the spectrum would focus on stability and security objectives, while looking ahead for future economic and social mobility. The key distinctions among these three groups are the (a) level of income or welfare of the household, (b) the time-frame applied in mobilizing and allocating short- or long-term resources, (c) the approach to risk management, and (d) the degree of diversity of activities or strategies (Chen & Dunn, 1996, 28).

Chen & Dunn discover, based on other studies, that coping strategies in developing countries parallel their framework. During lean periods of recurrent risk, the most frequently observed responses included diversifying livelihood or income sources; drawing on stored resources and social relationships; seeking alternative employment; borrowing; and if necessary, reducing or modifying consumption. After a lean season, households try to replenish their physical, financial, and social assets (Chen & Dunn, 1996, 21). While less is known about economic diversification strategies of poor microentrepreneurs in the United States, Chen and Dunn's research suggests that there is a conscious effort to diversify income streams. Thus far, research in the United States has simply documented that the poor "patch" together income to get by and may rely on social networks to stabilize household resources. Having numerous sources of income provides some income stability in the event an income source is lost (Edin & Lein, 1997).

Asset Theory

Asset theory (Sherraden, 1991) suggests that some psychological, social, and economic outcomes of microenterprise are a result of asset accumulation. That is, ownership improves how people feel about their future well-being. This applies not only to the microbusiness as an asset itself but also to accumulation of household assets resulting from business ownership. Michael Sherraden suggests that more than consumption is involved in household well-being and that assets yield important effects beyond consumption. This theory proposes that asset accumulation alters thinking and behavior in a number of ways resulting in increased personal efficacy and hope for the future, greater economic stability, greater community and political participation, and enhanced intergenerational welfare (Sherraden, 1991, 148; Page-Adams & Sherraden, 1996). The result is a different approach to the world that may result in a virtuous cycle in which asset accumulation and positive behaviors reinforce one another. Thus, asset theory suggests that people may choose to start a business because they want to own something and that the effect of ownership has positive economic and non-economic effects on their lives.

In sum, some theoretical approaches suggest that people choose self-employment because they are maximizing the economic advantage of their skills and available resources. Alternatively, some may turn to self-employment because they face limited opportunity and discrimination in the labor market. While some may do better by turning to self-employment, others will make little progress because racial and gender discrimination carries over into the self-employment sector. Other theoretical approaches suggest that people choose self-employment for non-monetary reasons, such as greater freedom, autonomy, and flexibility. In this case, workers may choose self-employment over wage employment despite possible lower earnings in self-employment. This trade-off may occur in the interest of maximizing satisfaction and utility, taking into account non-monetary rewards. Others may choose self-employment because there are more avenues and more resources available to support business ownership. Others may strategically combine a business with other earned and unearned income sources in order to diversify sources of financial support. Finally, asset theory suggests that the benefits of owning or accumulating assets may influence a decision to seek self-employment over wage labor.

Evidence on Microenterprise

What does the existing research on microenterprise in the United States tell us about why people choose self-employment and the results of that choice? Some studies have begun to shed light on microenterprise and its effects, although there is relatively little research given the extent of program development and enthusiasm for the idea of microenterprise. We believe research to date has been limited by several factors. First, the dual objectives of microenterprise programs, to promote both economic and social development, may have served to hinder researchers' interest. Microenterprise does not fit neatly into one disciplinary track such as business, economics, or social work, and so it may be viewed as a marginal topic in each discipline and thus an unlikely research topic. While *microenterprise* has become almost a household word in community development, it is less well-known among scholars. Second, the diversity and small size of programs makes research efforts challenging and

expensive. Third, the impact of microenterprise and self-employment is difficult to measure with accuracy because microenterprise often resides in, or
spills over into, the informal economic sector where official records are lacking. Microbusinesses are often home-based and are combined financially, spa-
tially, and in time with other community, family, and household functions.
Finally, there has been little money available for research. The field has grown
relatively quickly but with little support for inquiry.

A review of research suggests that study findings should be interpreted
with caution. With few exceptions (Benus, et al., 1995; Sanders, 2000, 2002),
most studies are cross-sectional in nature, lack control or comparison groups,
are descriptive, and sometimes fail to report findings with adequate interpretation. Moreover, it is difficult to parcel out program effects; that is, improvement
in household income or other economic well-being measures cannot necessarily be attributed to the microenterprise. Table 2.1 summarizes major studies
on microenterprise in the United States. The table can be used as a guide on
research to date and for further reading.

Business Survival

Survival rates for small business are known to be fairly low. The Small
Business Administration (SBA) estimates that almost a fourth (23.7 percent) of
small businesses close after two years and more than half (52.7 percent) close
after five years.[2] Although the estimates of microenterprise survival are less
comprehensive, several studies have suggested that the rates are similar, perhaps a little better. Data from a microenterprise demonstration project sponsored by the Department of Labor suggest a survival rate of 90 percent after
thirty-one months (Else & Gallagher, 2001). Findings from the Self-Employment Learning Project, suggest that almost half of businesses belonging to low-
income entrepreneurs were still open after five years, while more than half had
closed (Clark, et al., 1999).

Household Income

Most of the studies show modest income gains for the self-employed. Of
the two sites in the Unemployment Insurance Self-Employment Demonstration,
the Washington participants had significant self-employment earnings averaging $1,600 per year. In contrast, wages and salaries from employment in Wash-
ington decreased by about $1,800 per year. The research shows little impact on
total earnings. What participants gained in self-employment, they generally
gave up in earnings from wage and salary employment. Participants in the
Massachusetts site did not experience similar gains in income from self-employment. However, a positive impact on wage and salary earnings of more

Table 2.1

Major Empirical Studies on Microenterprise in the United States

Author(s)	Year of Publication	Sample Size	Research Method(s)	Key Findings
Drury, Walsh, & Strong	1994	Six-site demonstration. 645 participants.	Three-year evaluation of the Economic Dislocation and Worker Adjustment Assistance Act (EDWAA) on effectiveness of CDs in expanding employment through self-employment to dislocated workers. Four site visits to each site, telephone contacts, two conferences with grantees. Quantitative data on program participants collected by grantees.	Low earnings from self-employment not very feasible as an immediate wage replacement. Self-employment is a viable strategy for only a small subset of dislocated workers. Training without access to capital is not sufficient.
Spalter-Roth, Soto, & Zandniapour	1994	1,325 unweighted (SIPP). Four focus groups. Survey data (N = 140)(SELP). Interviews (N = 20).	Non-matched 4-group comparison using SIPP data: (1) self-employed welfare recipients; (2) self-employed former welfare recipients; (3) employed welfare recipients not self-employed; (4) non-employed welfare recipients. Focus groups and survey of low-income women participating in microenterprise training.	Limited earnings from self-employment contribute to household income, but not sufficient for self-sufficiency. Self-employed work more hours and lack health insurance.

(continued)

Table 2.1 *(continued)*

Major Empirical Studies on Microenterprise in the United States

Author(s)	Year of Publication	Sample Size	Research Method(s)	Key Findings
Benus, Johnson, Wood, Grover, & Shen[1]	1995	Washington: 755 experimental 752 control Massachusetts: 614 experimental 608 control	Two-site demonstration, classic experimental design with Unemployment Insurance recipients as participants.	WA: Impact on total earnings not significantly different than zero. MA: Increased annual earnings but driven by impact on wage employment. Both sites resulted in increase in time worked and likelihood of employment at second survey.
Raheim & Alter[2]	1995	Random sample of 120 participants of the Self-Employment Investment Demonstration (SEID).	Five-state demonstration with public assistance recipients. Post-program follow-up study. Telephone interviews.	Welfare recipients can successfully start businesses with knowledge, skills, and capital. Self-employment is a viable self-sufficiency option for some welfare recipients. At follow-up on average participants had experienced increases in business and personal assets that may or may not be a result of the program. Programs appear to influence positive psychosocial outcomes, such as increased self-esteem. Programs may increase self-employment among African Americans and decrease the failure rates among disadvantaged groups.

| Edgcomb, Klein, & Clark | 1996 | Seven SELP microenterprise development programs. | Three years of case study research (1992–94) examining program strategies, costs, effectiveness, and challenges for the future. | There is no single microenterprise model. Strategies vary but can generally be divided into credit-led, group lending, and training-led programs. Programs serve to a large extent, minorities, women, and the poor. Cost effectiveness measures compare favorably with other employment programs aimed at low- and moderate-income participants. Assessing effectiveness is an important component of program methodology and needs to be further advanced and refined. Greater stability in program funding needed. |
| Himes & Servon | 1998 | 2000 administrative survey data. 72 qualitative interviews. | Uses administrative data from ACCIÓN U.S. network made up of 6 micro-lending programs. Examines data at time of application and follow-up measures. Qualitative interviews conducted with ACCIÓN participants. | Study claims positive business and household financial outcomes on average. Qualitative findings reveal non-financial rewards surrounding human capacity as productive members of society and personal satisfaction of owners. |

(continued)

Table 2.1 *(continued)*

Major Empirical Studies on Microenterprise in the United States

Author(s)	Year of Publication	Sample Size	Research Method(s)	Key Findings
Servon & Bates	1998	Representative nationwide sample drawn from U.S. Census, Characteristics of Business Owners Survey (1991) for businesses with revenues of $5,000 or greater. Three microenterprise program case studies.	Analyzes cross-sectional quantitative data to examine kinds of small businesses most likely to help entrepreneurs become self-sufficient. Uses qualitative data from 3 case studies to examine the role self-employment plays in the economic situation of individual entrepreneurs.	Hard work and small loans are insufficient for business success. More educated and owners with specific skills are more successful in self-employment. Those who lack assets, skills, and support networks are unlikely to support themselves through self-employment. Programs that target clients carefully may help some escape poverty.
Clark & Kays, Zandniapour, Soto, & Doyle	1999	133 low-income participants of the Self-Employment Learning Project (SELP).	Longitudinal Survey (1991–95). Case studies.	Most households experienced gains in income over 5 years. Average household assets also increased. More than half moved above 150% of poverty line by 1995, and among them, the micro-business was an important source of earnings. Income from the business played an important role in the total income package of low-income households. Reliance on public assistance also declined substantially. Changes in income, assets and reliance on public assistance may or may not be a result of microenterprise, as no counter factual is included.

Raheim & Friedman	1999	819 program participants. 819 comparison groups.	Compares self-sufficiency outcomes of welfare recipients who participated in an entrepreneurial training program to other welfare recipients in the Iowa welfare reform program.	Factors associated with whether training participants started a business (N = 225) included prior business experience, prior work experience, and marital status. In addition to jobs created for self, 70 other jobs (mostly part-time) were created. Program participants received welfare for 20.2 months on average, compared to 20.6 for other welfare recipients.
Servon[4]	1999	Five program case studies.	Five case studies, in-depth interviews with program staff and client borrowers, analysis of existing program data, and non-participant observation of day-to-day operations.	Outcomes may be limited in terms of income generated and jobs created but other important outcomes result such as development of human and social capital and economic literacy. Gaining a stable income from self-employment can take many years. Safety nets are needed in the process, including public assistance that allows low-income entrepreneurs to transition toward self-sufficiency. Inter-program and intra-program networks empower borrowers and link them with critical services provided by other institutions.

(continued)

Table 2.1 *(continued)*

Major Empirical Studies on Microenterprise in the United States

Author(s)	Year of Publication	Sample Size	Research Method(s)	Key Findings
Dumas	2001	55 participants.	Case analysis of a microenterprise training program. Structured and semi-structured qualitative interviews conducted in focus groups at the beginning of the program and one year later.	Program empowered participants to begin moving toward self-sufficiency. Helped participants build business and life management skills. Influenced growth of locally-controlled businesses and helped to create new inner-city jobs. Implications include need for additional mentoring, networking and workshops; increased ethnic diversity among program users, better access to computers and training; better development of business plans.
Sanders[5]	2002	80 program participants. 109 non-participants. 242 non-self-employed wage workers.	Non-equivalent control group design. Study compares low-income SELP program participants to matched comparison groups drawn from PSID on economic outcomes between 1991 and 1995.	All three groups made economic gains in income and level of poverty. However, groups do not vary significantly, calling into question whether microenterprise development programs are having a program effect.

| Alisultanov, Klein, & Zandniapour | 2002 | 10 programs. 590 participants baseline. 295 participants 1 year. Follow-up. | Before and after survey design. Includes many sub-group analyses and also compares some findings to external studies and data sources. | The study notes increased employment activity including both self-employment and wage employment. Household income, income from the business, household assets, liabilities, and net worth all increased on average. However, a relatively few number of homeowners drive increases in assets. Use of TANF decreased dramatically between baseline measures and one-year follow-up. A small percentage (17%) moved above the official poverty line within the one-year study period. Findings cannot necessarily be attributed to microenterprise due to before and after design. |

[1] See also Benus, Wood, & Grover, 1994; and Schreiner, 1999.

[2] See also Else & Raheim, 1992; Raheim, 1996; Raheim, Alter, & Yarbrough, 1996; Raheim, 1997; Raheim & Alter, 1998.

[3] See also Clark & Huston, 1993.

[4] See also Servon, 1996, 1997, 1998.

[5] See also Sanders, 2000.

than $3,000 per year did occur in the Massachusetts demonstration (Benus, et al., 1994; Benus, et al., 1995).

Participants in Washington did not significantly increase the combined likelihood of employment in either a wage or salary job or in self-employment, although they did increase the time they worked per year and increased their likelihood of being employed at the time of the second survey. Massachusetts participants were more likely to find employment, increase the time worked per year, and increase the likelihood of being employed at the time of the second survey. Additionally, the participants combined annual earnings increased by nearly $6,000 (Benus, et al., 1994; Benus, et al., 1995). Most impacts, however, were driven by the impact on wage-employment not self-employment (Schreiner, 1999b).

After the Self-Employment Investment Demonstration (SEID), 55 percent of respondent families (n = 120) were earning their primary income through a job or self-employment compared to 9 percent prior to SEID enrollment. At follow-up, a total of 36 percent of business owners received regular income from their business. This included twenty-six who took in an owners' draw ranging from $20 to $1,500 per month (mean = $574) and eight who paid themselves a regular salary, ranging from $60 to $2,800 per month (mean = $798). A significant number of respondents (about 35 percent) who were unable to buy food and clothing on a regular basis prior to participation in SEID, reported being able do so after joining SEID. Some AFDC recipients (less than 10 percent) who opened a business reported that their family income was worse and that the new business placed additional strain on family finances, including incurring substantial debt due to poor business performance (Raheim & Alter, 1995).

Christina Himes and Lisa Servon (1998) in their study of ACCIÓN International, report that low-income program participants experienced significant increases in take-home income between the time of program entry and after receiving one to three business loans. Percent increases in take-home income averaged 29 percent after receiving one loan, 28 percent after two loans, and 15 percent after three loans.

Research conducted by the Self-Employment Learning Project (SELP) at the Aspen Institute also suggests that microentrepreneurs experience income gains over time (Clark & Huston, 1993). Between 1991 and 1993, 55 percent of the low-income participants (under 150 percent of poverty) in the study showed income gains and 25 percent had income gains large enough to move out of poverty. For those whose family incomes increased above the poverty line, the average increase in family income was $14,674. The average change in family income from the business was $6,723. The number of those whose income declined was not reported. By the end of the SELP study in 1996, 72 percent of low-income microentrepreneurs reported family income gains over a five-year period beginning in 1991, according to Peggy Clark and her colleagues (1999).[3] The average change was $8,484. Slightly more than half (53 percent) had gains large enough to move out of poverty. For those whose businesses remained open, an average of 37 percent of the increase in family income came from the business.[4]

Personal earnings, which represent all earnings of the respondent only, increased an average of $5,038 between 1991 and 1995. This increase was made up of $802 (16 percent) in earnings from the business and $4,236 (84 percent) in additional employment earnings. Reporting does not indicate the percent of total personal earnings that came from the business. For those low-income microentrepreneurs whose businesses remained open in 1995, the average increase in personal earnings was $5,049. Most of the increase ($3,159 or 63 percent) is a result of earnings from the business, while a smaller amount ($1,890 or 37 percent) came from other employment earnings.[5] While on average both family and respondent income did increase over the course of the SELP study, it is unclear to what extent the increase was an effect of microenterprise development programs.

A study by Cynthia Sanders (2002) builds on previous SELP studies by comparing low-income microenterprise program participants from SELP to matched comparison groups from the Panel Study of Income Dynamics (PSID), including low-income wage workers and self-employed workers not associated with development programs. Findings reveal that all three groups showed significant gains in family income and movement out of poverty between 1991 and 1995 (although 58 percent of the sample remained at or below 150 percent of poverty). However, the three groups did not vary much on economic outcomes over time, casting some doubt on whether microenterprise development programs are having an effect beyond what would have happened in their absence. On the other hand, SELP participants did not appear to have worse economic outcomes at the household level than other similar self-employed individuals or wage laborers, even though some theories would predict this. Study results also indicate greater household economic gains among Whites, households without young children, younger workers, and more educated workers. Men experienced larger gains in income from business than did women.

A study conducted by the Institute for Women's Policy Research' (IWPR), examines earnings and benefits among women engaged in part-time wage employment and self-employment (Spalter-Roth, et al., 1993). Economic well being was measured by three indicators: annual earnings, hourly wages, and employer-provided health insurance (or self-provided in the case of self-employed). The study, based on 1986 and 1987 panels of the Survey of Income and Program Participation (SIPP), found that self-employment provided smaller annual and hourly earnings than wage or salary work. Of the 10 percent of women who were self-employed, half combined self-employment with wage jobs or a second self-employment job. Workers who relied primarily on self-employment were much less likely to have health insurance.

A later study by IWPR examines the viability of self-employment as a strategy for alleviating poverty among women (Spalter-Roth, et al., 1994). Four comparison groups were generated from the 1984, 1986, 1987, and 1988 panels of the Survey of Income and Program Participation: (1) self-employed, current welfare recipients; (2) self-employed, former welfare recipients; (3) wage or salary packagers (on welfare and employed but not self-employed); and (4) non-employed welfare recipients. SIPP data were supplemented with data from focus groups, surveys, and in-depth interviews with low-income and/or AFDC recipients either contemplating or already engaged in microenterprise. The study is exploratory and groups were not matched. Nonetheless, findings shed some light on the self-employment experiences of low-income women.

Results reveal that self-employed former welfare recipients work more hours and weeks per year than other groups, have more hours of self-employment, have higher hourly earnings from self-employment ($4.37), and also have higher hourly earnings from other forms of work ($7.01). Self-employed welfare recipients also worked more hours and weeks per year than wage/salary packagers or non-employed welfare recipients. Almost half the hours spent working among this group were in wage work rather than in self-employment.

Results suggest that self-employment contributes to economic well being of AFDC recipients and former recipients but that the income derived from the businesses is a small portion of the family's income. Women who include self-employment in their income package also work more hours and weeks per year than other groups. Hourly earnings from wage employment were on average higher than earning from self-employment. Personal earnings (self-employment and wage or salary) comprise 26 percent of the family income of those who are not currently on welfare and are self-employed and 30 percent of the family income of self-employed AFDC recipients. The remainder comes from other sources and from other household earners.

Women who were self-employed and not on welfare were more likely to be married to a full-time working spouse who provided a substantial portion of the family income. This suggests that women who have spouses who work full-time may be in a better position to take the risks involved in self-employment. In terms of economic well-being (measured in terms of median hourly wages, median annual earnings, and employer-provided health benefits) wage and salary workers who were employed by a single employer and worked full-time, had the greatest economic well-being of all workers.

A more recent study that examines microenterprise as a welfare-to-work strategy (Alisultanov, et al., 2002) found, as with other studies, that household income increased over time on average. Household income from one year before program enrollment to the year after enrollment increased from an average of

$11,689 (median, $9,867) to an average of $15,068 (median, $12,936). Nonetheless, a significant proportion, 35 percent, experienced a decrease in household income. "Earned income patchers," those who drew income from both wage and self-employment had the highest incomes, compared to those with no earned income, wage employment earnings only, or self-employment earnings only. The number of income patchers was small relative to the other three groups. Of 113 respondents whose businesses were open one year after program enrollment, 51 percent reported personal income from the business with an average yearly income of $8,497 (median, $3,600). Of 167 respondents for which poverty status was calculated, 17 percent moved from poverty to above poverty during the course of one year. While in many cases self-employment played a role, income from a job was the most critical reason for movement out of poverty.

Income Diversification

Several studies provide evidence that poor families, especially those headed by women, use a small business as one of several sources of family income (Clark & Huston, 1993; Servon, 1996; Edin & Lein, 1997). For instance, the 1994 IWPR study finds that personal income—which includes self-employment and wage or salary earnings—comprises only 26 percent of family income of former welfare recipients and 30 percent of self-employed current welfare recipients (Spalter-Roth, et al., 1994).

The Self-Employment Learning Project (Clark & Huston, 1993) finds that, among a randomly selected sample of 302 from five microenterprise programs,[6] 30 percent of microenterprises managed their business while also holding down a job in 1991. In many households there were several different sources of income from several adults. The authors link this phenomenon to the growing number of working poor who cannot provide for their families with one, or even two, low-wage jobs. They note that microenterprise may serve an important buffer role, allowing families to have higher incomes than they would have if family members only held wage employment. Forty percent of microentrepreneurs relied solely on income from their business in 1991. A later study with a total of seven sites, reports that more than half of all respondents relied on the microbusiness as their primary source of earnings in 1991 but also continued to patch together more than one income source to make ends meet (Clark & Kays, 1995). These sources included other family earners, part- or full-time jobs held by respondents, and public assistance.

Overall, findings regarding household income gains from microenterprise are mixed. It appears that for people with low incomes, financial gains from microenterprise are modest, at least in the short run, but that income from the business may be an important source in a family's overall income package. Combining multiple sources of income is not unique to poor microentrepreneurs, as other studies have shown this to be a common economic strategy among poor women (Edin & Lein, 1997).

Household Assets

According to Salome Raheim (1996), participants of the Self-Employment Investment Demonstration had a number of household assets in 1993 that they did not have at the time of enrollment. The sum of assets in 1993 was $1,048,541, and average assets per participant were $8,738. However, because this was a postprogram follow-up survey, change in asset value is not reported, and the claim of increased assets appears to be based on subjective reports by study respondents. Additionally, since there is no comparison group, increases cannot be attributed to owning a business.

A publication from SELP reports an average increase in family assets among low-income microentrepreneurs of $15,909 over five years (n = 50, due to missing data) with 66 percent of poor respondents experiencing an increase (Clark, et al., 1999). Among respondents whose businesses remained open in 1995, the average increase in family assets was $26,400 (n = 25). The primary source of increased value was in homeownership.

The IWPR study found that self-employed former welfare recipients reported on average $2,600 in individual assets, while self-employed welfare recipients reported a significantly lower level, less than $400 on average (Spalter-Roth, et al., 1994). Welfare policies that discourage asset accumulation in order to qualify and maintain public assistance are likely to account for some of the difference (Sherraden, 1991; Orszag, 2001).

Ilgar Alisultanov and his colleagues (2002) report a more comprehensive examination of assets among participants in the Microenterprise Welfare-to-Work Demonstration and Evaluation. At baseline, participants reported an average of $5,865 in household assets. A year later, average household assets increased to $13,406. The growth in assets, however, is driven by a relatively small number of homeowners. Approximately 77 percent of growth can be accounted for by home value and most can be accounted for by home value appreciation. However, nine people did acquire a home within a year of enrolling in the program. Additionally, net worth increased on average. At baseline, study participants report a negative net worth on average and a zero median net worth. A year later, net worth averaged $1,891 (although median net worth declined to a negative $315).

The data suggest that asset holdings may increase with self-employment, but many questions remain. The data are not definitive, nor do they clarify the financial contributions of microenterprise to asset ownership and the mechanisms that lead to increases in asset ownership. Recorded increases may or may not be a function of owning a small business.

Reduction in Welfare Assistance

Raheim and Catherine Alter report reductions in dependence on public assistance among SEID participants (1995). Sixty participants had terminated AFDC benefits by 1993, a reduction of 52 percent. Use of food stamps decreased by 43 percent and reliance on food stamps as a secondary source of income decreased 62 percent. Of the 56 families who continued to receive AFDC payments at the time of the study, 32 percent were also generating income from self-employment. Reliance on AFDC as a primary source of income declined from 74 percent to 26 percent, a decrease of 65 percent.

Findings from SELP indicate that low-income microentrepreneurs reduced their use of government assistance by 61 percent over the five-year study period. On average means-tested benefits declined by $1,679 (Clark, et al., 1999). The percentage of low-income respondents receiving government assistance declined from 48 percent to 30 percent in 1995 (n = 61). Government assistance typically included AFDC and food stamps, but it also consisted of WIC and other food supplement programs, General Assistance, job training programs and other government allowances, SSI, and public housing.

The Rivercities of Iowa/Illinois Self-Employment Program (RISE), a study comparing outcomes from RISE with a comparison group of AFDC recipients, explored whether self-employment would enable AFDC recipients to move from welfare more quickly than other welfare-to-work programs (Raheim & Alter, 1998). The sample consisted of sixty-one pairs. However, there appear to be limitations in the matching process because RISE participants were on average older and more highly educated and it does not appear that these differences were controlled for in the data analysis. The authors report that 69 percent of RISE participants and 46 percent of the comparison group had exited from AFDC within the year following enrollment. Within two years, 90 percent of RISE participants had exited compared to 84 percent of the comparison group. After 30 months, 1.6 percent of RISE participants were on AFDC, compared to 6.9 percent of the comparison group, a statistically significant difference. However, because almost half of all individuals in both groups who had exited AFDC sometime after the beginning of the study returned to welfare before the end of the study, an alternative analysis of the data was also carried out. Although RISE participants received AFDC benefits for fewer months than did the comparison group, the differences were not statistically significant.

Other indicators of economic self-sufficiency were measured with the "Time and Money Management Skills" (TMM) questionnaire that assesses individuals' control and allocation of time, energy, and financial resources (Raheim & Alter, 1998, 54). Among RISE program participants, both those who started a business and those who completed training but did not open a business, showed significant improvements in their perceptions about their ability to control personal financial resources. However, individuals in the comparison group were not assessed on this measure, thus the researchers are not able to conclude that the microenterprise program was responsible for improved perceptions of economic self-sufficiency.

In another study by Raheim and Jason Friedman (1999), participants in an entrepreneurial training program in Iowa were compared to a similar group of welfare recipients under the Iowa's welfare reform program called the "Family Investment Program" (FIP). During the three years of the study, participants of the entrepreneurial training program received 20.2 months of FIP on average compared to 20.6 for other welfare recipients. While the authors report this as statistically significant, the difference appears to have little practical meaning.

The Microenterprise Welfare-to-Work Demonstration and Evaluation (Alisultanov, et al., 2002) examined movement off of Temporary Assistance for Needy Families (TANF) among participants of ten microenterprise organizations. At program enrollment, 94 percent of participants reported receiving TANF cash assistance, and one year later, only 35 percent reported receiving this assistance. This did not vary by whether or not respondents were operating a business.

The studies reviewed suggest that microenterprise program participants reduce their use of public assistance over time. However, because most studies lack a counterfactual with which to compare outcomes, findings cannot be attributed as unique to program participants. In fact, the average welfare stay, even prior to welfare reform, was around 12 to 13 months with a median of around 8 to 9 months (Blank, 1989; Pavetti, 1993; Morris, 1999). Additionally, a number of studies show 40- to 50-percent welfare caseload reductions within a 12-month period (Harris, 1993; Fitzgerald, 1995). It is not clear that microenterprise participants are doing better.

Non-economic Outcomes

In addition to economic outcomes, studies also examine non-economic outcomes of microenterprise such as changes in self-esteem, feelings of empowerment, flexibility, and sense of autonomy. For example, non-economic benefits resulted from participation in SEID. According to Raheim, based on self-report of SEID participants, increases occurred in self-esteem and confidence, ability to make decisions, respect from others, and reaching goals. Additionally, many participants reported improved relationships with spouses or partners and their children (1996).

Salome Raheim and Catherine Alter's (1998) study of the RISE program is the only study to utilize a standardized scale to measure the levels and changes in self-esteem. This was done at three points in time using the Index of Self-Esteem, which is easily administered and proven reliable and valid (Hudson, 1990). It revealed a small, but statistically significant, increase in participants' self-esteem. Both those who started a business and those who did not showed an increase in self-esteem. This may indicate that participation in the training program alone may produce increases in self-esteem. A weakness is that the authors did not administer the instrument at an even later follow-up date following business start-up, nor did they administer the test to the comparison group of AFDC recipients participating only in Iowa's welfare-to-work program.

Related to self-esteem, empowerment has also been suggested as an outcome of self-employment and microenterprise programs. Lisa Servon, using a case study approach that combined data from surveys, in-depth interviews, and non-participant observation, claims empowerment as an outcome based on her study of the Women's Initiative for Self-Employment (WISE). According to Servon, credit and training are used to facilitate greater economic options and to achieve individual empowerment: "The overarching goal at WISE is the individual economic empowerment of women, which has to do with increasing women's range of economic options on how to become self-sufficient and educating them about these choices" (1996, 34-35). Nearly half of the participants in the WISE program (whether or not they started a business) reported increases in indicators of empowerment including self-esteem, career options, work skills, and potential for success.

Similarly, when talking with both men and women at ACCIÓN International, Christina Himes and Servon (1998) report that most participants believed there were broader impacts of microenterprise. Outcomes included increased opportunity to start a business, sense of pride, confidence, independence, ability to manage finances, more financial security, and greater opportunities for social networking.

Social networking is another outcome of microenterprise. In case studies, Servon finds that MDP programs build social networks among borrowers within a program and among organizations. The first type, built through peer lending and training activities, results in customer referrals, building of social support, and increased access into business networks. The second type, created through contracts and informal relationships with an array of organizations, "begin to alter norms within these institutions," and help link participants to more resources (Servon, 1999, 112).

Flexibility in family responsibility, especially for female-headed households, is cited as one reason why women choose to start small businesses, especially home-based. For women with young children, microenterprise may facilitate greater flexibility for parenting and child care (Novogratz, 1992), but evidence of this is not yet established.

Turning to other possible effects on families, it is not uncommon for family members, including children, to assist in running the business. According to one study (SEID), thirty children of respondents had worked in these businesses on an unpaid basis (Raheim, 1996). Notwithstanding cautions about child labor, the experience of modest time working in a family-owned business may have important psychological and social benefits for children, including self-efficacy, self-esteem, and future economic self-sufficiency. This possibility merits future studies.

Overall, research has only begun to document motivations and outcomes for low-income workers who have chosen to enter self-employment. Most studies have focused on financial outcomes. Examining such outcomes is critical from the standpoint of knowing whether people are moving out of poverty, but they do not tell the full story.

Existing research also has done little to provide a connection between theory and empirical evidence. Lacking in current research is systematic in-depth examination of the experience of microenterprise from the perspective of participants, and how such experiences reflect on theory. This book contributes to the existing research evidence on microenterprise through a detailed accounting of microenterprise through the eyes of eighty-six microentrepreneurs. We explore why people undertake microbusiness, what they seek to accomplish, what they believe are the promising and problematic aspects of microenterprise, and how successful they are in achieving their goals.

Notes

1. If income sources are strongly correlated, that is, if they go up and down together, the ability to take risks is decreased.

2. A small business is defined as an independent business with fewer than 500 employees (SBA, 2003b).

3. This percentage is based on a sample of 61 due to missing data.

4. This percentage is based on a sample of 30, which is only about half of open businesses.

5. Findings from SELP should be interpreted with some caution due to missing data and outliers. Additionally, most findings in Clark, et al. (1999) are reported in percentages and means when numbers and medians would sometimes be more informative.

6. This includes both poor and non-poor self-employed.

CHAPTER 3

Who Wants to Be a Microentrepreneur and Why?

—Co-authored with Fred Ssewamala

Many Americans, at one time or another, have thought about opening a business. Some are struck with an inspired business idea. Others face dead-end jobs, an insufferable boss, or an inflexible work environment. In the end, most decide that the great business idea is too risky, and the job, while not perfect, is a better bet than trying to run a business.

For a variety of reasons, the entrepreneurs in this study did not back out. For some it was an opportunity that presented itself, and they decided to take a chance. For example, Terri saw microenterprise as an opportunity to get ahead, even though the idea of being a business owner had never occurred to her before: "*I was in barber college just about ready to graduate [when] I got a letter in the mail with [my] welfare check that said that they had the [microenterprise] program and they'll help you start your own business. So that's the only thing that gave me the idea. That was in 1990, and I haven't been on welfare since.*" For Terri, the idea of operating her own business was somewhat serendipitous, offering a way for her to use her new skills, a way that she had not previously considered.

Others decided to open a business primarily because of bleak job prospects. Mary, for example, saw in microenterprise a way to avoid a fruitless job search: "*I was going through a divorce, I was on welfare, baby-sitting and all, child care and stuff. What would I do? I didn't want to work in a factory and there wasn't really any other opportunity around this area at the time.*" So when she learned about the microenterprise development program (MDP), she decided to give her idea of a small liquor establishment a try. Other entrepreneurs, especially those living in rural Arizona and Arkansas and in other areas where scarce jobs were poorly paid and often temporary, had similar experiences. Self-employment presented a possible alternative.

Terri and Mary had not thought much about opening a business prior to learning about the MDP, but most of the entrepreneurs had given business ownership a great deal of thought. Possessed with a drive to own a business long before they heard of an MDP, they seized the chance to get some assistance. For example, Thomas's desire to own a business was deeply ingrained by the time he had opened his catering service: "*I wanted to try to start something on my own. It has been real successful so far. . . . Hustling has always been in my blood.*" Likewise, Glenn had always wanted to have his own business: "*I've been thinking about owning my own business since I was seven. I've always loved being my own boss . . . I don't like working for other people, and operate better if I have no one to answer to.*"

The Microentrepreneurs

The microentrepreneurs whose stories fill these pages are women and men, old and young, White, African American, Latino/a, and Asian. Some barely finished elementary school, while others had attended some college. Some live in rural areas and others in urban and suburban areas throughout the United States. Their businesses vary from small home-based resale enterprises to storefront retail establishments, to semi-professional and professional services. Some businesses are successful; others are not. But these entrepreneurs share three things: a desire to have a business, involvement in one of a growing number of MDPs, and low household income. This chapter introduces the eighty-six microentrepreneurs and explores their reasons for business ownership.

The entrepreneurs live in the seven states where the SELP (Self-Employment Learning Project) microenterprise programs are located: Arizona, Arkansas, California, Illinois, Iowa, Minnesota, and North Carolina. Compared to the U.S. population with low incomes, the SELP entrepreneurs are somewhat more likely to be non-white, female, and to have more education and higher incomes (Table 3.1).[1] African Americans and Latinos of Mexican descent make up almost half of the sample. Educational attainment is higher than among the poor generally, likely a result of self-selection. Seventeen (29 percent) have a high school degree, GED, or vocational degree. About a third had attended some college, although only eighteen (16 percent) had a college degree or more.[2] When the study began in 1991, the entrepreneurs had household incomes of less than 150 percent of poverty.[3] Household incomes ranged from $2,546 to $38,035 per year with a median income of $12,395.[4] More than a third (36 percent) owned their own homes, about the same as the poor overall. Although the entrepreneurs have slightly higher incomes, they are more likely to be receiving public assistance. Several MDPs targeted recipients of public assistance. As a result, thirty-six (42 percent) of the entrepreneurs in this study

Table 3.1
Demographic Characteristics of SELP Participants
and the U.S. Poor, 1991*

	U.S. Poor (Under 150% poverty)[a] (%)	Low-Income SELP Respondents[b] (n = 86) (%)
Race/ethnicity		
White	60	51
African American	22	31
Latino	13	17
Other non-Hispanic	4	1
Gender		
Female	50	78[c]
Male	50	22
Age		
18 to 20	2	0
21 to 29	28	11
30 to 39	29	33
40 to 49	18	38
50 to 59	14	12
60 to 65	9	7[d]
Education		
8th grade or less	15	12
Some high school	24	7
High school degree or equivalent	29	29
Some college	23	34
Bachelors' degree	6	16
Post college	2	2
Marital status		
Married	36	40[e]
Separated/divorced	29	35
Widowed	7	6
Never married	27	19
Household composition		
Average household size	3.1	3.5
Children less than 6	33	33
Income poverty		
At or below 100% of poverty	63	47
Home ownership	33	36
Government benefits		
Public assistance[f]	24	42
SSI	12	6

*All may not add to 100 percent due to rounding.

[a]1989 data based on 1990 decennial census public use microsample file, 1 sample for U.S. head of households excluding heads under 18 and over 65 (N = 13,775,791). Compiled by the Office of Social and Economic Data Analysis, University of Missouri.

[b]A few participants in the SELP low income sample had incomes over 150 percent of poverty. These are discussed in Chapter Four.

[c]Includes 22 married women who may or may not be considered the head of household.

[d]Includes 2 persons over 65 years old.

[e]Includes 2 entrepreneurs with live-in partners.

[f]Includes those who received either AFDC, Food Stamps, or both.

received public assistance and/or food assistance for at least one month in 1991, almost twice as many as the poor.[5]

In wave one of the study, 60 percent of the participants were single heads of households (separated, divorced, widowed, or never married). Most of these operated their businesses without the benefit of another full-time wage earner in the household. A third also had a child under six years of age. Almost one-fifth of the entrepreneurs were age fifty or over, including six over the age of sixty. Seven were disabled and received disability benefits, and another two had spouses receiving disability benefits. Some disabilities were the result of work-related accidents, such as Catarina's, whose severe back injury was the result of a farm labor accident. Several others had physical problems that made it difficult to acquire or keep a job, although they did not receive disability benefits.

Although the demographic profile suggests that the microentrepreneurs in this study entered self-employment with relatively low educational preparation and few household resources, they were older, more likely to be women and African American or Latino, and have higher educational attainment, and slightly more income, than the poor as a whole. Their marital status, household composition, and homeownership rates, however, were similar to the rest of the poor population.

The fifteen Latino entrepreneurs were older, more likely to be married, had less education, but also had more experience in business. Four of the Latino entrepreneurs were over the age of fifty-five and nine were married, larger proportions than among Whites and Blacks. The Latino entrepreneurs tended also to have less formal education. Thirteen (87 percent) had less than a high school education, including eight (53 percent) with less than eight years of schooling. Only two Whites and six African Americans had less than a high school education or equivalent. Less education may be a result of being older on average and the fact that several grew up in rural Mexico where access to education beyond elementary school is more limited. Latino entrepreneurs were more likely to have had prior business experience in Mexico and in the United States. Informal self-employment (e.g., child care, housecleaning, and laundry services), is a common income-generation strategy for Mexican immigrants as part of the household income-packaging strategy (Raijman, 2001). Discrimination based on language and ethnicity and limitations based on citizenship status may also have contributed to the decision to seek informal self-employment.

Opening a Business

Why did the entrepreneurs choose self-employment when it is well-known that small businesses have high failure rates? The demographic profile suggests that the entrepreneurs may have experienced disadvantages in the labor market that drove them to self-employment (Light & Rosenstein, 1995). At the same time, their household resources were relatively low, making business ownership challenging. What did the entrepreneurs say?[6]

Almost half (44 percent) said that having a business was a long-time dream. As Anne, a baker, said: *"It was one of those things I had thought about for a long time but never got it off the ground. . . . I wanted to be my own boss and earn money at something I liked doing."* While acknowledging the hard work involved, many of the entrepreneurs expressed a high level of motivation for business ownership.

Many of the entrepreneurs had prior exposure to business, including seventeen who mentioned that a family member owned a business at one time (Table 3.2). These included informal businesses, such as small home-based retail operations, and formal businesses, such as a sports facility. Early exposure to business offered the entrepreneurs an opportunity to observe, and, in many instances, to work in a family-owned business. Several talked about how they learned about business. In several instances, businesses were inherited from a parent. The link between entrepreneurial drive and family business experience was clear in Fred's case. He said that his business owner/father, was an *"inspiration"* to him. Peggy, who recently had merged her own business with her mother's, said: *"My mother has been a huge role model."*

Sometimes a single event, which Mokry (1988) calls an "entrepreneurial event," precipitated a decision to try self-employment. An important entrepreneurial event for some of the people in this study was change in welfare policy. As welfare-to-work policies gathered force in the 1980s and early 1990s, public welfare departments created strategies to move former welfare recipients into employment. Some states made new provisions that allowed for self-employment to qualify as a work option. In Iowa, for example, information was enclosed along with welfare checks inviting beneficiaries to attend information sessions on self-employment. Several individuals who previously had not been thinking about self-employment were intrigued and attended these sessions. Some decided to try their hands at business ownership, including Terri, who earlier recounted her decision to begin a business while she was training to become a barber, and Yolanda, who was interested as soon as she heard about it: *"It was the moment that it was announced. The ad talked about women who would like to open a business. But until seeing that ad, it had never occurred to me."* Many others also said that the MDP stimulated their interest in starting a business. In this way, policy motivated a significant number of entrepreneurs to open a business. The existence of a new kind of institution (the MDP) and policy change (welfare reform) created an opportunity that did not exist previously.

In addition to "pull factors" that draw people to self-employment, there are "push factors" that nudge them toward it (Messenger & Stettner, 2000).[7]

Table 3.2
Prior Exposure to Business as Motivation for Opening a Business

Business Ownership in Family of Origin Influenced the Decision to Open a Business (n = 17)[1]
- Mother owned flower arrangement business in Mexico
- Mother owned an art gallery
- Mother owned a janitorial business
- Mother owned a business (unspecified)
- Mother owned a business (unspecified)
- Mother owned a business in Mexico
- Mother owned jewelry business in Mexico
- Mother owned an antique store
- Mother owned a hair salon
- Father owned a "*side*" business (unspecified)
- Father owned craft business in Mexico
- Father and brother-in-law owned businesses (unspecified)
- Family owned clothing business in Mexico
- Family owned a sports facility
- Family owned an upholstery business
- Family owned crafts business, grandmother made and sold quilts
- Cousin owned a business (unspecified)

Entrepreneurs' Prior Self-Employment that Influenced the Decision to Open a Business (n = 12)
- Operated barbershop with husband
- Engaged in door-to-door retail sales
- Owned a bar
- Was a self-employed domestic
- Sold floral arrangements
- Sold clothing and toys
- Sold Avon and worked with husband's business
- Husband created business and she expanded with new retail line
- Owned a nightclub
- Made and sold wooden toys
- Was self-employed (unspecified)
- Owned various small businesses (unspecified) in Mexico

[1]The entrepreneurs identified these businesses when they were asked what motivated them to open a business. These are listed in no particular order. Level of specificity varies according to descriptions by the entrepreneurs.

For example, Marta, who had a home-based retail clothing business, said that her mother was a business role model who drew her to business, but she was also pushed toward business by a very unattractive job market: "*When I came to the U.S., I came, as they say, to 'work like a dog in a laundry'. . . . Even the mind atrophies when people work like a donkey. But I knew I had the potential to work for myself. My mom has always been a great salesperson, selling jewelry or anything she could in Mexico. I think I have inherited that trait.*"

Low wages and insecure jobs also encouraged the entrepreneurs to try self-employment. Among those reporting, eighty (93 percent) earned less than $10 per hour (Table 3.3). The fifteen higher-wage earners (wages above $8 per hour) appear advantaged in several respects. Nonetheless, they did not necessarily have good and stable jobs. Only eight of these top earners said they left their jobs of their own volition because they wanted to start a business. Five of them said they went into business at least in part because their jobs were terminated or they were laid off, including one who was fired because she would not work on the Sabbath. One was unemployed prior to starting a business and another was laid off before going back to school prior to starting a business. Another left his job in woodworking because it was *"too dangerous."*

Most of the other entrepreneurs held jobs with little stability or opportunity for advancement. Typical of what have been called "the working poor," most of the jobs were low paying, dead-end, with few or no benefits (Piore & Sabel, 1984; Newman, 1999).[8] The entrepreneurs said they lacked job security. Many had been terminated or laid-off from their jobs just prior to starting their businesses. For instance, Robert, who worked in meat packing prior to opening his business reported: *"I'd been working in a place twelve years, and it shut down, and every place else seemed to be shutting down too, so I did it more out of necessity. . . . It was just a bad time for trying to find a job, so I figured I had to create one somehow."* Vera lost her last position as a data entry clerk, and found she could not get another decent job even though she tried looking with the help of a job placement agency. She said that the available jobs were low paying and lacked benefits. Laurel worked in what she called the *"pink-collar ghetto"* for about ten years. She was tired of being classified and paid as a clerical worker, while she was skilled in editing, typing, desktop publishing, and producing manuscripts and documents. Although she often dreamed of owning her own publishing business, she did not have the impetus to do it until she was fired: *"So when I was more or less booted out to spread my wings, or go do this again somewhere else, I opted to spread my wings and start my own business."* Gwen said she *"would rather worry about running my business and have less money, than worry about losing a job somewhere else."* Cassandra said that while it is important to realize that *"You aren't going to make a big business overnight. . . . Nothing is definite anymore. Life is so mixed up. People get laid off all over."* At least *"when you have your own business, they can't fire you or lay you off."*

To many, self-employment also looked better than a job with no career opportunities. Ed felt exploited in his low-wage job: *"I couldn't find anything local that would pay more than minimum wage. I had worked for a number of different people. Over a period of time I wanted to be able to do something more than work for someone else and make them a profit. I wanted to make a profit for myself."* Marta quit her job at a laundry because, she said simply, *"it*

Table 3.3
Last Full-Time Job,* Hourly Wage, Adjusted Wage, and Business
Longevity, n = 86

Type of Employment	Hourly Wage**	Hourly Wage*** (1991)	Last Year Worked FT	Start-up or Existing Business
Director, health clinic	$21.63	26.88	1986	Start
Plant manager	16.03	15.56	1992	Start
Account representative	15.38	15.38	1991	——
Accountant	14.42	14.00	1992	Start
Legal secretary	10.00	10.98	1989	Start
Landscape consulting	10.00	10.00	1991	——
Self-employed (unspecified)	9.72	14.72	1973	Start
Store manager	9.62	9.07	1993	Start
Travel agency manager	9.40	9.40	1991	Start
Clerk	9.35	9.08	1992	Start
Food service	9.00	9.38	1990	Start
Administrator, nursing facility	8.65	9.50	1989	Start
Shop manager	8.55	9.39	1989	Existing
Cabinet maker	8.46	21.57	1987	Existing
Auto body technician	8.17	8.17	1991	Start
Sales manager	7.69	7.69	——	Start
Program coordinator	7.50	8.24	1989	Start
Claims clerk	7.21	10.81	1981	Existing
Pastry chef	7.00	8.06	1988	Start
Dispatcher	6.73	6.73	1991	Start
Specialist, activities department	6.73	6.73	1991	Start
Upholsterer	6.67	6.95	1990	Start
Salesman	6.60	6.60	1991	Existing
Meat cutter/packaging	6.50	6.50	1991	Start
Public relations	6.35	6.35	1991	Start
Instructor	6.25	14.05	——	Start
Janitor	6.25	7.20	1988	Existing
Line operator	6.25	6.51	1990	Start
Cashier	6.25	6.51	1990	Start
Accounts data entry	6.25	6.51	1990	Start
Manager	6.25	6.25	1991	Start
Food co-op	6.25	6.25	——	Existing
Beautician	6.25	8.19	1984	Start
Secretary	6.25	6.07	1992	Start
Firefighter	6.18	13.89	1977	Start
Self-employed nurse's aide	6.00	6.25	1990	Start
Information clerk	6.00	14.35	1976	——
Teaching assistant	5.77	6.64	1988	Existing
Apartment manager	5.77	6.64	1988	Start
Construction	5.71	5.95	1990	Existing
Youth counselor	5.50	5.73	1990	Start
Maintenance company supervisor	5.50	5.50	1991	Start
Community services caseworker	5.31	5.00	1993	Start
Field worker/machine driver	5.26	7.88	1981	Existing
Data entry	5.25	5.77	1989	Start
Seamstress	5.00	5.49	1989	Start
Carpet retail and installation	5.00	8.26	1980	Existing

(*continued*)

Table 3.3 (*continued*)
Last Full-Time Job,* Hourly Wage, Adjusted Wage, and Business
Longevity, n = 86

Type of Employment	Hourly Wage**	Hourly Wage*** (1991)	Last Year Worked FT	Start-up or Existing Business
Factory assembler	5.00	19.57	1968	Start
Subcontractor, janitorial	5.00	4.85	1992	Start
Day care center teacher	4.87	6.16	1985	Existing
Sales person	4.86	4.58	1993	Start
Mover	4.82	4.82	1991	Existing
Nurse's aide	4.81	4.81	1991	Start
Instructor	4.80	11.50	1976	Existing
Carpenter	4.80	5.27	1989	Existing
Clerk, bookstore	4.65	5.35	1988	Start
Retail clerk liquor store	4.57	4.76	1990	Start
Secretary, office manager	4.44	4.44	1991	Start
Drafting technician	4.38	4.81	1989	Existing
Cook	4.30	4.30	1991	Start
Self-employed	4.28	4.03	1993	Start
Administrative assistant	4.27	4.15	1992	Start
Waitress	4.00	4.39	1989	Existing
Head waitress	4.00	4.17	1990	Start
Machine assembler	4.00	8.99	1977	Start
Seamstress	3.85	3.85	1991	Start
Buyer	3.75	3.91	1990	Start
Receptionist	3.57	5.04	1982	Start
Domestic worker	3.57	4.11	1988	Existing
Maid	3.35	4.16	1986	Existing
Laundry worker	3.13	3.44	1989	Existing
Clerk	3.08	3.69	1987	Existing
Cashier	3.00	4.10	1983	Start
Field worker	2.57	2.57	——	——
Self employed	2.50	——	1965	Existing
Nurse's aide	2.35	5.28	1977	Start
Field worker	1.75	5.70	1972	Existing
Homemaker	——	——	1986	Existing
Manager	——	——	1982	Existing
Homemaker	0	0	——	Start
Full-time student	0	0	——	Start
Self-employed seamstress	——	——	Existing	
None	——	——	1989	Existing
Manufacturing	——	——	1975	Start

*Job titles as described by respondents. Many worked more than one job, but those that appear were the main source of income.

**Hourly wage figures were derived from entrepreneur reports of weekly wages divided by hours worked.

***In 1991 dollars adjusted using the CPI-U from the Bureau of Labor Statistics (BLS). Wages as reported by respondents and adjusted to 1991 dollars are listed because not all wages in all occupations changed at the same rate. This may be particularly true of low-wage service sector jobs (e.g., see "factory assembler") that may not have kept pace with inflation. In cases where the year is missing, dollars are unadjusted.

had no future." As she made the decision, she also thought about her children—she did not want her children to think that they would also end up in that kind of work.

Some believed that self-employment was the best option because of the harassment and discrimination they experienced in former jobs. Most were African American, Hispanic, women, people of advanced age, or people with disabilities. Sergio reported that he took his prior job with a janitorial company only as a last resort because he *"was desperate for work."* They did not pay well and *"we were mistreated. It was like the KKK [Ku Klux Klan]."* Outright discrimination convinced some to consider self-employment. Lessie said that race played *"a big role"* in her decision to pursue microenterprise. In her previous work as a police officer she was treated poorly because she was African American and a woman. She saw self-employment as a way to avoid biased treatment. A number of people living with disabilities chose self-employment because it offered more opportunities and greater dignity.[9] Kathleen, a masseuse, said that she was *"treated as a second-class citizen"* in former jobs: *"I was discriminated against because I am a woman . . . discriminated against because I am disabled, and . . . discriminated against because of my age."* She said her job options were so poor that even if self-employment did not work, it was no loss to her: *"I was already on rock bottom, so it didn't matter if it [the business] failed or didn't."* Catarina, who was disabled, found self-employment to be her only option for earning income other than low-paid, physically demanding work as a farm laborer: *"I worked for a while in the asparagus [fields] and different things . . . but when the heat picked up in April I thought I just couldn't tolerate it, so I found a little stand and began to sell."* Although she knew self-employment would pay little more than subsistence, she chose it because it would accommodate her disability and also it would offer self-respect. Similarly, Carol said that her physical difficulties, as well as those of her husband, made working in a job difficult: *"My husband always had health problems and I have rheumatoid arthritis and it's difficult for me to do a lot of things. . . ."*

Microenterprise Goals

Once the decision to open a business was made, what were the entrepreneurs' goals for their enterprises?

It seems logical that most people would start a small business to earn money. The desire to earn money, however, was matched or surpassed by other goals (Table 3.4).[10] Given the many routes to self-employment, this is perhaps not too surprising. The goals mentioned most often were a desire to make a living and to improve their quality of life.

Table 3.4
Primary, Secondary, and Tertiary Goals of Microenterprise (1996)

Goal	Primary (%)	Secondary (%)	Tertiary (%)	Total No. (%)
Make a living				
Full income	47.7	12.8	1.2	53 (26.0)
Partial income	15.1	12.8	2.3	25 (12.3)
Self-fulfillment and personal growth	8.1	18.6	9.3	49 (24.0)
Control and autonomy	11.6	23.3	1.2	31 (15.2)
Flexibility	11.6	7.0	5.8	20 (9.8)
Develop assets	3.5	10.5	8.1	18 (8.8)
Community service	2.3	3.5	3.5	8 (3.9)
Total	**86 (100.0)**	**64**	**22**	**204 (100.0)**

Secondary and tertiary goals do not total 86 because some entrepreneurs did not list more than one or two goals.

Making a Living

Making a living or supporting the household was the primary goal for half the entrepreneurs (Table 3.4). One group wanted to develop a business that would support their families. For a few, that meant making it "*big*" in business. Chester, who thought about owning a business for a long time, said that he believed he could benefit financially from owning a business: "*As time progressed, I moved up as a plant manager for a company. They were paying me an outrageous salary that I couldn't believe. I got to thinking, if these guys can pay me this kind of money, why not start my own thing?*" Most were more modest and just wanted to support their families (Tables 3.4, 3.5). Robert, for example, said he "*had to support [my family] somehow.*" Similarly, Gwen said her goal was "*to just be independent, to be able to support my kids and myself.*" Life circumstances had forced some to start a business, like Iris, "*to make ends meet.*" She had lost her husband just before opening the business, and hoped her business would provide income and hope: "*Losing my husband, it threw me into a downward spiral . . . but now, I'm on the road again and having positive thoughts.*" A few others tied their decision to open a business to trying to become financially independent of the welfare system.

Some entrepreneurs wanted only to supplement family income (Table 3.5). As Jeannette commented, "*I am not trying to do big business. I guess you would classify this as more or less a hobby, but every little penny I make helps.*" This was often true for older entrepreneurs like Jeannette, who said they wanted to supplement social security or disability payments. Out of the thirteen

Table 3.5
Types of Goals and Reasons for Microenterprise Goals

Make a living
- Full income: support family, financial independence, no job, job loss, quit job, no other income, lack of full-time/ year-round jobs.
- Full income: alternative to job/labor market, want to earn decent wage, need full-time, year-round job.
- Full income: Want to get off welfare, become self-sufficient.
- Partial income: Want to supplement existing family income, help with bills, pay for extras.

Flexibility (family, children, health)
- Time to deal with children, be at home for kids.
- In location to take care of children or other person.
- To work in a setting that accommodates poor health, can set own pace after accident, keep healthy.

Control and autonomy
- Autonomy: Be own boss, be in control, set own hours, run things own way, plan own life, work for self, have control of decisions (also, no interference from a boss, not work for someone else, not be tied to a desk).
- Lifestyle of entrepreneur, like "selling."
- Ownership: Always wanted to own a business, always wanted to do a particular activity, have something of my own.

Self-fulfillment and personal growth
- Pride: Run a business well, be successful, test abilities to develop a business.
- Do something they love, devotion to product, enjoys the business.
- Express creativity.
- Keep busy, meet people.

Develop assets (financial and/or human capital)
- Using business to learn skills, build human capital.
- Offer children an example (role model) and a way to build children's human capital.
- Future investment: Extra money to save for future use, pass on to children, save to buy a house.
- Want to grow a large business.

Community service
- Help others, provide a service to community or population group (e.g., children minority community), be a role model for others in community, mission or calling (religious overtones).

---

respondents over age fifty-five, six were seeking partial income. Doña Gloria noted: "*I am a widow and I live solely from my husband's Social Security, and I was motivated thinking about how I could get ahead on my payments. . . .*" An additional income source sometimes meant that quality of life might improve a little, or as Doña Chela, another older businesswoman, pointed out, "*when a person sells, they never lack a peso in their pocket.*"

Some younger entrepreneurs also planned to supplement household income. Marilyn started her business after her mother, who owned a salon, *"got some mail selling pocketbooks and T-shirts and all these things from the factory, and she sent in, and got a book. She told me 'here's some things if you want to do something on the side, make a little extra money.' I was in school at the time. So I decided to go ahead and do it."* Even Leticia, with her successful sewing business, said, *"the goal was to have an opportunity to earn some money to help my husband with household expenses."*

Some did not talk as much about making money, and some even emphasized that money was not the principal goal of their business. Donna said that she preferred a simple lifestyle and did not need much money. Clara viewed her business as more of spiritual mission: *"I did not focus on profits. I had blinders on when it came to money. But I thought I was going in the right direction at the time. I was very excited."* Among the entrepreneurs who said their first goal was to earn income, they said that other goals were also important.

Self-fulfillment and Personal Growth

Business owners expressed a desire for self-fulfillment, personal growth, and recognition. They wanted to be successful, to be challenged, to do something they love, to keep busy, to meet people, and to express their creativity. Heather *"wanted to succeed at something,"* as did Thomas who said, *"I wanted to try to start something on my own."* Shirley liked the challenge: *"I wanted to prove to myself that I could do it. I am that kind of person, always taking on challenges."* Others wanted to do something more interesting, including Eleanor, who articulated it this way: *"I was doing something positive with myself, not just sitting at home being a couch potato."* For Renée, her business allowed her to be at home with her son and to do something creative. Angie had worked in jobs for other people but *"they didn't give me the incentive to want to grow."* Sometimes the reward of being recognized for doing an excellent job was more important than a desire to make a lot of money.

Others believed that business would provide a way for them to help their children. Female and male entrepreneurs said that children absorb ambition and learn work skills through observation and that watching their parents work in a business would be good for them. Anita said she wanted *"to be a good example"* for her children. Stacy, for example, wanted her two young sons to know what they could accomplish in their lives. She especially wanted them to realize this before others came along and told them what they could *not* do. Marta wanted to teach her *"daughters how to work. . . ."* Theresa also hoped that her business would have a long-term impact on her child: *"I hope through my stumbling I will eventually walk and then run, as far as the business goes. And I hope that it will leave an impression on my son that he can not only work for somebody else, but he can do his own thing, that he can chart out his own course."*

Control and Autonomy

A sense of control was an important goal for many of the entrepreneurs. Poor work conditions and lack of decent pay and benefits led to a strong desire in many cases for greater control over work life. Like Lessie, who opened chapter 1, the choice between a job and being one's own boss was clear; she wanted to be *"independent."*

This yearning for independence was echoed in many interviews. Anita, who left her work in housecleaning to open her business, said, *"When you own your own business, you feel liberated."* John said that he liked being *"king of my own domain,"* while Yolanda wanted to be *"her own boss,"* and Doris also admitted that she liked *"to be the one in control,"* admitting that she was *"not a rules-and-regulations-type of individual."* Sara said, *"I've always been an independent person. I did not last long at jobs where I have a boss hanging over my head . . ."* Others emphasized a desire to set their own schedules. Paula said that she was *"tired of pushing a clock"*; as did Ed, who said, *"I don't like punching a time card. I like the freedom to be able to come and go as I please. That [is] one reason [why] I got involved in another business and I'll probably get involved in another business."*

According to Eleanor, the opportunity to make her own decisions were worth the economic risks of self-employment: *"I would rather work for myself because there is so much out there going on, you have to put up with so much. If I work for myself, I just have to put up with myself. If I make it good, it's good, and if I mess up, I've messed up."* Entrepreneurship offered an alternative to low-paid jobs and a variety of indignities. As Cassandra said, she chose business in part because: *". . . I did not want nobody to think 'you're stupid, and I'll give you two dollars and this is all you get.'"* Not only did business offer the possibility of more dignified work, it might also offer greater control over their future. As Marta said: *"In a regular job you have to work many years in order to retire. But with your own business you can decide the age of retirement. I would prefer my own business because I know that with my own business I have the potential to carry it forward. I am going to work more perhaps, but I can achieve more in my own business than in another place."*

Flexibility

Many participants said they wanted flexibility to meet their multiple responsibilities, including caring for young children and being available to participate in activities with their children at school and at other places; caring for other family members; or caring for their own health (Table 3.5).[11] Most of all, we heard about the need to have time and a flexible schedule to care for children. Lanette said she had always thought about opening her own business, but as she grew tired of working odd hours at a hospital and increasingly wanted to spend more time with her children, she *"just decided to . . . jump out there and do it. . . . I didn't want to return to a straight nine-to-five job and wanted to spend more time with my daughter."* As Leticia recalled:

> *Well, the motive that I had to begin working for myself was that I have two daughters who at that time were babies, and the problem was that I had no one to take care of them for me—they would not take care of them well—so I began to talk to my friends and tell them that I wasn't going to go to work [in a wage job], that I was going to stay at home, and if they needed any alterations or work done, that I could do it for them. It was my own choice because I knew how to do the work, and one day I thought to myself, "What would be a way to care for my daughters and at the same time work?"*

For people with disabilities, self-employment offered the flexibility to choose work that was more in tune with their physical limitations. Catarina who suffered from back pain and other health problems, and whose only job opportunity was migrant agricultural work, said: *"I had to work like a man. When the heat of April came along, I didn't know if I could endure it."* Self-employment offered her the option of working in conditions that were better suited to her health condition. Kathleen also suffered from chronic pain that prevented her from holding a job, but she wanted to *"start doing something"* because she had become *"shut off from society,"* and decided that self-employment would offer the kind of flexible work she needed.

Develop Financial Assets

Another reason why entrepreneurs began their businesses was to increase their families' economic assets. As Jackie pointed out, owning something tangible was important. She believed it gave her family a purpose that could not be attained through traditional employment: *"Every family should own something, even if it is a home-based business. The system is set up to keep you just getting by."*

Several hoped to pass their business on to their children. For example, Thomas's second-most important motivation, (after income), *"was having something that was owned by me and my family. Just having something that I could give to my kids."* As Renée asked rhetorically: *"You have to be focused on what it is that you really want. You have to look at long term and short term goals. Do you want to pass on the business to your children?"* Catarina also said that part of the reason why she opened a business was the question: *"When I die what will I leave for [my daughter]?"* Others wanted to have enough money saved from the business to pay for children's education, such as Gloria who said, "*I would like to be able to send them to college and stuff like that when they get older.*"

Two entrepreneurs started their businesses thinking that they would be able to earn enough money to purchase a home. As Rose said somewhat tentatively, "*And maybe I could even buy a house, you know?*" Nicole, too, asserted that "*one of my main goals was to get a house.*"

Some intended to save enough from their businesses to help them return to school. Sharon wanted to support herself but also to save enough to go back to school. Carlos was explicit about his goal: "*It was a transitional thing; I knew it wouldn't last much time. I wanted to have a career and afterward work in something better.*" Although he intended to return to Mexico eventually, the poor economic situation there convinced him that it would be better to save money and go back to school first.

Community Service

Some chose self-employment because it offered an opportunity to serve others and to make a contribution to the community. For example, Susan, who ran an adult day care center, said she realized that this kept older people in the community longer. Cassandra, too, opened her business in part because she "*was trying to help somebody*" by producing large-size clothing for overweight teens. Speaking of one of her customers, she said, "*If I could just make her a nice print, a nice pattern, and put a heart, or a flower on the pair of panties, and put some lace around it, she wouldn't mind changing clothes [in gym].*" Sometimes religious commitments influenced the choice of business, including Carol, who explained her motivation for opening her books-on-tape business: "*It's been more . . . a heart thing, . . . a love of helping kids.*"

Others had a desire to be a role model in the community. Fred stated that it was important to him to carry on the tradition and reputation of his father, who had started the family business. Stacy also wanted to be a role model, not only for her children, but also for the African American community as a whole. A number of people who shopped at her store had opened their own businesses, and she had provided guidance to several of them. Lessie, a hairstylist, chose her business partly to make people feel good: "*I made people look good, and that made people feel good. . . . How the people felt when they left, that was my number-one concern. True story.*"

Overlapping Goals

As Table 3.4 shows, many entrepreneurs had more than one goal. While the majority hoped to support, or help support, their household income, most had other goals as well. Glenn, for instance, wanted to "*work at home, be my own boss, have time for the kids, as well as make enough money to support that*." Renée wanted time to spend with her son, make money, work in a creative job, and serve others. Carol wanted to earn enough to exit welfare, gain a sense of self-fulfillment through her work with children, but also to find work that would accommodate hers and her husband's physical limitations. Catarina ranked income high on her list, but added that she wanted to avoid turning to welfare and Food Stamps and hoped to have a business to pass on to her daughter. Yvonne said that she started her business because she thought that selling cosmetics would get her out of the house, and it also let her care for her child and make a little extra money at the same time.

The Decision to Open a Business

How do these experiences help us better understand motivations for microenterprise? What theoretical perspectives are supported?

The decision to open a business took into account employment options, household financial necessities, personal goals, and family needs. Past business experience and opportunity pulled some toward business, drawn by positive memories of family businesses, past business experience, and the desired lifestyle of a business owner. Family members, friends, and MDP staff provided encouragement. At the same time, unpleasant job experiences, low pay, and poor job alternatives pushed many toward self-employment. Even those who earned relatively higher pay (over $8 per hour) in prior jobs reported that they felt insecure, and several had been laid off or fired prior to opening a business.

We find in this chapter that the entrepreneurs believed that business might offer opportunities for better earnings, an assessment that might support human capital theory. Although they believed they might be able to put their skills to better use in self-employment than in the labor market, an assessment of their skills and credentials suggests that they would have little human capital advantage in either business or labor market.

The extent to which several entrepreneurs saw self-employment as a way to make extra money also provides support for the idea of income diversification, or as it has come to be known, income patching. Several of the entrepreneurs said that they were not aiming to operate large businesses, but rather wanted an additional source of income. In support of asset theory, some entrepreneurs explicitly chose microenterprise as a way to increase their families' assets through business ownership and homeownership.

Another reason why the entrepreneurs chose business was because they faced disadvantage in the labor market. Just as Ivan Light and Carolyn Rosenstein (1995) say, some entrepreneurs choose business for "value" reasons, and others choose business because of "disadvantage" in the labor market.

Disadvantaged entrepreneurs choose business because they can make more money in self-employment than in a labor market characterized by discrimination and unfair treatment. As we have seen, many of the entrepreneurs in this study said they encountered discrimination, harassment, and other disadvantage in prior jobs because of age, race, ethnicity, gender, or disability. Some believed that microenterprise offered a way to avoid this treatment and possibly be more successful than they could in the job market.

We identify at least twenty entrepreneurs who said that they had encountered discrimination in the job market. The majority are women, lending support to feminist theory. A conservative estimate, these entrepreneurs mentioned discrimination among their reasons for choosing microenterprise. (These findings are striking especially because we did not ask directly about prior employment discrimination.) Among this group were eight African Americans, who referred to various difficulties in the job market because of their race, including five women, who said that gender compounded their difficulties in the job market. Two were also over the age of 65. Eight were White, including seven women who discussed various forms of gender discrimination. Three of the White entrepreneurs were over 55 years of age, including one man. Four were Latina, including one who was over 65 years of age, and another who had a physical disability.

Although most entrepreneurs aimed to earn full or partial income from their business, non-monetary goals were very important. As predicted by compensating differential theory, the entrepreneurs identified a range of goals that had little to do with earnings. The evidence here suggests that personal growth and development, control over work lives, and family well-being were important factors in choosing self-employment. Light and Rosenstein argue that so-called value entrepreneurs are not necessarily aiming to earn more than they could in the job market. In fact, they often earn less: ". . . those who have accepted financial disadvantage just to become entrepreneurs have demonstrated that social values (not money) prompted their occupational choice" (1995, 213). Most of the entrepreneurs in this study said that they had non-monetary goals for their businesses, such as personal growth and self-fulfillment, autonomy, control over their work lives, flexibility, being a role model for their children, and contributing to their community.

Because both groups sought monetary and non-monetary rewards, it is difficult to distinguish fully between "value" and "disadvantaged" entrepreneurs. For example, many of the entrepreneurs believed that self-employment offered them flexibility to care for their children and for other family members. They believed that choosing self-employment would provide their children with a chance to learn some work skills and also to acquire a greater sense of self-worth and self-respect. Value entrepreneurs and disadvantaged entrepreneurs talked about self-employment in this way, although disadvantaged entrepreneurs stressed the importance of self-respect and value entrepreneurs emphasized the benefits of modeling entrepreneurial work habits. This supports the idea behind compensating differential theory, that individuals choosing self-employment may do so for its ability to provide a way to earn a living that has dignity and that allows flexibility to care for family members (Blau, et al., 1998).

In sum, the initial circumstances and goals for business suggest that the decision to open a business reflected efforts to maximize earnings in a work world with significant disadvantages, including discrimination in the labor market. Overall, human capital theory by itself falls far short in explaining motivations of these microentrepreneurs. At the same time, non-monetary factors were key in the decision to try business. Thus, compensating differential theory seems very much in play as an explanation. To this we return with greater specification and insight in chapter 8.

Notes

1. Data from 1989 is based on the 1990 decennial census public use microsample file, 1 percent sample for head of households excluding heads under 18 and over 65. Compiled by the Office of Social and Economic Data Analysis, University of Missouri.

2. More education is also typical of the self-employed in other studies. For example, one study showed that almost 50 percent of the self-employed in Kalamazoo, Michigan, had a bachelor's degree or higher compared to 24 percent of wage and salary workers (Erickcek, 1997, 3). Similarly, in Cleveland, 31 percent of the self-employed had higher degrees compared to 22 percent among the larger labor force. Similarly, survey data showed that approximately 50 percent of small business owners had a bachelor's degree or higher (Erickcek, 1997, 3).

3. This figure, $18,229 for a family of three, represents 150 percent of poverty in 1991 ($16,290) adjusted to 1995 dollars. All income figures are in 1995 dollars.

4. We include three entrepreneurs in the qualitative analysis who were interviewed, but later omitted from the quantitative analysis in chapter 5 because they were just over 150 percent of poverty in wave one.

5. The number reporting is 79.

6. When the entrepreneurs joined the SELP study in 1991, almost a third (30 percent) had started their businesses earlier, including 21 percent whose businesses were at least three years old.

7. Dennis (1996) found that people tend to choose self-employment because they prefer it to wage employment. Our conversations indicated that there is a complex calculus that includes both the lack of desirable jobs and existence of discrimination, in addition to the pull of what they considered to be the attractions of self-employment.

8. Although the situation improved later in the decade, in the mid-1990s low-skilled working people had experienced sharp declines in real wages (Mishel & Bernstein, 1995; Newman, 1999, 312).

9. Evans and Leighton (1989) also found that people with disabilities had higher rates of self-employment.

10. The goals identified by this group of entrepreneurs are similar to the findings from a study of 3,000 new small business owners (Cooper, et al., 1990). The reasons given for forming a business included to "use my skills and abilities," to have "greater control over my life," to "build something for my family," and I "liked the challenge." While the wording differs, the ideas behind each of these correspond to reasons that emerge in the present study. However, only 13 percent of the Cooper study (1990) described self-employment as the "best alternative available," while making a living was most important among our low-income respondents. This suggests that low-income entrepreneurs may choose self-employment for what Dennis calls "the wrong reason," because they have no reasonable alternatives (1996, 648).

11. Devine (1994) notes that women in self-employment were increasingly likely to have young children between 1975 and 1990. Other studies have found similar reasons for starting a microbusiness (Keeley, 1990; Raheim & Bolden, 1995; Cohen, et al., 1996, 9).

CHAPTER 4

Getting Started:
Resources for Microenterprise

In the late 1990s, residents of Westminster, Maryland, rallied together for the "muffin lady" (Fisher, 1997; Shaver, 1997). Selling her homemade muffins for $1.25 apiece off of her Radio Flyer wagon to shops along her seven-mile route through the town's streets, she earned about $400 a month. Along with subsidized housing and child support, she was able to sustain herself and her teenage son. She thought she had found a way to get off and stay off welfare. However, Carroll County Health Department officials viewed her by the bootstraps efforts as a danger to public health and shut her down because she did not have a "department-approved commercial kitchen." Residents of Westminster rallied to her side. In the words of a fire fighter, who along with his colleagues, came to the muffin lady's aid: "Here was an individual trying to help themselves, but didn't want to come in and ask for a handout from welfare." She was offered a car, money for her business license, but most important, free access to a state-approved kitchen. She returned to her baking and selling, hoping to become self-sustaining by the following year. How many low-income microentrepreneurs find this kind of business support during their business start-up?

Many of the eighty-six microenterprises in our study were like the "muffin lady." Most were small, home-based, and owner-operated businesses. Businesses ranged from retail and wholesale sales (34 percent), to small-scale production and manufacturing (29 percent), household and personal services (21 percent), and low- and semi-skilled and professional services (16 percent) (Table 4.1).[1] Only a fourth of the businesses had an employee, and only eight had more than one.

Like the "muffin lady," the entrepreneurs lacked a variety of human, financial, and social resources. Asked about the principal challenges they confronted as they launched their businesses,[2] the most common challenge was a

Table 4.1
Types and Location of Businesses, n = 86

Retail/Wholesale, n = 29 (15 home-based, 12 shop-based, 2 vending carts)

Accessories* (2)	home-based
Appliances (used)	home-based
Arts and crafts (2)	home-based
Auto-cleaning products	shop-based
Boutique	shop-based
Boutique	home-based
Bridal shop	home-based
Clothing	home-based
Clothing	vending cart
Clothing and accessories* (5)	home-based
Comic book sales	shop-based
Cosmetics (2)	home-based
Floral arrangements and party supplies	shop-based
Florist (natural and artificial) (2)	shop-based
Health food	shop-based
Liquor	shop-based
Music store (CDs, records, and tapes)	shop-based
Party supplies	shop-based
Pawn shop	shop-based
Snacks	vending cart
Video rental	shop-based

Small-Scale Manufacturing, n = 25 (18 home-based, 7 shop-based)

Baked goods	home-based
Bakery	shop-based
Calendar publishing	home-based
Ceramics	home-based
Framing	shop-based
Handmade crafts	home-based
Jewelry (2)	home-based
Jewelry & pottery	shop-based
Sewing (5)	home-based
Sewing – embroidery	home-based
Sewing – lingerie	home-based
Sewing window treatments	home-based
Silk-screening custom printing and clothing	shop-based
Stories on tape	home-based
Textile products and sales	shop-based
Textiles	shop-based
Tie-dye clothing	shop-based
Toys	home-based
Upholstery (2)	home-based

(*continued*)

Table 4.1 (*continued*)
Types and Location of Businesses, n = 86

Household and Personal Services, n = 18 (13 home-based, 5 shop-based)

Auto reconditioning	shop-based
Barbershop	shop-based
Beauty shop (2)	shop-based
Beauty shop (never opened)	home-based
Car cleaning	shop-based
Catering (2)	home-based
Child care (2)	home-based
Hauling & lawns	home-based
House painting	home-based
Janitorial (commercial and residential) (2)	home-based
Janitorial and odd job	home-based
Tool sharpening	home-based
Wedding consultant	home-based

Low- and Semi-Skilled, Semi- and Professional Services, n = 14 (11 home-based, 3 shop-based)

Accountant	home-based
Adult day care	shop-based
Communication seminars	home-based
Corporate wellness training/workshops	home-based
Desktop publishing	home-based
Desktop publishing & copy editing	home-based
Educational consultant (scholarships)	home-based
Electronic repair	shop-based
Grant writing consultant	home-based
Illustrator/artist	home-based
Massage	home-based
Multi-level marketing (home accessories)	shop-based
Phone installation	home-based
Tax preparation	home-based

*Accessories include a mix of two or more of the following: jewelry, "what-nots," ceramics, toys, dolls, candy, home decorating items, floral arrangements, beauty products.

lack of financial capital for start-up and early expansion (Table 4.2). They also said they lacked business skills, especially management and marketing skills. Other challenges included family problems and personal issues, such as lack of self-confidence and time; inadequate business infrastructure, such as transportation and facilities; and contextual challenges, such as high poverty rates among consumers and competition from other businesses. Eleven others identified no challenges or their answers were unclear.

Table 4.2
Start-Up Obstacles, 1991

Types of Obstacle	Number	(%)
Financial capital	35	(40.7)
Marketing & sales	10	(11.6)
Infrastructure/Context		
Location/transportation	6	(7.0)
Competition	1	(1.2)
Personal issues		
Confidence	4	(4.7)
Other problems	1	(1.2)
Time	1	(1.2)
Skills, general	3	(3.5)
Employees	2	(2.3)
Equipment	1	(1.2)
Other	11	(12.8)
None or missing	11	(12.8)
Total	86	(100.0)

As we find in chapter 2, successful businesses require financial capital to get the business off the ground and to expand at the appropriate times, human capital to produce a business product, and operate a business, and social capital to leverage resources, support, and information. This chapter explores these resource requirements identified by the eighty-six business owners.

Financial Capital

Everyone had a common bond, and nobody had a lot of money.

—Shelby, child care

Conventional financing generally was unavailable to the entrepreneurs prior to joining the MDP (microenterprise development program). Reflecting on the reasons why financial institutions had denied them financing in the past, they said they lacked credit rating and collateral, had bad credit, were considered a high credit risk, operated a very small home-based business, and/or lacked adequate feasibility and business plans. Some entrepreneurs agreed with these assessments; others believed that gender, class, or racial discrimination also played a role.

Without conventional lending, the entrepreneurs typically turned to one or more alternative sources. Only one-fourth (27 percent) of the entrepreneurs

Table 4.3
Capital for Business Start, 1991, Number (percent)

	Number (%)	Range	Mean	Median	SD
Loans					
MDP/Financial institution/ Government	68 (81.0)	$488 to $40,000	$ 5,420	$ 2,500	$ 6,862
Family	19 (22.6)	$25 to $6,700	$ 1,528	$ 600	$ 1,881
Friends	10 (11.9)	$100 to $25,000	$ 6,375	$ 2,225	$ 9,044
Credit card	3 (3.6)	$2,000 to $4,000	$ 2,667	$ 2,000	$ 1,155
Home equity/second mortgage	2 (2.4)	$1,000 to $28,000	$14,500	$14,500	$19,092
Vendor credit	2 (2.4)	0 to $650	$ 650	$ 650	$ 650
Savings					
Personal funds	39 (46.4)	$50 to $19,600	$ 2,669	$ 1,200	$ 3,864

reported only one source of financing. Charles, a typical case, was turned down for loans by his bank and by the Small Business Administration, so he used his personal savings and a loan from his mother to start his business in 1988. A year or so later, he received a loan from the MDP, which provided loans over a six-year period.

The most common sources of capital were loans from MDPs, financial institutions, and government lenders. The average amount borrowed was a little over $5,000, although the median was less than half that amount (Table 4.3).[3] Ten microentrepreneurs received loans for $10,000 or more, including one person who received three loans totaling $40,000. MDPs provided or facilitated most of the loans.[4] Typical of other entrepreneurs, Marta had nowhere else to turn to scrape together the money to start her business. She explained that the small loan she received from the MDP was what made her business possible, *"because I don't come from a family with money, nor do I have money. . . ."*

Personal funds, including savings, earnings from sale of a home, or gifts, were the next most important source of funds. Almost half of the participants (46 percent) reported investing personal funds of between $50 and $19,600 in their businesses. (In many cases, as chapter 5 will suggest, additional household funds "seeped" into the business.) Most personal funds came from the entrepreneurs' savings, but some also received financial help from their families or friends. Sherri, for example, said that the loan she received from the MDP was too small to get her business off the ground, so she turned to her family for resources.

The next most common source of capital was loans from family members (22 percent) and friends (12 percent). Start-up loans from family members ranged from $25 to $6,700, but loans from friends were larger, ranging from $100 to $25,000. Anne, for example, received a $5,000 loan from the MDP, but she also turned to a friend for a large equipment loan. In three cases, loans from friends exceeded $10,000 and likely resulted in a business "partnership." Several declared that without the financial support from families and friends, the businesses would not have survived as long as they did.

There is evidence that very small businesses are often funded with credit cards (Ho, 1998). Only three businesses in the present study however, reported using credit cards for business start-up. Carl said that he could not wait for a loan from the MDP for business equipment, so he "maxed out" his credit cards to buy a computer, printer, copier, and furniture for his office. He regretted the high interest rate, but "*it's the way it goes.*" Two others established lines of credit with suppliers (vendor credit). For example, Ed turned to his suppliers for credit and paid off this debt when customers paid him: "*That helped considerably, because even after I had gone through the course [at the MDP], it was difficult to go through a financial institution*" because of the collateral requirements.

Some used their household assets as a way to generate capital for their businesses. Two entrepreneurs borrowed on their home, including one, who capitalized his business mostly with personal funds and a second mortgage. Susan said that she and her husband were "lucky" to have some assets to leverage capital for her business. She said, "*we put up our house; we put up everything we owned, [including] our . . . [car].*" They also "borrowed" in other ways from their household assets: "*We got very creative about coming up with equipment and furniture. I about cleaned out my house to supply the business. We supplied about $25,000 of equipment of our own. We were lucky that we could do that.*"

Five entrepreneurs reported that they received small grants from religious institutions or from a government agency, including very small grants of approximately $100 from Vocational Rehabilitation for entrepreneurs with disabilities.

Human Capital

"[I was] all fired up to get into it and get going, but I think I should have prepared more."

—Dan, car detailing

Most of the entrepreneurs were enthusiastic about their business idea and believed they possessed the skills to turn out a quality product. It was not long, however, before it became clear to many that they lacked business expertise. Successful entrepreneurship requires a broad range of "hard" and "soft" skills, including an ability to produce and market a product, to plan and manage a business, to make good decisions, and to network with others.

The eighty-six entrepreneurs brought very different levels of skill and knowledge, motivation and creativity, health, and other individual characteristics to their businesses (Becker, 1993). The entrepreneurs who had some college (42 percent) reported that learning skills and gaining a sense of confidence helped their business. For example, Carl had an accounting degree that he believed prepared him for his accounting business. Susan worked for many years with the elderly and then focused her college studies to help prepare her for her business in elder care. Others did not study business, but believed their college education was helpful. For example, Jackie said that scientific training prepared her well for the business world. As a result, *"Whereas some people would give up, I can deal with opposition because I have been trained to. It makes your whole life better, if your life is ordered. Nothing defeats me. I know how to carry things through, and get the conclusion that I want."*

However, as indicated in chapter 2, most of the entrepreneurs began their businesses with no business training at all. Like Doña Gloria who lamented, *"When I started my business I didn't know anything,"* they recognized that their business required more skills. In open-ended questions about the obstacles they encountered during their business start-up, thirty-four entrepreneurs (40 percent) believed that while they had good social skills and could produce a good product, they lacked business planning, management, financial, and sales and marketing skills (Table 4.2).[5] For example, Candy said that both she and her business partner were *"people people"* but that they were not used to business language and often did not understand fully what some business people were talking about. Sherri also said she lacked a variety of business skills: *"I was adequately prepared for the work ethic. In terms of having a plan, in terms of managing money, in terms of posting deposits and keeping files, hell no. I now finally post transactions every day and I learned how to do a closing for my store. My organizational skills are getting better, [but] I'm still not there."*

MDPs provided assistance in writing a feasibility study, creating a business plan, basic financial management, purchasing, and marketing skills and provided some individual technical assistance (Edgcomb, et al., 1996, 18–19).[6] Only four of the entrepreneurs in this study did not attend training sessions because of difficulties with child care and transportation. Among those who attended, only two said they did not find the training helpful (Table 4.4). Responses to open-ended questions about the MDP training also suggest more praise than criticism.[7] They particularly enjoyed sessions that grappled with nitty-gritty issues, provided practical lessons, and incorporated motivational guest speakers and businesspeople (Table 4.4). Several specifically mentioned that they liked the teachers' efforts to build their self-confidence. Regarding teaching methods, they preferred interactive and informal methods, especially facilitated small group discussions. Several mentioned the benefits of individual meetings with program staff.

Some entrepreneurs expressed frustration about certain aspects of training sessions, especially teaching methods. As Yolanda said, "*. . . all the time they just talked. I think the training lacked a lot for people just beginning.*" Some said that "hands-on" or experiential training is more useful. Some did not like the sessions that focused on writing business plans, and did not like the required "paperwork." Others were unhappy with ill-informed, disorganized, and gossipy trainers. Some instructors were not appropriate role models, as Doug pointed out:

> *A lot of people never could figure out why [some instructors were] teaching, because a lot of them [the teachers] had failed businesses. So they would say, "My business failed because of this reason or that reason" and we would be saying, "Why are you in here telling us?" We had this one guy who had two or three businesses that didn't go for whatever reason, but I was saying, "Jesus, why are you here?"*

Class composition contributed to some of the negative perceptions about the training. Peggy, for example, thought that the program made poor choices about participants and that microenterprise was in many cases "*a cop-out for lazy people on [welfare].*" She believed she was the only one who knew what she was doing in her class. She said the quality of participants affected the quality of the class, which she thought was boring and disorganized: "*The program should have helped 50 people who were really motivated rather than waste so much time on 500 who had no clue what they were doing.*" Even in her own case, she said one of the reasons why she participated in and stuck with the program was because she needed the medical benefits (Medicaid) that were part of the program.

Some complaints focused on the peer-lending groups, which most found boring, inconvenient, and too frequent. Members were sometimes uncomfortable with each other, personality conflicts surfaced in others, and mutual support was lacking. Group members had different goals and abilities and some did not treat group business confidentially. Program staff often did not monitor or facilitate the groups, and as a result, they were either monopolized by one person or were out of control. The requirements and goals of the entrepreneurs were different and made it difficult to work together.

Table 4.4
Entrepreneurs' Open-Ended Comments on Business
Training, 1991, n = 86

Positive assessment of training (n = 66)

Liked "all" of the training, did not specify	6
Content	
Feasibility study and business planning	10
Marketing and advertising	7
Financial management	7
General business training	6
Self-esteem building and empowerment	4
Bookkeeping and accounting	4
Banking guidelines	1
Collections	1
Saving	1
Process	
Small group discussions/social interactions	10
Good trainers/used illustrations and videos	4
Guest speakers	4
One-on-one sessions	3
Practicality of topics	1

Unfavorable assessment of training (n = 39)

Liked "none" of the training, did not specify	2
Content	
Working on business plan	5
Loan segment	2
Accounting/bookkeeping	2
Not enough business training	1
Market research	1
Process	
Trainers	7
Paperwork	6
Meetings (length, style, frequency)	4
Group process	4
Teaching methods	2
Group composition	2
Followup	1

(*continued*)

Table 4.4 (*continued*)
Entrepreneurs' Open-Ended Comments on Business
Training, 1991, n = 86

Wanted more training (n = 32)

Content	
Financial management/accounting/bookkeeping	8
Mentoring and one-on-one	8
Marketing and advertising	6
Networking and business representatives	4
Purchasing	2
Working with banks	2
Computers	1
Legal issues	1
Income taxes	1
Planning	1
Process	
Learn to work in groups	1
Longer training	1

Nonetheless, looking back on the training five years later, the entrepreneurs remained generally positive (Table 4.5). As Kathleen said: "*If I had not taken the class . . . I would have been totally unprepared.*" Diane said the training helped prepare her by exposing her to the range of skills she would need: "*. . . I would not have been prepared at all. I would have never realized any of the stuff I would have to do.*"

Of particular significance, many believed that the training in business planning was especially helpful. Writing a feasibility study and a business plan required focus and goal setting, as well as learning how to resolve basic time management and organizational issues in the start-up phase. For example, Iris remembered: "*They taught you how to make up a business plan, how to start your own business, how to look for the right type of location and building, and what to look for in the building. It was really very informative and very educational.*" Sara said that the training helped her clarify her business idea:

> *[The program] helped me get focused. At the time, I wanted to paint everything. I was doing T-shirts. I was doing cars. I was doing motorcycles. I was doing mailboxes. I was spinning my wheels because I wasn't really going forwards. I was getting disgusted because it seemed that nothing I was doing was clicking. It's not so much that [the MDP] was saying "focus on a subject" as it was saying "focus on an area that you want to do."*

Table 4.5
Entrepreneurs' Later Assessment of Training, 1996, number (percent)*

	Number	(%)
Training Strengths (n = 53)		
Basic business management	31	(36.0)
Business planning and start-up	12	(14.0)
Financial management and records	11	(12.8)
Marketing	3	(3.5)
Training Weaknesses (n = 33)		
Specific Content	18	(20.9)
Financial management	7	(8.2)
Product training	3	(3.5)
Marketing	2	(2.3)
Regulations	1	(1.2)
Management	1	(1.2)
Lack of follow-up/coaching	10	(11.6)
Poor teaching/class dynamics	6	(7.0)

*53 entrepreneurs commented on the training when asked about factors that affected their businesses' development.

In the process of setting goals, Leticia believed she gained insight into her potential:

> *Well, they helped me to think about the future, how to set goals, think more positively, and not to be satisfied with making only two or three dresses a week and receiving only the equivalent of minimum wage in a factory. That is, it made me see that I could have more opportunity working for myself. . . . They taught me how to promote myself. They gave basic training. They helped me a lot to feel more sure of myself and self-confident.*

However, thirty-three participants also addressed training deficiencies (Table 4.6). For example, some thought the training in financial management—including budgeting and accounting—was insufficient (7). This was one of the knowledge areas that presented the greatest obstacles for the microentrepreneurs. Even someone like Iris, who had fairly extensive training in accounting, said it took her quite some time to put that knowledge into practice: "*I went to night school and got a degree in accounting, and had been doing taxes for years. But the fact that I would not keep up and log how much money I was making [was a problem]. I kept up with it in a certain way, but there were no formal books. Now I list my clients, what service they got, what they paid, [and] I keep receipts."* Eileen said the program did not teach her how to track the cash flow and keep books, so she painstakingly created her own system of accounting. In general, although the training provided an introduction to financial management, more was needed. As Sara said:

> *They didn't train you in any skills. The only thing they give you, and they dwelled on, was how to propose to the bank a business proposal. They went step-by-step through that particular process. My business . . . I didn't need that. I paint a house, it costs X amount of dollars. I collect that up-front. [The program] did a lot of manicuring . . . your self-image, what you want to project, what kind of business person you want to be, what ethics are you going to put into this. If you borrow money, how to look at interest rates. They set the baseline for how a normal everyday business should be run.*

A few said that they needed more specialized training. As Diane said, MDP staff *"were a big help in providing the training necessary. However, they were all beginners and didn't know much about the craft business. They did as much as they could in giving me information. They were new and I was new."* Jennifer said she thought it was important to link entrepreneurs with resources who had specialized expertise, in her case, someone with knowledge of the health food business. The staff member who tried to help her had knowledge of the clothing industry, which *"wasn't helpful at all. It really brought us down more than it perked us up."*

Entrepreneurs mentioned two specific problems. First, they said that *production*, rather than *services*, were emphasized. Clarise said that, with the exception of child care, MDP trainers neglected service sector businesses:

> *But there was a downfall of the [MDP] when it came to the services provided. Most of the people who had some sort of service . . . they weren't doing that great. The program supported already established child care businesses as the only service-oriented program. There was a lot of education being done, but it stopped at a certain point. There was something missing.*

Second, ten entrepreneurs said that even though the training helped them in the early phases, it did not last long enough to help them develop their businesses (Table 4.6). As Doris said, *"After everything stopped, it was like you were just hanging out there. [The MDP] only gave you so much information and then cut you off."* Sherri drew an analogy between raising a child and growing a business: *"It's like . . . you have this foster child and you throw up your arms and say they're already successful or grown up, but they still need your treatment, they still need support. . . . I don't think [the program was] ade- quately prepared to deal with us."* Jennifer also thought the program should have lasted longer, especially for those with little or no previous experience:

> *We . . . [were at] the beginner's stage. We had an idea of what it was about. But in the long run I wish the program would've lasted longer to really get into . . . the knowledge of actual business running. We were told it just takes experience to learn this. But I think there could have been changes in the program. It basically taught us a business plan. As far as what to do after your business opens, that's where the lack of knowledge was.*

A lack of ongoing training gave the impression to some entrepreneurs that the MDPs were more interested in lending than in training. As Peggy said, more than money was needed to grow a business: *"They kept throwing 'let us offer you a small business loan' in our faces. . . . Loans don't help people . . . [the program] didn't teach anything to anyone."* Monica pointed out that *"more follow-up would've been helpful. Once you got financed, you are grad- uated and that's the end of the follow-up."* Joanne believed that the program would have been better if it continued to work with the entrepreneurs over time: *". . . instead of giving them a loan and sending them off. . . . You cannot give people a bunch of money then turn them loose without skills. It would have been great to have a one-on-one support system. They should take time each month to check up on how people are doing with their business. This is how they learn."*

Social Capital

The only person I have to help me is the Lord.

—Cassandra, lingerie production

The MDPs formed an important part of the network of support for the en- trepreneurs. To what extent were MDPs able to help entrepreneurs establish support networks and business connections? To what extent did entrepreneurs bring these resources into their businesses? Researchers have suggested that these social resources—or social capital—are a basic building block of successful entrepreneurship. As James Coleman wrote:

> If physical capital is wholly tangible, being embodied in observable material form, and human capital is less tangible, being embodied in

the skills and knowledge acquired by an individual, social capital is
less tangible yet, for it exists in the relations among persons (1988,
S100).

Despite its intangible qualities, social capital provides, in important ways, the
ingredient that makes it possible to put financial and human capital to work.
Furthermore, unlike financial capital, the more social capital a person uses
(like human capital), the more it increases (Light & Gold, 2000, 94–95).

Social capital comes in the form of obligations and expectations, information channels, and social norms (Coleman, 1988; Putnam, 1998). Without these
social resources it would be difficult to operate a successful business. Some
have suggested that social capital is comprised of "bonding" and "bridging" social capital. *Bonding social capital* unites groups in solidarity and mutual support (Gittell & Vidal, 1998; Putnam, 1998).[8] With bonding social capital people
may be able to survive, or in the words of Xavier de Souza Briggs, they may "get
by," but will likely not "get ahead" (1998). In other words, with bonding social
capital microenterprises may be able to subsist and bring in small amounts of
money that assist with basic economic survival. But they will lack connections
to larger networks that could help a business to thrive. Alejandro Portes and Julia
Sensenbrenner (1993) suggest that bonding social capital, by itself, actually may
be an impediment, and in the case of business, potentially high performers may
become overwhelmed with solidarity demands from the group. Reminiscent of
Mark Granovetter's "strength of weak ties" (1973), *bridging social capital*, or
networks of association across social groupings, can generate and leverage resources and opportunities from beyond the group and community (Woolcock,
1999). These social networks may extend to other low-income communities, to
wealthier communities, or to public and private institutions (Warren, et al.,
2001). As Michael J. Woolcock reminds us, development occurs when "people
are willing and able to draw on nurturing social ties" that link poor communities
to other more powerful social sectors (1998, 186).

Lisa J. Servon (1998) argues that not only are both types of social capital
important for entrepreneurs, but together they create a "virtuous cycle" that
empowers microentrepreneurs and builds capacity to link to other organizations. In other words, social cohesion within a group (bonding social capital)
makes it more effective in demanding and organizing for resources from outside the group (bridging social capital). And the more effective a group is in acquiring resources from outside, the more credibility and strength they generate
within. Research on business capitalization suggests that "embedded" or strong
relationships with a bank, as well as "arm's length" ties to information networks have positive impacts on acquiring loans at lower cost: "Social capital
explains how actors win individual and collective advantages through the intri-
cate webs of relations, obligation, and information channels in which they are
socially embedded" (Uzzi & Gillespie, 1999, 433).

If social capital is important for the development of successful businesses, how can low-income entrepreneurs develop it? Ivan Light and Steven J. Gold (2000) argue that there are two ways that entrepreneurs accumulate social capital: through inheritance and acquisition. Some people inherit their parents' business and business connections, a class-derived means to social capital (2000, 95). Others acquire social capital through the connections they generate in school, through memberships in business and other organizations, such as religious institutions and country clubs. Acquired social capital builds on and benefits from inherited social capital throughout a lifetime. As we have seen, relatively few of the entrepreneurs in this study grew up in families with businesses, and those tended to be quite small. Therefore, levels of inherited social capital are likely to be quite low. Acquired social capital derived from education, jobs, and other activities is also likely to be low because relatively few of the entrepreneurs completed college, had the types of jobs with powerful social connections, or lived in communities or belonged to organizations where promising business connections could be nurtured.

Was the level of bonding social capital among the entrepreneurs in this study sufficient to "get by" while they developed broader social relationships that could leverage greater opportunities (Lang & Hornburg, 1998)?

Family and Friends

There is ample evidence that the entrepreneurs relied on family and friends for financial and for other kinds of support. As discussed earlier, a large number borrowed from family and friends to start their businesses, but they also received other types of help. Of the almost two-thirds who said that they received assistance from family and friends, 24 received tangible support (other than financial), 12 received emotional support, and 17 received both tangible and emotional support (Table 4.6).

Tangible assistance included business and product advice, help with buying or selling, planning, transportation and deliveries, referrals, and cleaning and maintenance. This kind of tangible support often saved the money it would cost to purchase the help and was often assumed to be reciprocal (Stack, 1974). In exchange for help with the business, the entrepreneur often felt obligated to offer free services, for example, a child care business that provided free babysitting to a helpful relative, or children who earned clothing by helping their mothers' apparel business.

Family and friends also offered emotional support. Opening and operating a business was a demanding and often lonely experience, and having emotional support was important. Clarise said, *"I had a lot of support from friends and family members . . . so people would tell me you should do your own thing. I always had a lot of good ideas, going to work, raising my kids. I just went for it."* Some were dealing with personal and family problems at the same time. Monica's

Table 4.6
Entrepreneurs' Assessment of Family Support, 1991 and 1996, n = 86*

	Number	(%)
Tangible support only	24	(27.9)
Tangible & emotional support combined	17	(19.8)
Emotional support only	12	(14.0)
Total who made comments	53	(61.6)

*Includes all who commented on family support in the open-ended questions in the 1991 survey (Other than paid employees, who provides you the most assistance for the business? Has your family helped you in your business and how?) and in the 1996 in-depth interview.

friends in Al-Anon were like a family to her, providing emotional support which, in turn, she believed helped her with her business. Brenda's network of friends gave her moral support, but they also "*always let me know that if I needed them, they were there. If I needed to take off to [go to] a funeral, or a buying trip, one of them would watch the store until I got back.*"

The mutual support represented bonding social capital from the standpoint that it helped the businesses survive and helped the entrepreneurs persevere, especially through rough times. Did the reciprocal obligations build resources for the businesses? In some cases, the support was enduring and helped the businesses develop over time. But, in most cases, it was intermittent and crisis-oriented. There were few examples where family and friends provided access to expanded business opportunities (i.e., bridging social capital).

Microenterprise Development Program

MDP programs are designed to build solidarity and mutual support among a group of microentrepreneurs through peer lending and group training. As Servon observed in a case study of a large MDP, Working Capital, group meetings help "to combat the isolation that many self-employed people experience" (1998, 120). To what extent did the MDPs in our study build social capital among entrepreneurs?

MDPs provided tangible support. Fifteen entrepreneurs described ideas, advice and coaching they received from MDP staff. For example, Cassandra, who had experienced several deaths in her family in a short period, was grateful to staff who helped her with sales in order to pay off her loan. Geneva said staff were understanding and helped her adjust her loan payments after her husband was laid off his job.

Table 4.7
Entrepreneurs' Assessment of MDP Support, 1991 and 1996, n = 86*

	Number	(%)
Positive comments		
Emotional/moral support	32	(37.2)
Tangible assistance (not training/lending)	15	(17.4)
Support for business networking	6	(7.0)
Total who made positive comments	54	(62.8)
Negative comments		
Not responsive or supportive	22	(25.6)
Lack support for business networking	4	(4.7)
Total who made negative comments	24	(27.9)

*Includes all who commented on program support (excluding training and lending) in a series of open-ended questions in the 1991 survey (e.g., What did you like/dislike about being part of a borrowing group? Other than paid employees, who provided the most business assistance? What group business activities did your group undertake? Why or why not did your business expand after you participated in the program? Has the program helped in other ways? What is the most important way the program helped your business?) and in the 1996 in-depth interview.

Many more (32) reported emotional and moral support from the MDP that led to increases in their determination and self-confidence (Table 4.7). For example, from the beginning, Jamie said she felt supported: "*You sat through so . . . [many classes] and then you had homework at night. They went through everything with me. They stopped every month or every other month to see how everything was going. . . . They were there for everything. . . . They are real good.*" Heather explained that the staff treated her as a "*unique individual*" and that they continued to offer support by calling her occasionally. Robert said the staff tried to help in any way possible and the counselor he worked with the most was "*fantastic.*" Sara appreciated the personal approach and availability of the staff:

> . . . *They let you know that, no matter what the stumbling block, you could pick up the phone and call. If it is the disaster of the day or the disaster that's going to stop you from going forward, you can call. It didn't matter to them what you thought was a disaster or what you thought was terrible. They were not opinionated. They were just there*

*to help you out. [My case manager] was super. How she did all the
things she did was beyond me. Everything about her was just wow!*

At the same time, twenty-two were not satisfied with MDP support. Jennifer, for example, believed that her MDP offered a lot of *"false promises,"* but
"when it came down to the actual 'help part,' they weren't there." Dan pointed
out that his counselor tried to help, but his advice was not helpful or did not add
much to what he had learned in class: *"One time, he said, 'No matter what you
do, don't close the doors, even if you have to work somewhere else, flipping
hamburgers.' And I thought, 'Well, I got two kids, I can't flip hamburgers all
night and work at the [business] all day.' I got disappointed because he did not
offer anything that I could use."* Only nine entrepreneurs said that the MDP
worked with them past the initial training period.

To what extent did the MDP build the entrepreneurs' social capital? One
could argue that the connection to the MDP itself represented social capital for
the entrepreneurs. For example, four entrepreneurs said they received help in
securing waivers from the welfare department so that they could continue
receiving public assistance after they started their businesses.

MDPs are also designed to generate bridging social capital through access to strategic information and linkages to social welfare, financial, and
business organizations. Six entrepreneurs mentioned that the MDP offered
opportunities to network with established business owners. Some MDPs
brought in businesspeople from the community to teach parts of the entrepreneurship curriculum, and a few programs included mentoring through
programs such as the Service Corps of Retired Executives (SCORE). But
these rarely transformed into ongoing relationships. Among those who said
that the program lacked support for business networking, Susan said she
needed help at the outset developing connections with other businesses in the
field of elder care so that she could learn from them. In fact, there was a striking absence of comments about how the MDPs helped them link to business
organizations and networks. Few entrepreneurs talked about making contact
with networks of suppliers and distributors or groups engaged in product development, sources of capital, and training outside of the MDP. These findings suggest that the social capital gains during the program may have been
relatively short-lived.

Peer Group

While peer *lending* was generally unpopular, the entrepreneurs believed
that the peer group itself was helpful (Kibria, et al., 2003). The greatest benefit
was the opportunity to, in the words of participants, *"interact," "discuss,"* and

"*exchange ideas*" with a group that has a "*commonality of purpose*." They appreciated an atmosphere that allowed for "*constructive criticism*." Several referred to the "*sense of community*" in the group, including one who called the group "*a big cooperation*." In these ways, MDPs brought together people with common interests and problems together.

This interaction provided emotional support (Table 4.8).[9] Among the twenty-five who mentioned emotional support was Cora, who said it felt good to help others and also to share her business challenges: "*I enjoyed inspiring other people to keep on going and let them know what I went through*." Laverne said that other participants' stories were encouraging and made her feel "*if they can do it, I can do it too*." Sharon said her group members gave one another more moral support than the teacher. Lanette recalled that they talked every Wednesday night and brainstormed ideas for their businesses: "*It's been great to have someone who knows exactly where I'm coming from*."

A smaller group (18) said that the peer group also provided tangible assistance. For example, Clara said that members of her group "*were . . . helpful, and very supportive, and would come out and help with some of the projects. And some of them were wonderful on bringing their life experiences, and skill*

Table 4.8
Entrepreneurs' Assessment of Peer Support, 1991 and 1996, n = 86*

	Number	(%)
Positive comments		
Emotional/moral support	25	(29.1)
Tangible assistance (not training/lending)	18	(21.3)
Negative comments		
Meetings	7	(8.1)
Lack support in group	5	(5.8)
Group composition	3	(3.5)
Total who made comments	46	(53.5)

*Includes all who commented on peer support (excluding peer lending) in a series of open-ended questions in the 1991 survey (e.g., What did you like/dislike about being part of a borrowing group? Other than paid employees, who provided the most business assistance? What group business activities did your group undertake? Why or why not did your business expand after you participated in the program? Has the program helped in other ways? What is the most important way the program helped your business?) and in the 1996 in-depth interview.

into our group." Amy said that one of the women in her group helped her with her résumé. Eleanor said group members exchanged information and ideas; they all got to know each other, had similar needs, motivated each other and shared experiences, even the bad ones. Some found the peer group a good way to build business networks and to generate more business for themselves. Brenda stated: "*Oh, yes, [the other participants] were real good. They would come around and buy from me. We would pass around our business cards and help to advertise for each other.*" Vera said that a group member helped her market her product by producing her résumé and business flyers and Doris exchanged information and ideas on marketing with group members.

To what extent did family, friends, MDPs, peers, and others help to mobilize indigenous resources and leverage outside resources for business start-up? Theoretically this is an important question because it is possible that microentrepreneurs might have a fighting chance of business success even without high levels of financial and human capital (Light & Gold, 2000). Most of the social resources provided by family, friends, and the MDP involved bonding social capital rather than bridging social capital. Family and friends provided tangible and emotional support. The MDPs helped to build solidarity among the entrepreneurs through peer group training and through other activities. And for a short period of time, they provided access to information and training. But there is relatively little evidence that their social capital linked the entrepreneurs to business organizations or created alternative structures of business support.

Resources for Business

In summary, the entrepreneurs began with product skills, energy, and enthusiasm, and they devoted themselves to building their businesses. But from the outset they lacked an array of resources, including financial capital, skills, and social resources. As Roberto said, "*I have always wanted to work for myself. The problem is that I don't have the resources to work for myself.*"

Timothy Bates asserts that small businesses are unlikely to succeed without financial and human resources. Speaking about minority-owned businesses, he writes that "Management, money, and markets are the essential building blocks. . . ." (1997, 257). Other researchers suggest that even with relatively low levels of human and financial capital, it might be possible to compete as a low-income entrepreneur (Waldinger, et al., 1990). Ivan Light and Steven J. Gold suggest that some ethnic groups, for example, are able to "reduce the costs of doing business and provide investment capital, advice, raw materials, training and access to customers" (2000, 128). Were families, friends, MDPs, and other contacts able to provide the kinds of resources to burgeoning businesses that coethnics provide in refugee and immigrant communities?

Overall, the evidence in this chapter suggests that the financial, human, and social capital resources of entrepreneurs were insufficient. While the entrepreneurs said that MDPs provided vital financial resources, training, and technical support to help them get their businesses off the ground, it was not enough to provide a solid foundation for continued business growth and development. Regarding financial capital, the entrepreneurs were able to patch together capital from family, friends, the MDP, and various other sources to open their businesses, but many financial needs remained unmet. Entrepreneurs with some assets were *"lucky,"* as one of the entrepreneurs aptly stated, because a savings account, a home, furniture, tools, a car, or another asset provided a way to generate more resources for the business without going into too much debt. Second, they approached their businesses with helpful, but often insufficient, human capital. The learning curve for business is steep and requires ongoing assistance and training. The MDPs provided useful orientation and training, but often left them *"hanging"* with little additional training resources. Looking at how well the businesses performed over a period of five years, we do find that that those operated by an entrepreneur with at least two years of higher education performed better than those with less education.[10] Moreover, those who had received significant loans (over $3,000) from financial institutions were also likely to earn greater income from the business compared to those with informal sources (e.g., loans from family and friends).[11]

Finally, the social capital available to the entrepreneurs was largely a "bonding" type that provided support and encouragement and some instrumental support. This helped them cope with the stress and hard work involved in business ownership, but they generally went into business lacking the "bridging" type of social capital that might provide access to resources outside of their immediate social networks.

In sum, there is substantial support for theories of resource constraints, and MDPs were only partially effective in overcoming these constraints. These research results should give considerable pause to proponents of microenterprise as an anti-poverty policy that could be used by a large percentage of the poor.

Notes

1. Some of the businesses operated more in the informal sector than in the formal business sector (i.e., they paid taxes, used financial institutions, followed industry regulations, and followed labor laws), although we did not seek to determine level of formality. There are advantages to each. Informality allows businesses to avoid taxes, circumvent business and welfare regulation, and use family labor without paying payroll taxes, but informality also precludes retirement savings through social

security, and restricts markets and access to financial services (Microenterprise FIELD, 2003b).

2. This was an open-ended question asked in 1991 ("When you started the business, what obstacles to success did you encounter?").

3. Sources for loans and loan amounts are derived from surveys conducted by the Self-Employment Learning Project (SELP). Commentary is derived from open-ended survey questions in 1991 and from in-depth interviews in 1996.

4. This included loans from the MDP, financial institutions, and government because participants were unclear where their loans originated. In some programs, for example, financial institution officials came to the MDP and signed loan documents with participants on site. Other times, they went to the financial institution. As a result, participants often did not know the origin of their loans.

5. The types of factors mentioned sometimes straddled categories. For example, one person mentioned that her small town provided only a limited market and she also confronted stiff local competition. Because of her emphasis, we counted this as an obstacle of business context and competition, not as marketing skills.

6. Our interviews suggest no consistent patterns by program, including participants' assessments of program services or outcome measures, such as business earnings.

7. Open-ended questions asked in 1991 by SELP included: which training activities participants liked and disliked the most, and why, and which training activities were not offered that they would like to have.

8. Social capital can also impact negatively. For example, gangs offer bonding social capital, providing short-term security and group identity, but have negative longer-term impacts.

9. Of the fifteen entrepreneurs who made negative comments about the peer group, the reasons usually had to do with not liking or trusting other group members. For example, one person complained that she knew all the people in the group were "*born-again Christians*," and another said group members made her feel "*uncomfortable*." Some worried about confidentiality, some said there was too much "*criticism*," and one said that some members "*took too long to decide anything*" and the group "*stagnated*" after the initial training.

10. In 1995, among those entrepreneurs with an open business (N = 52), those with a two-year college degree or higher (N = 16) had a significantly higher income from the business on average ($10,718) than those with less schooling (N = 36, $4,932, t = -2.28, df = 50, p $\leq$ .05).

11. Regarding formal loans, entrepreneurs with formal loans (MDPs, banks, and government loans) of $3,000 or more (N = 20) had significantly higher income from the business on average in 1995 ($9,906) compared to those with less loans (N = 32, $4,716) (t = -2.14, df = 50, p $\leq$ .05).

CHAPTER 5

The Bottom Line:
Business and Household

Blurred Boundaries between Business and Household

In this chapter we examine the entrepreneurs' business and household income over a five-year period. Income is the typical measure of microenterprise success, but as we demonstrate, measurement presents a number of challenges. We also expand the discussion of financial position to include assets, liabilities, and net worth. Although often overlooked in anti-poverty research, these are appropriate outcome measures for research on enterprise, even very small enterprise.

> *Everything just went into the pot, and then everything came out of it.*
>
> —Judy, retail textiles

In many cases, business and household are not distinct financial entities. Sometimes the entrepreneurs said they made no profit, but later talked about what they did with their business "profits." Some admitted that they did not keep "books," often because the businesses were so small they could keep track in their heads. Others tried to keep books, but acknowledged reaching into business accounts to pay for household expenses or reaching into household accounts to pay for business expenses. In many cases, there was only one pot of money, sometimes kept in the bank, and other times kept at home. Sometimes these financial transactions were carefully tracked and/or recorded, but quite clearly in many cases they were not. Because of the imprecise nature of financial records, confusion and difficulty in reporting financial outcomes, and the blurring of boundaries between business and household, it was difficult for many of the entrepreneurs to say with certainty whether they made profits and how much.

Collecting accurate data on personal and business finances is a challenge. A variety of problems, including accuracy of recall, misunderstanding of terms, awareness, social desirability, and beliefs that finances should be private can reduce the reliability of financial data. In our conversations with the entrepreneurs we found that the most serious issues were confusion about terms and blurred boundaries between the business and household, both of which made it difficult to generate a clear picture of financial outcomes. Indeed, based on this experience, we have serious doubts about the quality of most survey data on the financial position of microentrepreneurs.

Anita's case illustrates the difficulty of measuring business and household finances. The way she talked about her bookkeeping at first led us to conclude that she kept finances entirely separate: "*I had no profit left after I paid for the loan . . . and the rent and other expenses I had to cover. I kept a register and the accountant also kept records on our profits (although there weren't any). I finished paying the loan with my income from my job.*" But she later said she used her job income to cover household and outstanding business expenses. It was clear that she subsidized her business from her wage income, but it was difficult to assess if finances were mingled and unaccounted for.

Based on the measurement problems exemplified by Anita's case, we divided the entrepreneurs into three groups, using the following rules to distinguish the level of financial separation between business and household. "Separate" suggests that three conditions were met: (1) there were separate accounting systems for business and household; (2) the business was not subsidized by household funds without accounting for it (an exception to this is made in the business start-up phase when they were learning how to keep separate accounts); and (3) household expenses were not covered by business funds other than through salary or draw or without accounting for it. Returning to Anita's case, we determined that she kept separate accounts because she kept separate bank accounts, she paid her children for working for the business (she took no "draw" herself), and because she demonstrated understanding and basic implementation of separate accounts. (Whether or not it was a good idea to subsidize her business to the extent that she did was a separate matter.)

In thirty-two cases (37 percent) the entrepreneurs kept household and business records separate. Cora said that in the beginning she borrowed from her business to pay for household necessities and then paid the business back, but then she said, "*I think I took out more than I put back though, . . .*" However, by the time of the interview, she reported having separate accounts and keeping finances strictly separate. Sherri had also improved her accounting practices:

There were times last year that I ended up spending—writing checks out of my own account and then trying to reimburse them. This year

I've had good separation. The only thing that would get somewhat overlapped is that I now have a pocket check for the business account, but let's say I don't have any money and I use it, I would write that in as an owner's draw versus a business expense.

In twenty-seven cases (32 percent) finances were "likely mingled," because they said they used business funds to pay household bills or household funds to pay for business bills, without clearly accounting for them. Many used a single bank account for business and household. For example, Renée had one bank account for business and household and said that she sometimes took a "draw" from her business, but then continued in a way that suggested that her finances might be mingled:

Sometimes I do, and sometimes I don't. Basically, I try to be sure my bills are paid, that's a must—the rent, the lights, etc. After those are paid, then if there is something where I can give myself a salary, fine. But then if there is something that the business needs, then my salary might go toward the business. Most of the time, I give myself something.

Similarly, Monica said that she had separate bank accounts, but she generally took $75 to $100 a month from the business to pay for household expenses before she calculated profits. She did not call this a "draw," saying she took some when she *"needed it."* Angie also felt it was necessary to take money from the business to pay for household expenses.

In twenty-five cases (29 percent), finances were "mingled" because there was little or no distinction between the household and business finances, including an apparent lack of accounting and separation of business and household funds. Allison observed that *"everything trickles down through the business,"* and what is left went to personal expenses. In response to a discussion about bank accounts, Yolanda said, *". . . there is no separation for the business and for the household."* Or in another case, even though Linda had separate bank accounts for her business and household, when asked what she did with her profits, she said, *"I would pocket the extra money. I would use it for paying bills or purchasing supplies."* In Doña Gloria's case, it was clear that there was total financial blurring between household and business. She asked rhetorically, *"Did I make a profit in 1995? The truth is, I didn't keep track. I'm not going to lie to you, I didn't keep track. But yes, it was going well. I remember that I made good money, but exactly how much? I don't remember."*[1]

Although the entrepreneurs typically understood the importance of separate accounting (*"That is where I screwed up,"* said Sharon), they found it difficult to keep accounts. The businesses were small and many operated at home, and often were carried out at the same time as household and family duties. In fact, we find that boundaries are statistically more likely to be mingled in home-based businesses compared to shop-based businesses.[2] The businesses frequently realized very low profits and total household income often did not cover families' monthly expenses. Many had too little income to pay all the bills when they came due, so keeping business and household revenues and expenses separate was an ordeal. As Doris said: *"When someone paid me—whatever bill was due, I just paid that bill."* Or Yvonne, whose business closed in 1994, said that *"If I had some profit, and I had a bill to be paid, I just paid it. That's what I mean when I say I wasn't very good on my accounting, because I didn't keep it separated like you are supposed to have done."* Sometimes there was too little money to warrant the effort. As Doña Gloria said: *"I don't have books. Listen, why would I? Why spend money buying books to carry accounts if I don't sell anything?"*

Others seemed to not understand accounting terms or even the reasons for keeping accounts separate. Although Lessie knows "the difference now," she recounted her initial difficulties with financial accounting:

> *When you say profit, that throws me. If you would have said what do I do with the money from my business, I would stop by the grocery store. That's different from profit for me. But that would be money from my business. . . . Profit would be how much money I made over the receipts that I had to show for what I did with my business . . . used it for everything, it was just random money. . . .*

Other possible reasons for poor financial record keeping are welfare regulations and taxation policies that are relatively inflexible about the earnings of start-up businesses. Proper reporting of business earnings could threaten some with reduced welfare benefits and also could place some households in higher tax brackets. One entrepreneur admitted that she counted all of her "work-related expenses" carefully for tax purposes. As she explained (contradicting data from earlier surveys that showed her making a profit),

> I try *not* to [make a profit]. That sounds terrible. At this point and time in my life, everything that I do, and this is literal, is work-related. My home is nicely painted. We entertain a lot of people. My vehicle is essentially work-related. Nine times out of ten, if I go out for an evening, it may not start off being work-related, but it ends up being work-related.

It should be understood that given the extent of "likely mingled" and "mingled" finances, calculations of business earnings, profits, and household income are approximations. Nonetheless, these data are as good or better than data from other studies of microenterprise because they are derived using several waves of survey data, in addition to evidence from in-depth interviews.

Diversified Household Income

Hustling has always been in my blood. I have always worked two jobs for all my life, and tried to do things for my family, I wanted them to have the best.

—Thomas, catering

Like many low-income households in America most of the entrepreneurs and their families relied on more than one source of household income.[3] While some lived on income derived from their business and perhaps the earned income of a spouse or partner, many patched together multiple sources of income to make ends meet. For example, Jackie earned a part-time salary, received honoraria for her artistic works, and collected retirement, in addition to her business earnings. She lived in a house owned by her mother so Jackie only had to pay utilities. Sometimes her roommate helped with household bills. If finances got really tight, she sold off a few stocks or bonds. Another entrepreneur worked a wage job and served in the National Guard, brought money in from the family farm, sold Avon, and rented out a vehicle.

Cash Income

The entrepreneurs identified many different sources of cash income, including earned (e.g., business or jobs) and unearned income (e.g., child support, welfare assistance, or social security) (Table 5.1).[4] Some earned income came from stable and reliable sources, such as wage employment, while others, such as odd jobs, were less consistent. The entrepreneurs described between one and six sources of cash income averaging 2.6 sources (median, 3).[5]

EMPLOYMENT. In 1995, of the 52 open businesses, three-quarters reported some earnings. Twelve (23 percent) also held a full-time job, and 6 (12 percent) reported part-time jobs. Of the closed businesses, 20 (67 percent) of the former owners held full-time jobs, 7 held part-time jobs, and two held 2 part-time jobs. Overall, 47 (57 percent) of the participants reported earnings from other employment in 1995. Moreover, 31 (38 percent) of the entrepreneurs had a spouse or partner who contributed to household income through their employment,[6] including 5 whose spouse or partner had their own business as well. Fourteen (17 percent) received income from another household earner such as

Table 5.1
Diverse Sources of Household Income and
In-Kind Support (N = 82)

Source	Percent
Earned Income	
Respondent full-time job	39
Respondent part-time job	18
Spouse/partner job	38
Business income (n = 52)	75
Odd jobs	13
Asset income	15
Unearned Income	
Other household member (family/roommate)	17
Government income	37
Child support	16
Other miscellaneous cash source	22
In-Kind Support	
Government	34
Non-government in-kind	15
Housing assistance	12

a family member or roommate. Sometimes teenage children contributed earnings from after-school and summer jobs to their parents. For example, when her husband left, Sandra said her older children worked and helped out with household expenses.

ODD JOBS. In addition to full and part-time jobs with a regular employer, a number of entrepreneurs also took on odd jobs to make ends meet. Of the 82 entrepreneurs who reported detailed income, 11 (13 percent) did odd jobs, including baby-sitting, selling snacks, transporting friends, doing hair, hauling trash, snowplowing, and lawn mowing. Some entrepreneurs also earned extra money selling Tupperware, Amway (a multilevel marketing organization) or cosmetics, such as Avon or Mary Kay. These jobs were seen as desirable because they helped families make ends meet but also left time flexible for business activities. Robert, for example, combined income sources to support his family until he was forced to close his business and get a job: "*I had a family so I had to support them somehow. I do odd jobs, I do carpentry work for people and just about anything. . . . I could just to make money and that was just another way to make money. But now I've gotten a job that pays good money.*"

Rich's business revenues sometimes did not cover his business expenses and he had to use money from odd jobs to help support the business during slow times. On occasion, he also took on odd jobs to care for his family. Lois said that due to the seasonal nature of her business she worked for a "temp" agency in order to make ends meet when business was slow. She also utilized Food Stamps and Medicaid for her and her daughter. Susan occasionally typed college papers for students or received payments for speaking engagements. Renée sold herbs. Sandra sold snacks to people in the community. Doug said he sometimes hauled rubbish and mowed lawns. Laverne made a little money through baby-sitting, as did Cassandra, who also did hair, sold cosmetics, and ran errands.

When asked about income sources on prior surveys, many entrepreneurs did not identify, nor calculate, income from their odd jobs. However, odd job income came up in the qualitative interview when we asked how they made ends meet. There are two ways to interpret this. First, microentrepreneurs might not have reported this income earlier because they were accustomed to keeping it hidden from public welfare officials (who might reduce their welfare benefits), or from the tax man (who might take some away), or if it was illegal (and they would be afraid of being caught). Second, survey methodology may not be the best way to learn about informal income.[7] Based on their relative openness about reporting multiple job sources, we believe most were forthcoming, although we cannot be sure. Either way, it is not possible to assess exactly how much total income is generated, but the amount is probably relatively small because of the types of jobs held.

SOCIAL ASSISTANCE AND SOCIAL INSURANCE. Unearned income sources included social assistance and social insurance benefits. Only ten (12 percent) said they received pre-welfare-reform assistance, Aid to Families with Dependent Children (AFDC), at some point in 1995. However, over a third (37 percent), relied to some extent on at least one public assistance program, including Social Security, Disability, AFDC, Supplemental Security Income, Veteran's pensions, Unemployment Insurance, and General Assistance.[8]

Several entrepreneurs combined earned income with income from social services support. For example, Iris needed additional income after her husband's death in 1989, so she started an arts and crafts business. She became ill working two jobs, and henceforth disability payments had been her main source of income, along with the small earnings from her home-based business. Shelby also said she never would have been able to make ends meet without welfare. It was a relief to know she always had her basic household costs covered: "*Then the money I made from day care, I put back into day care.*"

SUPPORT FROM FAMILY AND OTHERS. The entrepreneurs also relied on other sources of cash income, including child support and help from family members living outside the household. An important source of income for thirteen (16 percent) of the entrepreneurs was child support payments. For instance, Candy said due to child support and income from her hospital job, she had been able to begin paying herself a little on a regular basis from her business. It also helped that she was *"extremely good with money."* Kim also found it easier to make ends meet because of child support payments from her ex-husband. Child support was also important to Anita, even though it took some time for the state to track her ex-husband down and draw directly from his paycheck. Several others were unable to get the child support, including Clarise, who commented, *"That guy got away 'scott free.' He never paid one penny. Not one dime."* But she was reluctant to seek assistance from other sources, declaring, *"I am very independent. I do not ask anybody for anything."*

Although many of the entrepreneurs shared Clarise's independent streak, eighteen (22 percent) of the entrepreneurs reported receiving unearned income from family, neighbors, friends, and religious groups. Family members some-times provided more or less regular financial support. For example, after the death of her husband, Catarina received financial help from her brother and neighbors and she lived rent-free with her sister. When Kim said that she needed extra financial help, her brother-in-law let her work for him moving houses and her father lent her money. Sherri reported that she received ongoing financial help from her father, who had invested a substantial sum in her business, and who paid for medical insurance for her and her child.

In other cases, family or friends picked up occasional bills or made dona-tions in times of need. Monica's family sent clothing and paid for an occasional dentist or eye appointment for her children. Family, friends, and neighbors also helped Laverne with personal, not business, expenses during hard times: *"That's for my personal [use]. My business takes care of itself."* Others received gifts in response to family crises, such as a death in the family or an illness. Carol said they benefitted from a strong church network, who knew that she and her family were struggling, and occasionally gave them $50. When her car broke down some parishioners arranged to have it repaired. Others bought groceries or clothes for her new grandchild. Her landlord also allowed her to be late on her rent payments from time to time and her pastor and his wife invited her to work at the church camp for two weeks during the summer where she earned almost $2,000.

INCOME FROM ASSETS. Assets holdings provided some additional income, includ-ing real estate rentals, interest on savings, and returns on stocks and bonds. Twelve (15 percent) entrepreneurs reported receiving some cash income from assets. Some added to household income by leasing business space or a room in their home. As Sherri, who owned her home, said, *"For me I needed to have a roommate. It was a financial thing."* Allison, who had earlier brought in some income by caring for three foster children, had taken in a roommate for the same reason the day before she was interviewed for this study. Four entrepreneurs discussed savings or other investments that paid small monthly dividends, although in at least one case the entrepreneur was reinvesting the income.

LUMP SUM, IRREGULAR INCOME. Others received lump sums that contributed to household income, including receipt of money from insurance settlements from accidents or deaths in the family, selling a house or other property, and withdrawal of savings. Some had also received or were planning to receive inheritances. For example, despite a slow business start, Allison thought that she was more stable because she owned her home, thanks to her inheritance and her parents' help with the mortgage: "*I was fortunate because of inheritance and because. . . . I owned my own home. . . . Because of the trickle up effect, I am more financially secure than I was . . . my assets have increased since I moved into this house. Since I have passed the five-year threshold, other businesses and banks will take you more seriously.*" Jackie said that because of her inheritance and her business, she feels able to take greater risks: "*I am the sole heir . . . I can live on the edge. . . . Not everybody can say that, but I can. Therefore, a lot of times, I will live on the edge and give real close to my last (dollar) because I know that I have a business and if I need to create money, I can. For people working for others, it's harder. . . .*"

In-Kind Support and Swapping

In addition to financial support, over half (55 percent) of the entrepreneurs stretched income and reduced expenses through in-kind support. The most common form of in-kind support came from government sources. Twenty (24 percent) entrepreneurs reported receiving one source of in-kind support from the government and eight (10 percent) reported two sources. The most common type of in-kind support was Food Stamps, which 15 (18 percent) entrepreneurs received at some point in the prior year.

Twelve (15 percent) of the entrepreneurs also reported receiving in-kind support from non-governmental sources, including friends, neighbors, and religious organizations. Child care and transportation from friends and family members were common forms of in-kind support. Some family and friends helped with projects, such as Fred's family, who helped with renovations. Others received food and gifts from friends and religious members, including Allison, who not only received help with child care, but also surplus from a grocery store and occasional cash gifts.

Housing was another important form of in-kind support. Ten entrepreneurs (12 percent) reported receiving some form of housing assistance including government-subsidized housing or rent-free living from a family member or friend. For example, Carlos stayed rent-free with his relatives, although he contributed money here and there. Shelby, who ran a children's day care, traded child care for free rent when she moved in with her boyfriend.

Advantages and Disadvantages of Combining Sources of Income

> *When you have one source of income you put all your eggs in*
> *one basket, which I don't like. The way things are today nobody*
> *knows how long you're going to have a job.*

—Shelby, day care

When factoring in all sources of relatively steady income (cash and in-kind), the entrepreneurs had from one to seven sources, with an average of over three.[9] Overall, the entrepreneurs tended to think that diversified income sources were beneficial. A few said that having several income-earning activities offered greater variety. Judy liked the mixture of activities that multiple income sources provided, and Loretta commented that she liked doing several different things because "*I am the type of person that does not like to be in the same place for a long time.*" Cora said she liked "*having my own business and work for someone else part-time.*" She enjoyed managing the income as well: "*I like getting a lump sum here and a lump sum there and then spread it out for the whole year and do a budget.*" A few also thought that holding a job in addition to operating a business provided a way to learn more. Candy pointed out that having a job takes time away from her business, but because she works in a professional setting, she is able to use it to do "*on-the-job role plays*" that she believes contribute to the quality of her business product.

But most thought multiple income sources were a practical financial matter. Simply put, for many, having more than one income source was prudent because if one source falters, the other(s) would be there to stabilize household income. For example, Judy's business was so financially unpredictable that she held two outside jobs, one sewing and one taking care of an elderly woman. She thought that three sources of income gave her control and good money, but it also caused fluctuations in her business because of the time squeeze. A full-time job might not leave enough time to devote to a small business, so having a part-time job along with the business worked well for Charles. For Fred, having a single source of income was too risky because "*if it slows up, then there you are. If you got more [than] one way of money coming in, when one gets slow the other may take up the slack.*" Similarly, having more than one income source, according to Toni, "*is an advantage . . . 'cause if you fall short in this one, you got something else there to pick you up.*"

Others said an advantage to having more sources of income was the amount of money coming into the household and business. Jamie said that more income sources means "*you can do more things.*" Cassandra mentioned that she would occasionally do hair, sell cosmetics, or take people shopping. Why? "*I'd take that money and keep gas in the car.*" Brenda was relieved that she had added income: "*If I need extra money, I don't have to ask anyone for it. If I come up short, I don't have to take anything away from the household because my husband takes care of the bills.*" Some said that health insurance was available through their jobs. Jobs sometimes offered more income and greater security. For example, Loretta said that she received regular increases in her bus-driving job and her home care job, and at the same time, one of them also provided health insurance.

Unearned income had its own advantages. It took less time and, in the best of circumstances, was regular. Examples are social insurance and child support. Social assistance was often minimal and time-consuming, but conferred important benefits, such as health insurance. Entrepreneurs who lost Medicaid when they lost their welfare benefits were sometimes forced to take wage jobs in order to obtain health insurance. Although Candy acknowledged that her job took valuable time away from her business, she needed the health benefits after she lost her Medicaid coverage.

Many entrepreneurs said there were disadvantages in patching together income. This was especially true because multiple income sources usually meant more jobs requiring time and energy. For example, Shelby said that patching "*means you put your time out in multiple sources*" and "*you're going in four different directions.*" Candy said that having multiple income sources meant there was a "*never ending battle of juggling time and priorities. It's hard to work all week and then work all weekend.*" Jennifer said she hoped to start working in a full-time job because of time conflicts between family and multiple jobs.

Similarly, some entrepreneurs commented that having many income sources made it difficult to focus. As Fred pointed out, an advantage of having just one source is that it is easier to stay "*focused and working hard.*" Brenda liked having the extra income, but was concerned that during the time she worked at her job, she was losing business:

> *The only disadvantage is that I leave at two o'clock every day . . . and I don't get back until four o'clock. Usually I have my daughter filling in for me, but I would love to be there myself. I have considered giving up that job, but I haven't done it yet. I enjoy the kids, and love the job, and the income helps out. But I hate leaving during the peak season when it's real busy, and I think I might lose some sales from not being there all the time.*

Some alleviated this problem by cutting out one job, while others cut back their hours. Clarise decided to work fewer hours on her job making more time for her business, saying that while a full-time job "*was an advantage because it was more money . . . it was a disadvantage because I would be at work five days a week, nine to five, and I couldn't get out to do my business.*"

Combining earned income with social services support caused some to worry about running afoul the law or welfare regulations. The disadvantages sometimes outweighed the benefit of regular extra income. For instance, Carol ran her business, mowed lawns, delivered newspapers, managed property, and still made time to volunteer in the local hospital: "*. . . when people need a sitter, I sit with them and I'm on call at the hospital to do hospital sitting with people.*" She spoke emotionally about her desire to be honest with the social service authorities and the challenge of making ends meet at home:

> *I do have principles and high moral values. There were times I literally felt like I had to lie about any income reported in small ways. At that time the waiver hadn't yet gone through. We were so scared if we made a sale and reported it, we had so much debt hanging over our head, that we would lose Food Stamps, that we'd lose medical. There was always a fear factor. . . . We're not on that help now, and I can report my lawn mowing. During those times I was afraid to report lawn mowing and stuff because we could not live on what social services was giving us. I was so gut-honest at first I reported every birthday gift my kids got and then I would lose that much in Food Stamps. That killed me.*

Sara commented that while she had "*received assistance in the past*" for food and rent, it was very difficult to balance her business earnings with the regulations for welfare:

> *It taught me how to be dishonest. It taught me how to use the system. There was no way that I could support the family on what I was making. Things were just too unsure. I might have one . . . job one week and then not have any thing for six weeks. Then I'd have to go through the whole [qualification] process of thirty days and ninety days. . . . By that time another job might come in—you just have to really juggle things around to make them look right. Maybe I was not quite as honest as I could have been. But then other times . . . I was lower and needed the money more. I had to keep that even keel.*

Candy also said that welfare income was difficult to count on. Public assistance was helpful because it was steady, but it was "*scary*" every time she had a review. She said she felt like she was "*on the edge from year to year.*" But she did not want to lie about her earnings; she wanted to do it by the "*letter of the law.*" For Stacy, the welfare department offered so little, it was not worth pursuing. She qualified for continued public assistance, but said "*It is so little money, it is more of a slap in the face.*"

Overall, entrepreneurs offered considerable evidence on the practice and meaning of income diversification, to which we return in the conclusion.

Financial Outcomes

In this section we present quantitative data on financial outcomes. This information is of crucial importance in understanding microbusiness performance, though some readers may be a bit overwhelmed with the amount of data. If the detail is not useful, we suggest turning to the summary of economic outcomes of microenterprise at the end of this chapter, or focusing on the financial tables in Appendix D.

Financial outcomes are based on a sample size of 83 of the 86 microentrepreneurs interviewed. (Three cases had large amounts of missing data). Eight households were above 150 percent of poverty but are retained in these analyses because their incomes were close to 150 percent of poverty (income to need ratios ranged from 1.01 to 1.24) and each was receiving at least one source of public assistance, indicating economic hardship.[10] All 1991 dollars have been adjusted to 1995 dollars to assess for real change between 1991 and 1995. As of 1995, 52 businesses (63 percent) were still open. Descriptive statistics for business outcomes in 1995 reflect only open businesses. The likelihood of a business remaining open in 1995 did not vary significantly by race, gender, marital status, presence of young children, or poverty status in 1995. Descriptive statistics for financial outcomes are provided in Tables 5.2 through 5.8 in Appendix D. Standard deviations associated with each variable are large, which indicates that values are widely dispersed, and thus the means are somewhat crude representations of the entire sample.

The Business

BUSINESS REVENUES, EXPENSES, AND PROFITS. Some of the entrepreneurs did not provide figures for business revenues or expenses. Therefore, these results should be interpreted with caution. In 1991, participants reported average revenues of $25,425 (median, $6,517). For businesses that remained open in 1995, revenues averaged $28,618 (median, $9,450) in 1991, and increased to an average of $30,075 (median, $11,840), a statistically insignificant increase. (See Table 5.2 in Appendix D.)

In 1991, average expenses were $22,617 (median, $9,646). Businesses that remained open through the study period averaged $25,146 (median, $10,037) in expenses in 1991, decreasing slightly to $24,600 by 1995 (median, $7,704).

Business profits in 1991 averaged $3,130 (median, $209). Half of the businesses (34) broke even or showed a loss and half (35) showed a profit in

1991.[11] For businesses that remained open through the study period, average profits were $4,092 (median, $489) in 1991. Among those, 43 percent broke even or showed a loss in 1991, and 57 percent showed a profit. Profits increased in 1995 for open businesses to $5,061 (median, $1,066), though not significantly. Twenty-nine percent broke even or showed a loss in 1995, and 71 percent reported profits. Average dollar change in profits declined among participants with open businesses by $3,449, with a median increase of $800. Forty-seven percent of businesses showed a decline in profits between 1991 and 1995, and 53 percent showed an increase in profits.

Although business revenues among whites and non-whites did not vary significantly in 1991, non-whites experienced an average decline in revenues and whites experienced gains during the study period. By 1995, whites had significantly more revenues than did non-whites. Average business expenses did not vary significantly by race and ethnicity. Average business profits did not vary significantly in 1991, but by 1995 business profits for whites averaged $7,426 compared to $2,616 for non-whites.

Business revenues were significantly smaller among women's businesses than men's businesses in 1991 and 1995. However, in terms of change, women saw significantly greater gains in business revenues compared to a decline for men. Regarding business expenses, men had significantly greater business expenses in 1991 and 1995, and greater increases in expenses between 1991 and 1995, compared to an average decline in expenses for women. In 1991, men had significantly larger profits compared to women, but by 1995, profits did not vary by gender. Men experienced a significant loss on average compared to an average gain by women.

Married participants had significantly higher business revenues in 1991 and 1995, as well as significantly higher expenses. Married participants also had significantly higher profits compared to non-married participants in 1991. However, between 1991 and 1995, married microentrepreneurs experienced losses compared to non-married microentrepreneurs. By 1995, profits did not vary significantly by marital status, although married participants continued to have higher profits on average.

Households with children under age six and under had significantly greater business revenues in 1991 and 1995 than did households without young children. The average change in business revenues, however, was greater for households without young children than for those with young children. Business expenses in 1991 and 1995 were significantly higher for households with young children than those without. Households with young children had higher profits on average in 1991 than those without, who showed a business loss. By 1995, there was no significant difference in profits for open businesses with and without young children, because dollar change in profit between 1991 and 1995 was greater for those without young children than those with young children. Since microentrepreneurs with young children are also significantly more likely to be married, this pattern somewhat parallels that observed among married versus not married microentrepreneurs.

BUSINESS ASSETS, LIABILITIES, AND NET WORTH. Again we offer the caution that a number of participants did not provide figures for assets, liabilities and/or net worth. Business assets in 1991 averaged $12,250 with a median value of $3,259. (See Table 5.3 in Appendix D.) For businesses that remained open through the study, business assets in 1991 averaged slightly higher, $12,921, with a median of $3,462. By 1995, business assets increased on average to $18,163 (median, $5,342). Average change in business assets between 1991 and 1995 was $3,391 (median, $600). Almost as many businesses declined in business assets as increased between 1991 and 1995 (49 and 51 percent, respectively).

In 1991, business liabilities averaged $6,040 with a median value of $953. For businesses that remained open, liabilities increased to an average of $6,827 (median, $0) in 1995. Between 1991 and 1995, liabilities increased in 13 businesses and stayed the same or decreased in 30 businesses.

In 1991, business net worth averaged $5,935 (median, $1,608). Twenty businesses (28 percent) had zero or negative net worth and 51 (72 percent) had positive net worth in 1991. Among open businesses in 1995, net worth increased to an average value of $9,657 (median, $2,914) compared to an average value of $8,045 among the same businesses in 1991. Twelve businesses (29 percent) in 1995 had a zero or negative net worth and 29 (71 percent) had positive net worth. While business net worth did increase on average it did not do so significantly. The proportion of businesses with negative net worth was about the same in 1991 as 1995. On average, business net worth increased by $359 (median, $400). Twenty businesses had no change or a decline in net worth, while 21 had an increase in net worth between 1991 and 1995.

Outcomes varied by demographic characteristics. Whites entered the study with significantly greater business assets than non-whites, but also more liabilities. By 1995, whites no longer had more business assets but continued to have significantly more liabilities. Non-whites experienced large gains in business assets between 1991 and 1995 compared to whites. While not statistically significant, whites on average had greater business net worth in both 1991 and 1995.[12] However, it is worth noting that the average change in net worth between 1991 and 1995 declined for whites while increasing for non-whites.

Turning to gender differences, men had significantly greater business assets on average than did women in 1991 and 1995. They also had significantly greater liabilities in 1991 and 1995,[13] and liabilities increased significantly more for men between 1991 and 1995.[14] Interestingly, while men continued to have more assets on average than did women, men experienced a small decline in business assets between 1991 and 1995, while women experienced a substantial increase.[15] Also, while men had significantly greater business net worth in 1991,[16] men and women did not vary significantly on average business net worth by 1995. Women had experienced a significantly larger increase in net worth than men, who on average had a decline in net worth.[17]

Married microentrepreneurs had significantly more business assets in 1991 than did non-married microentrepreneurs, but by 1995, there was no significant difference by marital status.[18] Married microentrepreneurs on average experienced a decline in business assets while non-married entrepreneurs experienced a substantial increase on average.[19] Married participants also had significantly more business liabilities in both 1991 and 1995. In 1991, married participants had greater business net worth,[20] but by 1995, non-married participants had experienced a greater increase in net worth than married participants,[21] resulting in no significant difference on average.

Households with children under six years old experienced an average decline in net worth between 1991 and 1995, and net worth was similar for both those with and without young children in both 1991 and 1995.[22] Neither education level nor age was significantly correlated with business assets, liabilities, or net worth.

Those are the main findings. (See Tables 5.2 and 5.3 for greater detail.) We draw conclusions on these business financial outcomes at the end of the chapter.

Impact on Household Income and Poverty

HOUSEHOLD INCOME FROM THE BUSINESS. In 1991 when the study began, average personal income drawn from the business was $4,257, with a substantially lower median of $895. While 49 participants (59 percent) reported earnings from their business, 34 (41 percent) reported no earned income from their business in 1991. For those whose businesses remained open in 1995, income from the business in 1991 was $5,236 on average, not significantly different from the average of $6,712 drawn in 1995. This indicates that on average those remaining in business did not experience a significant gain in income drawn from the business between 1991 and 1995. In 1995, of 52 entrepreneurs with open businesses, 39 (75 percent) reported personal income from the business. (See Table 5.4 in Appendix D.)

On average, about 30 percent of household income came from the business in 1991. The median was substantially lower at less than 1 percent. Participants whose businesses were still open in 1995 drew a significantly higher percentage (35 percent) of their household income from the business in 1991 than did participants who businesses closed by 1995 (21 percent). For those whose businesses remained open in 1995, approximately 34 percent of the household income was derived from the business. In 1995, 21 (40 percent) of the open businesses experienced no increase or experienced a decline in income drawn from their business during the study period.

Earnings from the business differed by various demographic characteristics. Some groups did better than others in terms of personal earnings from the business. Interestingly, non-whites drew significantly more income from their businesses than did whites in 1991. However, by 1995, for those whose businesses that remained open, whites drew significantly more income from their businesses than did non-whites. Change in income from the business was significantly greater for whites than for non-whites and, in fact, non-whites on average experienced a decline in income drawn from the business between 1991 and 1995.

While average business income for men and women did not vary significantly in 1991, men experienced significantly greater gains in income from their business than did women by 1995. On average, men drew $14,110 in 1995, significantly more than women who drew an average of $4,951. Similarly, married microentrepreneurs drew more from their business than did non-married microentrepreneurs by 1995. While not significantly different, those with children under six years old in the household drew more on average from their business than did those without young children.

Younger entrepreneurs also realized more income from the business than did older entrepreneurs. Age was significantly and inversely related to income from the business in 1995, as was change in income from the business between 1991 and 1995.[23] Age was also inversely related to percent income from the business in 1995 and change in percent income from the business.[24]

In general, whites, men, those who were married, and younger entrepreneurs faired better in terms of income drawn from the business. We return to these findings in the conclusion.

TOTAL HOUSEHOLD INCOME. Mean household income for the 83 participants in 1991 was $14,915 (median, $12,395). In 1995, mean income was $20,893 (median, $18,793). Both those with open businesses and those with closed businesses experienced significant gains between 1991 and 1995. The average change in household income between 1991 and 1995 was $5,978 (median, $4,471). However, 30 of the 83 households experienced a decline in their income between 1991 and 1995. (See Table 5.5 in Appendix D.)

Non-white microentrepreneurs had significantly higher household incomes in 1991 compared to whites. However, white households had significantly larger gains between 1991 and 1995 than did non-whites. By 1995 household income on average did not vary by race.

Married couple households had significantly higher household income than did non-married households in 1991 and in 1995. This is quite likely a function of larger household size and more income earners in the household. Households with children under six years old had significantly higher household incomes than those who did not in 1991, but by 1995 there was no statistical difference.

Education was significantly and inversely related to household income in 1991.[25] It was not significantly correlated in 1995, but change in household income between 1991 and 1995 was positively correlated.[26] That is, those with lower education start out with greater household income but those with more education experienced greater gains in household income between 1991 and 1995.

POVERTY STATUS. As noted earlier, with the exception of eight cases that fell slightly above income poverty in 1991, all households began at or below 150 percent of poverty in 1991. (Income poverty for the purposes of this study refers to families that fall at or below 150 percent of the national income poverty line.) By 1995, 39 (47 percent) had moved above income poverty and 44 (53 percent) remained below.[27] (See Table 5.6 in Appendix D.)

Another way to portray poverty is through an income-to-needs ratio. This expresses a family's income as a proportion of the official poverty line (for a family of that size) and gives a more complete picture of relative poverty, not just whether a family is living above or below poverty. A family with income exactly at the poverty line, for example, is at 100 percent of poverty and has an income-to-needs ratio of 1.00. The measure is computed by dividing the total family income by the poverty level for the appropriate family size. Income-to-needs ratios among the participants in this study ranged from .14 (i.e., 14 percent of the 150 percent of poverty income based on household size in 1991) to 1.24 (i.e., 24 percent above poverty). The average income-to-needs ratio was .70 and the median was .71. Among businesses that remained open all five years, the average income-to-needs ratio was .68 in 1991. As of 1995, 53 percent of households remained in poverty while almost half (47 percent) had moved above poverty. The income-to-needs ratio ranged from .13 to 4.47 (the next highest is 2.0). Average income-to-needs ratio in 1995 was 1.05 (median, .96). The average for those with open businesses was 1.07.

Average income-to-needs ratios in 1991 and 1995 were significantly different both for the group as a whole and for those whose businesses remained open, indicating households on average made significant gains in income-to-needs ratios. (See Table 5.7 in Appendix D.) The average change in income-to-needs ratio between 1991 and 1995 was an increase of .35 (median, .25). However, between 1991 and 1995, while 64 percent of households experienced a gain in income-to-needs ratio, 36 percent experienced a decrease.

Income-to-needs did not vary significantly in 1991 or 1995 by race, gender, marital status, presence of young children, or by whether or not the business remained open in 1995. By 1995 whites were significantly more likely to have moved above poverty than were non-whites.[28] Movement out of poverty by 1995 did not vary significantly by gender, presence of young children, or marital status.

Age was inversely correlated with income-to-needs ratio in 1995,[29] and amount of change in income-to-needs ratio between 1991 and 1995.[30] Education was positively correlated with income-to-needs ratio in 1995 and change in income-to-needs ratio.[31] Those who moved above poverty by 1995 had a higher average education than those who remained in poverty (13 and 11 years respectively).[32]

HOUSEHOLD ASSETS, LIABILITIES, AND NET WORTH. Based on a small sample size, participants reported an average of $26,350 in household assets in 1991 (median, $4,407). By 1995 assets had increased on average to $39,495 (median, $21,256). The average change in value of assets was $10,796 (median increase, $2,897). Thirty-one percent of 68 participants reported a decrease in household assets, while 69 percent experienced an increase. Those participants whose businesses were still open in 1995 had a significantly greater change in household assets between 1991 and 1995 than households where the business closed. Average change in household assets for those with open businesses was $15,925, compared to $1,974 for those whose businesses had closed. Those with open businesses had average assets of $25,333 in 1991 and $42,967 in 1995. Additionally, those with businesses that remained open all five years of the study were more likely to own their homes in 1995 than those whose businesses had closed.[33] (See Table 5.8 in Appendix D.)

In 1991 non-whites had significantly higher household assets on average than did whites. By 1995 household assets no longer varied significantly by race, although non-whites continued to have higher household assets on average. Non-whites were significantly more likely to own their homes in 1991 and in 1995.[34]

Married couple households had significantly greater household assets than non-married households in both 1991 and 1995. This may be a function of homeownership as married households were significantly more likely to be homeowners than were non-married participants in both 1991 and 1995.[35] Households without young children experienced significantly greater gains in household assets between 1991 and 1995 compared to households with young children, who experienced a decline on average in household assets.

Household assets did not vary significantly in 1991 or 1995 by gender. Between 1991 and 1995, average dollar change in asset value was significantly greater for women ($13,286) than for men ($1,190).

Age was positively correlated with household assets in 1991[36] but was not so in 1995, suggesting that younger participants made substantial gains in household assets between 1991 and 1995.

The average amount of household liability in 1991 was $10,734 (median, $4,345). The amount of debt in 1995 was significantly higher with average liabilities of $16,302 (median, $11,073). However, this varied by business status.

Those with open businesses in 1995 had average household liabilities of $10,675 in 1991 and significantly greater household liabilities in 1995 ($17,226). For those whose businesses had closed by 1995, average liabilities did not differ significantly between 1991 and 1995. Of 71 reporting, half (35) declined in liabilities and half (36) experienced an increase in household liabilities.

On average men's household liabilities declined $5,737 between 1991 and 1995, while women's increased by $7,831. In 1991 married couple households had significantly more household liability than did non-married households. However, between 1991 and 1995 non-married entrepreneurs had a substantially greater increase in liabilities compared to married entrepreneurs, and by 1995 average household liabilities did not vary significantly. In 1991 average liabilities did not vary by whether or not young children were present in the household but between 1991 and 1995 households with young children reported an average decline of $4,004, compared to an average increase of $9,833 for those without young children.

For those reporting both asset and liability figures in 1991, the average household net worth was $14,938 (median, $1,086). Thirteen percent of the participants reported a negative household net worth while 87 percent reported positive household net worth. In 1995 average household net worth had increased to $20,365 (median, $4,859). Thirty-five percent had a negative net worth in 1995 and 65 percent report positive net worth. Net worth figures for participants reporting in 1991 and 1995 are not significantly different. On average assets and liabilities increased, but net worth did not. Of 65 reporting, 45 percent report a decline in household net worth between 1991 and 1995 while 55 percent reported an increase. Looking only at those with open businesses, average net worth in 1995 ($21,818) was significantly greater than in 1991 ($12,619), while those with closed businesses did not vary significantly in level of net worth in 1991 versus 1995. Average dollar change in household net worth was $9,005 compared to an average decline of $3,027 for households in which the business had closed. It may be that those with more successful businesses were able to invest more in household asset accumulation. Or, it may be that household finances were otherwise better or more stable for participants whose businesses survived.

Non-whites had significantly larger household net worth in 1991 than did whites. However, between 1991 and 1995 whites experienced an average gain of $6,958 compared to $967 for non-whites, so that by 1995, the difference was not statistically significant.

Male entrepreneurs averaged higher household net worth than female entrepreneurs throughout the study period. Married households had significantly more net worth than non-married households in 1991 and 1995. While not statistically significant, households with no young children report a substantial gain in household net worth on average ($6,826), compared to an average decline ($1,550) for households with young children.

Age was significantly and positively correlated with household net worth in 1991; however, by 1995 there was no significant correlation, suggesting that younger participants made substantial gains in net worth.

Economic Outcomes of Microenterprise

We turn now to reflect on the meaning and applications of this data, both qualitative and quantitative, on economic outcomes of microenterprise.

Boundaries

Interviews with low-income microentrepreneurs in this study suggest that only slightly more than one-third kept clear and separate accounts for businesses and household financial dealings. This does not necessarily mean that those whose accounts were mingled did not have an idea as to how much income came from the business or from other income sources, but only that they combined all their income and drew from a central pool of funds to pay whatever business or household bills came due. The degree to which household and business finances were mingled suggests, however, that financial data over the study period are often approximations more than exact amounts. Possible reasons for blurred boundaries include a lack of financial management skills, a desire to keep business accounting informal for tax or convenience purposes, and costs of record keeping and financial services.

The high degree of financial permeability between business and household suggests a need for greater financial education with microentrepreneurs, and better tracking methods for research.[37] Regarding research, this issue is so pronounced that it casts a shadow on this and on previous studies that purport to describe economic outcomes of microenterprise. It would be reasonable to conclude that existing knowledge of economic outcomes rests on a suspect foundation.

Diversification of Income

Diversification of income streams may reveal the resourcefulness of these low-income families. Household income included earned and unearned income from full-time, part-time, and odd jobs; from social insurance and social assistance programs; and from other forms of financial and in-kind support. Entrepreneurs reported on average three different sources of cash income at one time, and about one-third of households relied on some form of in-kind support. Some enjoyed the variety, learned skills in various jobs, and increased their overall household income by doing so. However, most used multiple sources to make ends meet, to cope with job unpredictability, and to make a little extra for hard times. Unearned income was viewed as a good thing because it acted as a supplement and sometimes came with benefits. However, given the choice, many would likely have preferred a full-time job or business that provided a stable source of income. The advantage of diversifying may be to insure income in the event one source is lost, but the disadvantages include expending energy in multiple activities.

Theoretically, this study perhaps makes a contribution to understanding labor income diversification as a protection rather than simply as an inefficiency. The unpredictability of income streams for people with low-skills, may make diversification a rational choice for disadvantaged workers. Nonetheless, diversification of income has costs. The balancing of protection against costs suggests that low-income entrepreneurs may be continually making complex financial calculations that workers with "good" jobs typically do not have to make.

Business Economic Performance

A small group of businesses realized substantial financial benefits from their businesses, but the majority made small or no financial gains over the study period. In 1991, about half of the open businesses were making a profit, and by 1995 about two-thirds were making a profit. This finding may have important policy and program implications. It may be possible to evaluate fairly quickly which businesses are "growth" businesses and which are likely to remain small or to close.

White, male, and married entrepreneurs tended to have better financial outcomes from the business. One interpretation is that these groups may benefit from similar advantages in business as they do in the labor market. Conversely, women, minorities, and single entrepreneurs may experience disadvantages similar to those in the labor market. Disadvantages may include market discrimination against women and minorities and constraints on choices of business for women and minorities. Household and child care responsibilities may impede business growth for women. Access to capital may impede business growth for minorities.

Generally, financial outcomes for businesses among non-whites (African Americans and Latino/as) followed a pattern that was positive in the beginning, but less positive relative to whites by the end of the study. This pattern may suggest that minorities are continuing to experience discrimination in accessing resources for developing their businesses.

Interestingly, business financial results do not suggest any clear connection to formal education. If human capital matters in business performance, it may not be the kind of human capital that is offered in the schooling that was available to these entrepreneurs.

One thing is very clear from in-depth interviews: a full-time income earner or a business partner in the household is a big support for a nascent business. Fred said that the best of all worlds is to have a working spouse who can help shoulder responsibility for income generation. Juanita said that her husband's rising income helped the household survive and her business to do well. Clarise wished for a partner: ". . . *I would really like a change to take place, like [having] a partner, but it would have to be someone who is really motivated like me to get things done. I would like to have a husband so he could go into a partnership with me, or just a business partner.*"

Quantitative data bear this out. Married entrepreneurs had greater business revenues, profits, assets, and net worth in 1991. However, some of these differences faded by 1995.

Household Economic Outcomes

The businesses in this study contributed one-third of household income on average. Average household income from businesses did not increase significantly over the study period. Generally, businesses that remained open were associated with more financial resources in households. Entrepreneurs with open businesses drew a higher percentage of household income from the business early on. These findings suggest that the more viable businesses (those that remained open through the study period) were able to make greater contributions to household well-being.

Consistent with prior research, men had greater income gains from their businesses than did women. This may be an indication that men were expanding their businesses more than women, and taking greater business risks. Or alternatively, women might have faced greater obstacles in running their businesses or may have been operating businesses that were stereotypically "female" low-revenue businesses, such as child care, sewing and alterations, and domestic house work.

Younger entrepreneurs surpassed elderly entrepreneurs in realizing more business income by the end of the study period. This may be explained in part because many of the older entrepreneurs received guaranteed income from pensions and disability, and were not necessarily interested in increasing the size of their businesses. This pattern also coincides with a leveling off of the earning curve in older workers compared to younger workers who hope to see an increase in income.

Overall, household incomes increased over the study period, whether businesses were open or closed. Higher household income and open businesses were positively related. Average change in household income did not vary significantly whether the business stayed open or closed, but 48 percent of those whose businesses closed also experienced a decline in household income, while only 29 percent of those with open businesses experienced a decline. These are rather mixed indicators that microbusinesses can sometimes improve household income. Despite overall improvement, a large number of households (36 percent) experienced a decline in household income over the study period.

While movement out of poverty was limited, there was improvement on average. Without a control group, it is impossible to say whether the rate of movement out of poverty would be the same or different in the absence of microenterprise. This is a finding that warrants further study. Using 150 percent of the official income poverty line as a marker, less than half of the entrepreneurs moved above poverty, while the rest remained in poverty. Rates did not vary whether or not the business remained open.

The income-to-needs ratio improved from an average of 70 percent of the poverty line in 1991 to 105 percent in 1995. While most households experienced an increase in income-to-needs, about one-third experienced a decline. Consistent with income gains, Whites were also more likely to move above the poverty line than were Blacks and Latinos. Younger and more educated entrepreneurs experienced larger gains in the income-to-needs ratio. These findings are consistent with general business performance.

An association between formal education and household income by the end of the study suggests that the financial gains from education emerged over time and helped support movement out of poverty. Thus, human capital seems to be a better predictor of household financial performance than of business financial performance. We suspect that human capital, when assessed by a single measure (typically, years of schools) is an oversimplification. It may be that this construct will eventually develop into a number of dimensions that have distinct explanatory capability. If so, what are the dimensions that may explain business performance? There is some indication that modeling (e.g., other entrepreneurs in the family) and experience (e.g., a prior business failure) may be as or more important than years of schooling (Edgcomb, et al., 2002).

Conclusion

Overall, modest earnings in microenterprise—even for those businesses that remained open through the study period—suggest that many of the entrepreneurs may have gained other benefits from microbusiness. Otherwise, why would they risk attempting it? Why would they persist? To the extent that the entrepreneurs might have been able to earn more in the labor market, these findings suggest that compensating differential theory may be relevant. To be sure, given the blurring between household and business, it is possible that some business earnings were hidden. But it is unlikely that the amount exceeded income from a full-time job. There must be other reasons why the entrepreneurs persisted. We turn to these reasons in chapter 7.

Notes

1. There was too little information to determine which of these three categories best described the accounting situation in two additional cases.

2. $X^2 = 9.69$, df $= 2$, p $\leq .01$.

3. Considering the issue of blurred boundaries between household and business, it is impossible to determine how much of the income discussed in this section actually stayed on the household side. Many of the entrepreneurs mentioned that they subsidized their businesses, in one form or another, from the household.

4. These numbers are derived from eighty-two of the eighty-three entrepreneurs who reported their household income. One entrepreneur did not provide detailed sources. The sources of income reported here include those that entrepreneurs mentioned when asked about their total household income and income earned in their businesses in 1995. Additional sources disclosed during the interview, but not necessarily considered formal or stable sources of income, are also discussed.

5. This includes income from full-time, part-time, temporary, and intermittent wage employment, and businesses.

6. This includes full-time work, part-time, and temporary jobs, as well as ongoing but intermittent work, such as the National Guard.

7. This is easy to understand. Asked to report jobs and income, it is relatively easy if there are one or two sources, but it is more difficult if there are many sources, some part-time, some seasonal, and some odd jobs. As Edin (1993) found, it can take considerable time and trust to uncover multiple income sources, including informal sources.

8. In 1995, of eighty-two entrepreneurs who reported detailed sources of household income.

9. This is derived from interviews with eighty-three entrepreneurs and does not include credit from home equity, credit cards, and other loans.

10. After reviewing data from earlier survey waves and hearing the participants discuss their confusion about financial accounting, we decided to recalculate all of the financial outcomes. With copies of the original survey instruments, we recalculated business and household financial figures for all eighty-six participants (although three were ultimately excluded due to missing data). In some analyses, we also omitted outliers, believed to be entry errors, because they skewed results. As a result, our findings differ from other analyses (Clark & Kays, 1999). (See reference section.)

11. Based on N $= 69$ reporting data on revenues and expenses in 1991.

12. When excluding one outlier (extreme value) of $145,698 in business net worth for 1995, average business net worth in 1995 is very similar for whites ($6,191) and for non-whites ($6,344).

13. When excluding one outlier of $145,231 for business liabilities in 1991, men and women do not vary significantly in average business liabilities.

14. When excluding one outlier of $54, 394 for change in business liabilities, men continued to show a greater positive change in liabilities compared to women, however not significantly so.

15. When excluding two outliers in change in business assets of $132,117 and $120,388, men had a significantly larger positive change ($22,001) than women ($729) (p ≤ .01).

16. This relationship does not hold when excluding an outlier of $135,943. Men no longer have significantly greater net worth in 1991.

17. When excluding two outliers in change in business net worth of $−115,443 and $136,626, men and women did not vary significantly in average dollar change and both had on average a slight decline.

18. When excluding one outlier of $145,698, business assets in 1995 vary significantly by marital status with married entrepreneurs having significantly more business assets ($26,584) than non-married (p ≤ .01).

19. When excluding two outliers of $−132,117 and $120,388 for change in business assets, both married and non-married entrepreneurs experienced a positive dollar change on average.

20. When excluding an outlier of $135,943, married entrepreneurs continue to have greater business net worth in 1991 but not significantly so.

21. When excluding two outliers of $−115,443 and $136,626, dollar change in business net worth did not vary by marital status.

22. When excluding an outlier of $135,943 for business net worth in 1991, those without young children have significantly greater business net worth than those with young children (p ≤ .05). In 1995, when excluding one outlier of $145, 698, those with young children have on average a negative business net worth compared to those without young children (p ≤ .10).

23. $r = -.28, p ≤ .05, r = -.39, p ≤ .01$.

24. $r = -.28, p ≤ .05, r = -.35, p ≤ .05$.

25. $r = -.38, p ≤ .01$.

26. $r = .23, p ≤ .05$.

27. The eight cases that were above 150 percent of the poverty line in 1991 are counted as moving out of poverty if they experienced at least a .04 gain in income to needs ratio, as this is the minimum change between 1991 and 1995 in income to needs ratio among those moving from 150 percent of poverty or below to above 150 percent of poverty.

28. $X^2 = 3.63, df = 1, p ≤ .05$.

29. $r = .19, p ≤ .10$.

30. $r = .19, p ≤ .10$.

31. $r = .21, p \le .05, r = .20, p \le .10.$

32. $t = -2.04, df = 81, p \le .05.$

33. $X^2 = 4.70, df = 1, p \le .05.$

34. $X^2 = 9.99, df = 1, p \le .01, X^2 = 3.24, df = 1, p \le .10.$

35. $X^2 = 10.91, df = 1, p \le .01, X^2 = 6.25, df = 1, p \le .01.$

36. $r = .27, p \le .05.$

37. In an international context, Daniels (2001) has examined different measures of profit and net worth that provide a useful approach to evaluating methods and for optimal approaches to defining and measuring financial outcomes.

CHAPTER 6

Microenterprise Performance

In this chapter the entrepreneurs discuss factors they believed affected their business performance. To begin, we take a closer look at businesses that have done well and others that have done poorly. These cases illustrate the range of factors that influenced performance.

Allison's Home-based Sewing Business

Many years ago, Allison had made a satisfactory but unrewarding living as a seamstress, before going overseas to work as a volunteer. She returned home to sell her house, earn some money, and return overseas, but in the meantime, decided to support herself by sewing and selling bedroom accessories. There was a building boom in the area and before she was able to sell her home, her business snowballed. So instead of moving, she enrolled in a microenterprise course and developed her business. She liked the independence that her business offered her: "*If I wanted, I could totally leave it behind, and [it] would not mess up someone else's work schedule. One of the reasons to stay doing it was that if a door opened to go to another country, I could close down the business, go to the foreign country and come back and open it [back] up.*" She had not traveled as she had hoped, but she had no regrets.

Allison generated most of the capital for her business from savings and credit cards. She kept her start-up capital needs low because she already owned much of the sewing equipment. And she learned the business from her former boss, who had built a small home-based sewing business into a large one with many employees.

Allison felt supported by friends and family, and although her mother did not always show it, "*I guess that my mother is proud, deep down.*" Her parents purchased her first house ("*something I never would have been able to get at that point in my life*"), and let her keep the equity when she moved into her second

117

home. This allowed her to qualify for a larger loan for a larger house to accommodate her business. She was also part of a national religious support group that helps people out with their health expenses through a type of pooled "insurance" fund. She treated it as an insurance premium, even though she understood that it was not really insurance and would only cover a limited amount of expenses. Over time, her local church had provided several small cash gifts to help her as well.

Support from the microenterprise development program (MDP) was helpful, especially in the beginning. The MDP provided a small loan that she used to pay off the credit card debt she had from purchasing a sewing machine. The peer group and training provided basic information, but it *"kind of fizzled. . . . If the group had functioned more like it should [and] been more active in arranging for guest speakers, [we] could have benefited from it further."*

Over time, the proportion of revenues that went toward paying off her expenses had gone down, and she was able to pay herself a larger salary. The only thing that slowed things down was when she brought in three foster children who took up much of her time while they lived with her, although they also brought in a little additional income that helped at the time.

In addition to having a marketable skill and an outward-looking and entrepreneurial nature, Allison attributed much of her success to her business choice and location. There were many new homes in her area and although she advertised, her business mostly sold itself. Former customers stayed with her. Her success made her *"a little bit more positive in my outlook,"* she said.

> *I remember back [when I was] working for someone else, and the fact of the daily grind, of always living from paycheck to paycheck, and never seeming to get ahead, and wondering how on earth I will be able to replace it when it dies, it seemed to me more like a heavy cloud of gloom and now, in a way, I am not much better off than I was. But my outlook is better. Somehow, I think it is all going to work out.*

Lanette's Wellness Training Business

With only a high school education, Lanette had worked as a semi-professional manager in a hospital prior to opening her business. She always liked administrative work, and her job paid well, but she had always thought about starting her own business. Moreover, she had a strong and independent personality and she disliked her working hours. Finally, she *"decided . . . to jump out there and do it."* She wanted to be at home more with her daughter and her long-term dream was to build a *"large company."*

The business started as an all-purpose career planning center but it had become more focused, as she searched for her niche: *"Now my focus is more concrete—as before it was just to do wellness programs for everyone and anyone. Now it has evolved into an interest in . . . health [issues for Blacks in the corporate sector]."* The business was doing well, although she still did not make much money—especially compared to her previous job. Not long before the interview, however, a large franchise had called her to do a wellness program and she was finding that her style worked well in the corporate business world.

She understood when she started the business that she had excellent management skills from her prior work experience, but poor sales skills: *"I did not know how to sell the business. My management skills have allowed me to survive, but I think I would be in a tremendous profit area right now if my selling skills were as good as my management skills."* Marketing was costly. Although she took out a loan from the MDP, she did not have enough money for advertising. Ever the entrepreneur though, she was *"trying to do a contract now to get some funds to do a regular radio show."*

Lanette received crucial financial support from her father, who, although he opposed the business while he was living, left his house to her when he died. Having the house helped and she also felt freer to do business without his pressure and judgmental attitude, and had consequently more of *"a sense of direction."* She also received assistance from her daughter and support from another entrepreneur with whom she shared ideas: *"It's been great to have someone who knows exactly where I'm coming from."* She believed that the African American community was not as supportive as it could be of Black-owned businesses (*"a barrier we have to overcome"*), but it did not hold her back: *". . . I don't let it get to me."*

Lanette said she never felt particularly welcome at the MDP because their focus was on helping women transition off welfare to business ownership. The MDP helped her with her business plan and gave her a loan, but she needed more assistance with marketing and sales.

She hoped to move in some new directions. One was to continue teaching and consulting, and the other was to open a non-profit entrepreneurial institute to teach women how to be entrepreneurs: *"I would not want a woman to go through what I went through trying to get where I am with my business. I feel I could have gotten there a long time ago with the right assistance."* Nonetheless, she liked the way things were going for her, saying that she was much stronger, had more patience, and was determined to succeed.

John's Office-Cleaning Service

When John searched for a way to make a living, he turned to the family's janitorial business. As a child John learned the business, but he had not grown up thinking he would ever take it over. But the jobs open to him offered low wages, while his father's janitorial service offered a good source of income. His mother encouraged him to take over: "*She encouraged me to pursue [the business], and thought it might be a nice supplement to any real work I might ultimately find. . . . The income has been good. . . . And it's not very taxing. The income has been solid, and met all my needs. It has allowed me to pursue other interests.*" John bought the business with his personal savings, turning down the opportunity for a loan because, he said, he does not like debt. The business gave him a steady, but modest, income. "*As long as I keep doing this, I will have some reliable income.*" He believed he could take on larger contracts if he really wanted them.

When he had questions, he called his father for advice. His friends also had been helpful by giving him names of potential new customers. He kept his living expenses low because he had no children and lived with his grandparents. Every month and a half or so he drew $1,000 to $1,500 to cover household expenses. The boundaries between household and business were somewhat blurred, although he kept separate business and household checking accounts. He said the MDP training was helpful in this regard. He had set aside savings, reasoning that "*money will always have value later in life, but the investments I make in a car or computer will devalue almost immediately. Investments can be more of a long-term consideration. There is no wear involved, no long-term devaluation.*" He also reinvested in his business on a regular basis.

John took a low-key approach to business. He did not "*wear a tie, and sometimes [doesn't] give the impression of a responsible business owner,*" but he acted professionally when dealing with clients, and over time, he found it easier to develop business relationships. He had adopted a rational business style. He thought about the mistakes that he had made along the way, such as pricing contracts too low or buying supplies for clients without payment up front, assessed what went wrong, and then changed his practices. He became proficient at the job: "*It's a trade I cannot get out of my head now, because I have done so much of it. It's not like it requires special skills, just a sense of determination to fulfill the obligations of the contract . . . [and] people always need to be cleaned up after.*" His ambivalence about the business appeared to be connected, at least in part, to the kind of work, which he said was physically challenging and sometimes dangerous. It had never been a dream:

> *Sometimes, when I am not in a particularly upbeat mood, it's hard to get motivated and that will sometimes affect the quality of my work. . . . It has not been my favorite thing in the world, quite frankly, but I suppose that's why they call it work. The money which I have gotten, a better sense of self-esteem, not due to the quality of the work, but because I*

am the king of my own domain. I think that I could start a company with more grandiose prospects, now. I think I could pull that off, the hand-shaking duties, as well as the more technical things.

He was sure that he preferred to own a business rather than work for someone else, despite certain advantages of labor market employment:

There seem to be some advantages to working for an employer, which in some ways compensate for the reduced wage—like insurance perks, or job security, tax issues. But a lot of that seems to be fading these days. I am glad to say I can put my security in myself, rather than in my employer. . . . When I look around and I realize that there are so many people around making . . . [a lot of] money, or riding the government dole, I really feel privileged to be able to write my own ticket and not have to answer directly to a boss.

John was investing in equipment and beginning to prepare himself for a new consulting business.

Jennifer's Natural Foods Business

Jennifer had worked in housecleaning for many years and had hoped to expand it with assistance from the MDP. Despite her personal goals, program staff and her business partner convinced her to open a specialty food store instead. The shop opened in 1992. By 1993, it closed.

According to her feasibility study, the idea of a specialty foods store was not a bad one. There was a market and it appeared to Jennifer that it could raise her family's standard of living. But things went badly from the beginning. Neither Jennifer, nor her business partner, had the knowledge to succeed in the specialty food industry. Then the landlord raised the store's rent: *"The overhead was a big killer for us. A real big killer."* They had to move the business, which cost more than $1,000. Although her family was helpful—her husband helped on the home front and her older kids helped in the store—there was *"no one to fall back on"* when the kids got sick and her grandmother became ill. So, occasionally she had to shut the store for a day or two at a time. Her business partner quit after a few months. Finally, her mentor at the microenterprise program was fired. Despite these setbacks, Jennifer worked hard and substantially reduced her business debt. But in the end, without more help and without the capital to resupply the store with new and better products, she had to close. Although her business had promise, she was afraid to take on the kind of debt that would have been required to keep it open.

Because she had to stop cleaning houses and her business never turned a profit, Jennifer had no income. At the same time, her husband's work hours were cut, making it increasingly difficult to make ends meet at home. In fact, for a time they were underwriting the business from household income at about $400 per month. When they closed the business, the family income increased substantially because she took on two part-time jobs. Given the circumstances, Jennifer felt that she and her family were much better off not owning a business and she expressed no desire to start anew. As a mother with two children, she also felt guilty about trying to operate a business and be a "*part-time*" mother.

In retrospect, Jennifer believed that the choice of business and the timing were poor and that she should have spent more time gathering information, making connections, and developing support from the MDP. Her mentor at the program "*did what he could, but when it came down to the actual 'help' part, they weren't there.*" Jennifer believed that given her previous experience and her skills, she would have been more successful owning a housecleaning service. Even so, she believed she could have overcome these limitations if her partner had not quit and if the MDP continued to assist the business after her business mentor departed. Assessing the potential of microenterprise, Jennifer believed that it could help a family get ahead "*if the family head has knowledge and stamina. This is not for everyone. It takes a lot of financial backing. It should be explored to its fullest. . . . Most importantly, get support.*"

Doña Gloria's *Dulces y Jugetes*

Doña Gloria used to sell a little homemade candy out of her home until her daughter-in-law inspired her to add small toys and knickknacks to her inventory. The daughter-in-law helped her by traveling to a larger city to purchase inventory. At first the business went well. But because it was home-based, the business was limited by the small space. Then, her daughter-in-law stopped doing her purchasing and Doña Gloria did not have a car to buy and transport inventory herself. Nonetheless, she bought merchandise when she could, especially on trips to Mexico, to sell in the United States.

Many people in her area were employed in seasonal agricultural work. When agriculture is down—as it had been around the time of the interview—Doña Gloria said unemployment was high and there was little money in people's budgets for extras: "*I am selling very little because everything is dead [around] here. Everything. There is no work. . . . Dear God. Everything is ugly, ugly here now. There was not a large enough crop this year [because] the harvest finished in February rather than April.*" Customers owed Doña Gloria money. Payment for $2,000 in merchandise remained outstanding. She was waiting to see if her customers would pay her, but she did not insist on payment because she knew they were going through tough economic times.

In addition to the local economic downturn, she suffered with a heart condition that slowed her business. She also had been a "granny" to a friend's young child for almost two years. Her friend needed her help with child care and the young child was good company. She did not charge anything for caring for the child.

Despite the challenges, Doña Gloria kept her business open. She made her loan payments on a regular basis, sending $89 a month, which she paid out of the social security income that she had been receiving since her husband died. She found the staff at the MDP helpful and they treated her well. She had no checking account either for her household or for business, she carried no business accounts, and paid no taxes on her business. She said she made so little money that she did not see a need to formalize her accounting system.

Nonetheless, she said her business supplemented her meager income from social security, supplemental security income (SSI), and Food Stamps. She lived in subsidized housing and kept expenses low by living very frugally. With no car or access to public transportation, her children drove her wherever she needed to go. On the day before the interview, she grossed five dollars.

Laverne's Bakery and Catering Service

When Laverne was diagnosed with a heart problem, she gave up her job cleaning at a local hotel and opened a catering business. She had been encouraged by friends, relatives, and church members to try cooking for a living. She obtained a microloan and began making and selling items such as cheese biscuits, sausage biscuits, and potato jacks on a seasonal basis during the holidays. Her business made little money but she also managed not to lose money in the process and enjoyed doing it.

Like Doña Gloria, transportation was a problem because she did not own a car, so she settled for baking for local nursing homes, churches, and individuals mostly around the holidays. Support from fellow church members and from her pastor made operating her business easier. Her business showed a slight but steady decline over the years that she attributed to buying too much of the wrong kinds of food before knowing what her customers wanted.

Although she typically used her business profits to buy more food, she sometimes had to use them to pay the electric bill. Her business did not contribute much to her household income; she lived off of her widow's pension and disability checks. Despite low profits, Laverne was satisfied with her business. She enjoyed the work and felt that she could parlay her love for cooking into a small enterprise, although she still dreamed of owning a small restaurant someday.

What Explains Growth and Decline in Microenterprise?

What do the experiences of these entrepreneurs tell us about why some microenterprises do well and some do not? Allison's success is explained by a combination of creative talent and skills that helped her to reach out to a booming local market. Moreover, her inherited assets provided a location for her small, but successful, sewing business. Lanette's ability to work with people, skills from a prior job, and goal-directness helped her find a niche and grow her business. She also received invaluable support from others along the way, including inheriting a house, like Allison, which provided a location for her business. Like Allison and Lanette, John also inherited an important asset. Although he paid for the business, he believed the deal was a good one. And despite his nonchalance, John was succeeding in his business. He kept expenses low through careful planning and management and looked forward to launching a different kind of business in the future.

In contrast, Jennifer believed that she made the wrong business choice. Although the MDP encouraged the idea of a specialty food store, she did not have the resources or the product knowledge to compete successfully. The business also suffered setbacks when her business partner left and she had to relocate her business. Doña Gloria lacked a constant source of supplies and transportation, but perhaps most importantly, a poor local economy meant that people did not have extra income for the candy and knickknacks that she sold in her home-based business. Laverne's bakery and catering service barely broke even, although she did not live in an area as economically depressed as Doña Gloria. Without a car, she had difficulty marketing her baked goods. She earned enough to pay her high electric bills and she enjoyed the small business, but she did not count on her business income to survive financially.

Growth and decline are the result of a variety of factors in these cases. On one hand, business growth appears to be associated with well thought-out goals, opportune choice of business, product and management skills, financial support, and a good market. On the other hand, business decline is associated with poor product choices, a poor local economy, poor business skills, and lack of business infrastructure, especially access to markets and transportation. What do all eighty-six business owners say? To help the entrepreneurs focus their comments, we asked them to reflect on the factors that help explain the times when their business was making a profit, and what helped to explain the times when their business was losing money.

Business Growth

Table 6.1 lists the factors that entrepreneurs said contributed to business growth. Those mentioned most often were the entrepreneur's own skills and

Table 6.1
Explaining Growth: Primary and Secondary Facilitators
Identified by Entrepreneurs

	Primary Facilitator	Secondary Facilitator	Total Facilitators
Business skills[1]	20	6	**26**
Social support[2]	7	8	**15**
Business infrastructure[3]	11	3	**14**
Business capital[4]	8	2	**10**
Economic and social context[5]	2	1	**5**
Personal strengths[6]	2	2	**4**

[1]Business skills refers to the range of business attributes of the entrepreneur.

[2]Social support refers to availability of tangible and intangible support from others.

[3]Business infrastructure refers to the range of elements that support a business in its immediate environment.

[4]Business capital refers to availability of loans and other sources of capital for the business.

[5]Economic context refers to the environment in which the business operates.

[6]Personal issues refers to positive personal and family qualities or benefits.

business decisions, support from others, and availability of capital. In some instances entrepreneurs mentioned more than one factor. In these cases we ranked them as primary or secondary, according to the entrepreneur's emphasis. Some participants did not identify any facilitating factors, either because they did not articulate a reason for rising profits or because they did not perceive that their business had ever done well.

Business Skills

Many entrepreneurs attributed times of higher profits to their skills, including their ability to produce a quality product, their business talents, or their *"good business sense."* What do these mean? Most refer to confidence and pride in being able to produce a quality product (Table 6.2). As we saw in chapter 3, many entrepreneurs chose to open a business because they wanted an opportunity to do something they liked. Therefore, it is not surprising to find that many believed they produced a quality product. Pride is palpable in Sara's comment: *"It really feels good to spend a week, a day, an hour, and look back when you're finished with a product and know, 'That's a damn good job.' It just makes me want to go do more. I give myself a lot of pride."*

Table 6.2
Explaining Growth: Business Skills (n = 27)

	Number of Entrepreneurs
Selection and quality of product[1]	16
Marketing and networking[2]	5
General business[3]	6

[1]Selection and quality refers to the nature of the choice of product and ability to produce a quality product.

[2]Marketing and networking refers to their ability to market and develop the networks necessary to sell the product.

[3]General business skills refers to those who mentioned skills, but did not specify which ones.

They learned their skills from parents, in former jobs and businesses, in school, and through a variety of life experiences. Fred inherited the upholstery business from his father, who had built a solid reputation that Fred proudly upheld: "*Through my father's reputation and the reputation I have for doing quality work, clientele find me from the suburbs and everywhere. See, once I do a job for someone out there, then they make sure that they can find me. It's not a big business, I just make sure I do everything right.*"

Some said their business management skills helped their businesses succeed. For example, Sara previously had managed a 7-Eleven store: "*I have previously had jobs that gave me bookkeeping skills. What I do today is a reflection of all the experiences of all the jobs I have had throughout the years.*"

Others believed that they had the ability to time their business decisions well, to take advantage of a good market. For example, Monica thought she was making the most of demographic changes that supported her child products business because there are "*major babies*" right now. Susan said that her elder care business may have come a little early, but she was certain her business ultimately would benefit from demographic trends: "*Demographically, my studies have proven that we're in the heart of a population that could be coming to us any day. We're a little before our time, but we know the wave is coming.*"

Skills in marketing and sales contributed to business profits. Good communication skills, social skills, and ability to network helped businesses. Iris said loyal customers were essential: "*Orders from special customers that have come back in years past. I have a couple of ladies that continuously call me for special occasions. I get re-orders. It's not so many new customers that I have. It's just the old customers that are re-ordering.*" She calls her customers often and asks if they ever need anything. She is good at informal marketing and communication. She puts ads in free papers, gets her business known through word-of-mouth, and posts flyers at the community center and religious institutions around town. Sara also spoke of the benefits of word-of-mouth advertising:

> *There is a tremendous amount of competition. I never really advertise. I don't run my number in the Yellow Pages. It has just been a solid foundation of mouth-to-mouth referrals. There was a time that I tried running an ad in one of the free shoppers. I ran that ad for three months. I didn't receive even one call off that ad. I said, "This is baloney." If you are good at what you do, people talk. The referral, mouth-to-mouth, is 100 percent fantastic.*

Thomas also built his clientele through his involvement in the community. He donated his catering services in the aftermath of a destructive storm in order to help people and also to reach a wider clientele:

> *Like when the storm came through. . . . I asked a lot of other businesses and the Chamber of Commerce . . . we all got together and set up different booths in the park and fed the city employees, and their families, and gave them a day of appreciation for how hard they worked. There were about 600 employees, and 10 or 12 restaurants fed them all.*

Not only was he proud to help his community, it was also "*a lot of free advertising.*"

Social Support

While being a sole proprietor of a microenterprise takes a great deal of personal motivation, in reality, it is not "*something you can do on your own,*" as Doris said. Fifteen entrepreneurs said that tangible and emotional support were among the key factors that contributed to their business success. Support mostly came from family members and friends, but a few also mentioned MDP program staff and employers.

Spouses and partners supported some households while businesses were developing, making up for lost wages during start-up. Candy's husband, like several other spouses in this study, supported her business by covering household expenses with his salary while she reinvested all of her profits back to the business.

Allison said that her parents' assistance in buying a house provided much-needed support for the business. In her estimation, her standard of living did not fall when she started the business because "*even though I was bringing home less than $200 per week, I owned my own home.*"

Others received assistance that helped their businesses grow. Dan's brother helped him start his car-cleaning business: "*He really busted his butt [for free] to make that place go. He was out putting flyers on people's doors and doing all sorts of things. He was a positive influence.*" Brenda said that her friends helped staff the business. "*They always let me know that if I needed them, they were there. If I needed to take off to a funeral, or a buying trip, one of them would watch the store until I got back. . . .*" Shelby said her landlord lent her money, helped her find a car, and then let her use her rent deposit to purchase it. "*It was a car that wasn't the greatest, but it was nice enough and got me where I was going and started my day care.*" Friends in her apartment complex also helped care for the children in her day care: "*There was a grand-mother across the hall who was on-call—where if something would happen and I had too many kids, she would take the leftovers.*" Shelby also said she "*couldn't have done it without*" her mother, who helped run the household and the day care.

Valuable advice and emotional support also came from friends and family. For instance, Candy said that two friends from college provided advice, encouragement, and mentoring. Specifically, she said they help her set her prices and avoid undercharging her clients. In other cases, entrepreneurs said that friends and family offered emotional support that the entrepreneurs believed contributed to business growth. For example, Sara said that her boyfriend was helpful. After particularly difficult days, he advised her:

> "*OK, calm down. Maybe you should try this or maybe you should try something else.*" *He's been in the military for twenty years. He just has a way of saying,* "*OK, it's not as bad as it seems. Why don't you try taking it from this angle.*" *He's really the backbone of the business. . . . He calms me a lot. He has helped me the last three years tremendously. I don't think I would have been as successful at this point and time without him.*

Some viewed their businesses as family enterprises. Instead of receiving support here and there from family members, family were involved in business operations. When it came to his catering business, for example, Thomas believed that the family was "*all in it together.*" "*It's just a family thing. We plan our lives and our things around what we have to do.*"

Table 6.3
Explaining Growth: Business Infrastructure (n = 14)

	Number of Entrepreneurs
Good location	6
Existing business	4
Low overhead	3
Microenterprise program	1

Business Infrastructure

There are several business infrastructure factors (i.e., the range of elements that sustain a business in its immediate environment) that helped businesses grow, including a good physical location, acquiring an existing business, and minimizing overhead expenses (Table 6.3). Some entrepreneurs located their businesses where potential customers already existed. Carla, for example, operated a comic book shop in a downtown location near where the kids hung out and where there always was "*a lot of walking traffic*" that fed her business. Brenda also had a great location, "*right downtown on a main street*" where she was visible from the street and four doors down from the town's most popular restaurant. Diane's framing business benefited from being located in her family's art gallery. Heather considered herself lucky because she found a prime location "*right in the square*" and Terri moved her business to a location where "*almost all my clientele is walk-in business.*" Ed benefited from being near a major source of customers for his furniture. "*It was good because north of where I was at was a big campground that was open all year round where people would buy their lots and put a trailer on it or put up a fence. So we had a lot of people coming out from [the city] and they'd go right by the house and that's where I got a large portion of my business.*"

Some bought existing businesses that already had a reputation. Like John, who owned the janitorial business, Shawn believed that buying an existing business helped her profits. Peggy took over an existing business in a "*touristy*" part of town so she "*didn't start from scratch.*"

Others kept overhead low. Like Allison and Lanette, who opened this chapter, some kept expenses down because they operated out of buildings they owned. Linda's costs were low because she "*had enough space in my house. I had an office space in one of the bedrooms of my home. I also had some garage space where I kept the woodcrafts.*" A local service club owned the building where Jo ran her hairstylist business and, although she was responsible for rent and supplies, the equipment was included in her rent.

Business Capital

Several participants said that having capital available was important to business growth. For instance, Sergio said that obtaining financing was "*always positive—I received loans from [the MDP and the bank]. . . .*" Lessie used MDP loans to upgrade her hair salon and buy supplies, including a chair, hair, a manicuring table, storage, and upholstery. Laurel said that her $5,000 loan and ongoing public assistance permitted her to keep her business open.

When conditions are right, financial capital can help generate business growth. Diane said that receiving the MDP loan was cost-effective because "*The first loan I got with the help of [the program] was just the boost I needed. With that money I could buy wholesale and save a lot of time and money. This was the best thing I did.*" Similarly, Sara said that she had "*enough capital to keep the business going continuously. . . . Ever since that happened, the business has been growing and growing.*"

Allison said that inheriting a house offered financial security, a place to conduct business, and collateral for capitalizing her business.

> *I was fortunate because of the inheritance and because of my parent's house, that even though I was bringing home less than $200 per week, I owned my own home. But that was only because I had the benefit of my parents holding the mortgage, which I never would have been able to get at that point in my life. Because of the trickle up effect, I am more financially secure than I was. Now, my assets have increased, since I moved into this house. Since I have passed the five-year threshold, other businesses and banks will take you more seriously.*

Economic and Social Context

A few entrepreneurs pointed out that a strong local economy was critical to their business success. In most of these cases, thriving local or regional tourism provided opportunities for business growth. Like Allison's sewing business discussed at the beginning of the chapter, Judy's textile arts business was bolstered by local tourist development and by new art galleries moving into the area that brought in customers. Jeff also reported that there were plenty of potential customers. He did not have to advertise; he found all of his 225 customers through word-of-mouth.

In a few cases, racial, ethnic, or gender solidarity worked to the advantage of a business owner (Light & Gold, 2000). Leticia said her ethnicity helped her develop her sewing business, because "*the majority of my clients are Latinos.*" Although she quickly added, "*but I've had Black [customers]. I've also had a few [white] Americans*." Similarly, Theresa targeted her marketing efforts toward African Americans, saying that race was central to her business, helping talented young Black students obtain funds for college.

Personal Strengths

While personal strengths often translated into good business skills, some entrepreneurs specifically singled out their personal attributes, especially a clear vision, as the reason for business successes. For some it is an ability to see the "*bigger picture*," like Susan, who pointed out, "*I'm very much a person that looks long-term not short-term*." Jackie, a silk-screener, said she was optimistic about her business's future partly because she set her goals carefully and because she was comfortable with herself and her beliefs:

> *I have looked at what others have done, and I have used wisdom, and the business has come to me. I do not advertise, it comes to me every day through word-of-mouth, through the agencies. It has really not been the money. But I will use [my business] as a major income producer. . . . And I will provide jobs, which has always been my heart's desire. It should be very profitable. . . . People want to deal with someone who is talking the truth . . . They want to know that there is not something up your sleeve. That's the reason really why. . . . Some of the millionaires in town call me by my first name. I am respectful of all people. It has gotten me in a lot of doors. . . .*

Sandra also had a clear sense of her goals—and her limitations—which she believed helped her business do well: "*I am a person with a lot of ideas. . . . I could make whatever I wanted to. I would turn people down in a minute. If I couldn't see where I wanted to go, even though I was qualified, if you had something you wanted to make me do, and if I didn't want to tackle it, well, I would just send you to someone else.*"

Business Decline

Many of the same factors came up as entrepreneurs discussed reasons for business decline (Table 6.4). Sometimes entrepreneurs identified aspects of one factor that contributed to their business success and other aspects that contributed to decline. For example, as Lanette's case suggests, business skills can go both ways. Her management skills helped her business develop, but her lack of marketing skills made it difficult to grow fast enough: "*I did not know how to sell the business . . . . My management skills allowed me to survive, but I*

Table 6.4
Explaining Decline: Primary, Secondary, and
Tertiary Barriers Identified by Entrepreneurs

	Primary Barrier	Secondary Barrier	Tertiary Barrier	Total Barriers
Economic and social context[1]	25	9	6	**40**
Business skills[2]	18	15	5	**38**
Business infrastructure[3]	17	15	5	**37**
Business capital[4]	8	18	9	**35**
Life events[5]	9	11	2	**22**
Personal issues[6]	8	5	7	**20**

[1]Economic and social context refers to the economic, political, and social environment in which the business operates.

[2]Business skills refers to the range of business attributes of the entrepreneur.

[3]Business infrastructure refers to the range of elements that support a business in its immediate environment.

[4]Business capital refers to capital available for the business.

[5]Life events refers to specific personal and family episodes.

[6]Personal issues refers to personal and family impacts.

think I would be in a tremendous profit area right now if my selling skills were as good as my management skills."

Economic and Social Context

Many entrepreneurs believed that their communities had been bypassed by economic growth that was taking place in other parts of the country. Forty entrepreneurs thought that poor profits were related to the economic and social context, including a poor local economy, intense competition, seasonal fluctuations, and discrimination (Table 6.5).

The Mexican peso devaluation of the early 1990s resulted in a local economic slump that negatively affected businesses in the border area of New Mexico and Arizona. As Doña Gloria pointed out, people had little money in the wake of the devaluation. For a while, she kept selling, but then had to stop because people had no money to pay: *"If there is no money, why be battling to make them pay me? Better that I store it away. Now they owe me $2,000. One owes $100, another owes $150."* Similarly, Marta, a clothing retailer, said: *"With the devaluation in the peso, [our town] was badly hurt economically. The borderline is open to both communities—USA and Mexico—for temporary vis-*

Table 6.5
Explaining Decline: Economic and
Social Context (n = 40)

	Number of Entrepreneurs
Local economy	19
Competition	15
Discrimination	3
Seasonal fluctuation	3

its. [There is] exchange of goods and services between [Mexico] and [our town]. People left owing me lots of money and I couldn't collect."

Weak local economies were not confined to the Southwest. Paula, who lived in the Midwest, noted that for a period of three years it was difficult to sell anything in her community because it *"has been so depressed with a lot of lay-offs."* Mary also noted that factories had closed in her community, causing retail outlets like hers that served factory workers to close. The impact of the loss of business was pronounced and families moved away. In a more competitive en-vironment, larger businesses and organizations began cost-cutting measures that impacted microenterprises, some in very direct ways. Doris, who relied on con-tract development work with larger businesses, commented bluntly on the im-pact of cost-cutting: *"I could see myself making money, but people started using resources right within their own organizations. Nobody wanted to pay an out-sider to do anything unless they were in deep [trouble]"* Towns dominated by one or two industries were particularly vulnerable when economic downturns led to factory closings. Gwen said that business fluctuations were felt immedi-ately by her microenterprise because *"if people start to get scared about losing their jobs or [if] there are layoffs,"* they reduce consumption, especially of non-essential items.

Local economic downturn was so extreme in some places that poverty in-creased and reduced consumption among current and potential customers.[1] For example, Catarina reported that she had to be careful about what she sold because people had so little money. She began to stock inexpensive gifts like little cars and dolls for children. Some participants suggested that increased poverty led to more customers wanting lower prices and purchasing on credit. Business owners wor-ried; they often knew these people well, many were friends and family, and they found it difficult to turn them down.

Changes in welfare exacerbated the challenges of running a business. The Family Support Act of 1988, the waivers that followed, and the Personal Re-sponsibility and Work Opportunity Reconciliation Act (PRWORA) allowed states to deny clients benefits if they did not work. Some entrepreneurs said that they had noticed that their customers' purchasing power plummeted or that they delayed payments when their public assistance was trimmed by these measures. At one time, Doña Chela permitted her customers to purchase fairly large items "*on time*," but she began to insist on payment at the time of purchase.

Competition created problems for many businesses. Especially damaging for microenterprises were firms that sold similar but lower-priced products. For example, Dan said he had more competition than he originally anticipated in his car-cleaning business. Eleanor, who operated a small boutique, reported that there is "*so much competition out there. There are places for people to go, to get more variety and selection—their costs are lower. Once you get your costs up, you lose your customers because they can get things [cheaper elsewhere]*." Charles pointed out that although his merchandise was not high quality, it was the "*hot fashion*" for local customers. "*As long as Wal-Mart didn't have it,*" he did fine; however, when another boutique opened nearby, he was forced to close.

International competition was difficult for others, including Chester, a textile business owner, who said that the North American Free Trade Agreement (NAFTA) doomed his once-thriving business: "*After they passed that free trade thing from Mexico, there was a lot of equipment going there, and there were lots of imports. Our best customer went out of business. Another big customer switched their business over to a different line than what we were doing. That hurt us. We show a loss for the last two years and a big loss for this year.*"

Small local competitors made it difficult for microentrepreneurs, but large corporations that sold similar or competitive products more inexpensively were particularly challenging. Javier reported that people were "*shopping at big chain stores, they go to stores like Wal-Mart and Home Depot*" where merchandise is offered at lower prices, leaving the small businesses—including his electronics shop—unable to compete effectively. Leticia, the seamstress, said that she did not know how to "*compete with the stores that run 'specials' and have prices that are appealing to people.*" Anne's bakery suffered losses competing in a small town with large supermarkets and commuters who shopped out of town.

Seasonal fluctuations in business, due to weather and flow of customers (e.g., tourist seasons and university schedules) challenged some business owners to plan carefully for increases in work and revenues at certain times and slowdowns at other times. In businesses with very low revenues this was difficult, and sometimes they could not accommodate these fluctuations and went under. Long down-cycles strained businesses such as Shawn's small party store. Her business peaked in December and February and then bottomed out in the summer. In the Southwest, open-air businesses slumped during the months of intense summer heat.

Although racial, ethnic, and gender solidarity helped a few businesses, other business owners said there was little support from their own community. Angie, like Lanette, observed that locating their business in an ethnic market was difficult: "*sometimes . . . our own people don't want to patronize the business because of jealousy.*"

Several of the entrepreneurs talked about challenges presented by discrimination. For example, Cassandra said that being "*a black woman. . . . That's two strikes against you from day one . . . buying things and trying to get someone to maybe lend you money or even fix your home. It's a hard job.*" One person complained of discrimination in a MDP; she believed the program and staff were racist and directed their assistance to white entrepreneurs. Lessie said that she encountered difficulties when she joined an all-male barbershop: "*Things go on in a barber shop that are unmentionable to a women. It is not an atmosphere where they would want a woman invading their privacy—it had been a barbershop for so long.*" A few women said they found the attitudes of some male customers to be irksome and taxing. Peggy, who frequently encountered sexist comments, was most annoyed by male customers who assumed that a man—perhaps her husband or father—was the business owner. Similarly, Carla said that people sometimes came into her store assuming she was the owner's wife, sister, or daughter. Although it is impossible to measure the impact on business development, such actions may have a cumulative negative effect.[2]

Even some of the men agreed that gender discrimination affects business performance. Thomas believed that men have an advantage over women in running their own business: "*Men, we can open a few more doors than women can, whether we are Black or White. A lot of times you can get in to talk to people that a woman may not do.*" Carl, an accountant, thought that being a male accountant gave him an advantage in working with male clientele: "*Not to be prejudiced, but. . . . I do not think a lot of my male clients would go to a female. I don't know, for whatever reason, that's just my feeling.*"

However, MDP programs and affirmative action laws appeared to protect the entrepreneurs from discrimination's full impact. Two women pointed out that they believed opportunities were slowly expanding for women. Eileen said it was easy to feel intimidated in an industry dominated by "*big old-boy business*" where women are "*not the decision makers,*" but affirmative action had helped her obtain contracts. Renée also had a sense that opportunities for minority women in business were expanding, in large part because of the existence of the MDPs: "*Yes, things are changing now, so that minority women are getting to do things that years ago they couldn't.*"

A number of entrepreneurs drew a distinction between the reality of discrimination—which they readily acknowledged—and their ability to overcome the barriers. For example, Sara believed that being a woman hurt her business at first, but with time, she was able to overcome it. As a woman in the construction trades, she said her abilities were often questioned. Men were surprised when she would show up to do a painting job and hesitated to hire her. However, Sara pointed out that once she had overcome the initial barriers that sexism placed before her, she believed that being a woman might have helped. She was unique— a woman working in the trades—and she slowly built her business through word-of-mouth. In time, men began to send jobs to her. After completing work on a construction site, she said her fellow workers often would hire her to do work in their own homes. At this point she did not believe that discrimination was a serious problem for her business development.

We heard similar descriptions from others. In building a customer base, the entrepreneurs explained that their efforts to build a customer base were color-blind. For example, Charles, who is African American, said his town is "*70 percent Black, 26 percent White, and four percent Spanish.*" He had white and Black customers, while his wholesalers were often Korean. He thought that there were "*pretty good relations*" between the different races. Likewise, Eleanor, who was white, had Black and white customers; she said it did not matter to her. Laverne said that she has all kinds of customers although they are interested in different products: "*I have white customers who buy my biscuits. Black people mostly buy my sweet potato jacks.*" Jo said that sometimes being Black created a problem because her white elderly customers often had questions about whether she could do their hair, but she did not believe they were being racist. Brenda said: "*I get along with everybody, . . . I have all [kinds of] customers that are black and white and Hispanic. I just don't see any difference. . . .*" Fred, who is African American, believed that "*some whites will not go to blacks, and some blacks will not go to whites.*" His clientele was 75 percent white. In this sense, he believed that his reputation overcame racial bias and he was able to draw people from across town, not just from his immediate—and mostly Black—neighborhood. He emphasized that it was quality, not race, which made the difference. Amy asserted that she treated everyone the same; they are all customers. They come from all over the state and from out of state as well. She advertised in the phone book and had friends, neighbors, and family spread the word. Her customers always returned. Shoving aside the idea of differences, she said she had only three words that she works and lives by: "*Friendship, truth and honesty.*"

These examples illustrate that although many of the entrepreneurs recognized the existence of discrimination, racism, and sexism, and believed that they had suffered its consequences to some degree, they distinguished between dynamics operating outside their businesses and those within. They underscored the importance of maximizing their market—whoever or wherever their customers might be. In short, they were interested in selling a product to anyone interested in purchasing.

Table 6.6
Explaining Decline: Business Skills (n = 38)

	Number of Entrepreneurs
Marketing/advertising	14
Business planning & management	9
Product choice and skills	7
Bookkeeping & financial mgt.	4
Purchasing and pricing	4

Business Skills

Business owners were more apt to believe in their ability to make a product or deliver a service (although a few were unsure of even these product skills), than to have confidence in their ability to manage the business side of the work. Marketing, management, bookkeeping and finances, pricing, and purchasing were especially challenging (Table 6.6). Thomas articulated the difference between having a product skill and knowing how to make it into a business. While he had a knack for cooking, he laughed when we asked him how prepared he felt to run a business, he said, "*Not really. I went out on a 'rooster.' I was searching. . . . Like I told my wife, I know how to cook, but getting out here and knowing how to serve and how much food to fix, or how they are going to eat, or whatever the case may be. . . . [that's the problem]*"

Many felt under-prepared in the area of advertising and marketing. As Carl said: "*Every advertising venture that I have ever done, I have never made squat on. I have never even gotten one [job] out of it. It is terrible. . . .*"

Marketing skills in a global economy presented other challenges. Eileen began to export her handmade toys, but ran into problems with an international trade deal in which she lost money. She believed she needed better understanding of how to market internationally and how to protect her investments.

Good marketing also meant keeping in touch with old customers. Leticia, whose sewing business was doing well, noticed that her sales fell after her family moved. "*Then my sales dropped in the first few months quite a bit, and I remembered what I had failed to do . . . I realized that . . . I had not called my old customers.*" Once she contacted them, her business began to grow again.

Some entrepreneurs had to learn how to charge for their services. Carol explained how difficult it was for her to market her product: "*I'm not one to sell myself. Even when we get [jobs], I shy off from the money part of it. I'm not yet what I want to be in terms of promoting, I'm very accommodating with people.*"

Or as Lessie described, "*I was prepared to do the work, but not the business. I was not prepared to charge people. . . . I have difficulty in accepting my money from you. I don't understand it, but that's the way I am.*"

Although most entrepreneurs believed they produced a quality product, some believed they either needed more product training or had made a poor product choice. Jennifer and her partner had only a "*basic survey knowledge*" of the specialty food business. In retrospect, she concluded that they needed another year of training. Robert said customers at first liked the idea of bringing their tools to him to be sharpened, but once the novelty wore off, and tools became cheaper, they began to purchase new tools instead: "*Well, when everybody first heard about it they liked the idea. Then . . . everything changes and everybody goes for something new. [They] started buying . . . throw-away [tools].*" In hindsight, he believed that his product choice was misguided. Similarly, Dan said self-employment can work, but the choice of business has to be realistic. Looking back, his was not:

> *I don't think that the car wash was one that was meant to work out. Your hands were kind of tied. Either you stay there and work by yourself all day (and it would take you most of the day to do one car if it was a complete job—and you would make $80). That was the best-case scenario. But if you hire someone to help you, then you are not making any money either.*

Others reported that they lacked management skills. In Javier's case, for example, this meant the ability to supervise his store managers: "*Everything was in the store, everything was paid for, all the managers had to do was walk in and sell and get a commission.*" Unfortunately, they did not report all their sales and inventory and pocketed the profit from sales. As a result, for a period of time, Javier said he was left with no profit and a damaged reputation as well.

Lack of skills in financial management, accounting, and bookkeeping created problems for others. For example, John said that he had problems "*keeping on top of billing.*" He had to learn from experience, accommodating the idiosyncrasies of certain clients, including those who would only pay in cash. Yolanda conceded that she lacked financial management skills: "*Well, it seems that I didn't have a good orientation, as a financial manager and also in purchasing things.*" Efforts to make sure that the entrepreneurs formalize their bookkeeping procedures apparently did not overcome Jo's reluctance to use banking services. She kept her money at home: "*The banks have done a number on me. So I don't like banks anymore . . . I want to keep my own money.*"

A few business owners said problems with purchasing and pricing led to business losses. Leticia found purchasing for her successful bridal dress business difficult especially at first, before she learned where to shop for less expensive materials. Another entrepreneur, Cassandra, was prepared for design and sewing, but did not feel skilled in setting prices. If a customer did not have enough money, she just cut the price. She had other sales experience—with Avon and Fuller Brush—and found the selling easy, but pricing was trickier.

Business Infrastructure

The entrepreneurs suggested that business infrastructure problems—such as poor location and facilities; high overhead; lack of transportation, parking, and equipment; lack of information about low-cost suppliers; and problems with employees—affected business performance (Table 6.7).

High rents and poor building quality were problems for several entrepreneurs. High rents hurt Doug's vending cart business in the mall, especially during the holidays when retailers make most of their annual profits. Moreover, he could not always get assigned a good location within the mall, further affecting his revenues. Thomas's first facility and location negatively affected his business: *"The location where I was at was hurting me. Everything was closing down there, in a predominately Black neighborhood. It went downhill. I had a lot of break-ins one year."* The health department had given his business a poor rating because of the condition of the building (not because of the food or cleanliness), which caused him to lose business until he was able to relocate. Eleanor's business was a victim of theft: *"It was close to Christmas. The weather was bad out. I ordered an inventory—a large one, for a person like me—and set it up on display. People came and shopped, and bought . . . [but then] someone came overnight and took some things."* After that she was fearful of working in the little trailer where she located her business. She said she neglected the business and it went downhill.

Operating from home often helped to keep overhead low, but it sometimes caused other problems. Amy said that family members got in her way, the house was always a mess, and it was difficult for her to keep financial boundaries clear between home and business. If she could move into her own shop, she believed she *"could go highly above and beyond what my [current] expectations are."*

Other infrastructure problems included lack of parking in front of businesses and lack of transportation. Steven's business was located in a congested part of downtown where customers had difficulty finding a parking space. He believed this took a significant toll on his desktop publishing business. Vilma could not get to her customers because she did not have a car. Her business had begun to make a profit, but then it ran into trouble when *"One day it started downhill . . . I didn't have any transportation . . . a friend used to take me, but he had a problem and from that date I haven't had transportation. . . . This is my worst obstacle."* Lois, an artist who lived some distance from the region's art

Table 6.7
Explaining Decline: Business Infrastructure (n = 37)

	Number of Entrepreneurs
Facility and overhead	6
Microenterprise program	5
Transportation	5
Location/parking	5
Employees	4
Market and network access	4
Equipment and supplies	3
Security	3
Business partner	2

center, said that transportation was a large expense for her and she could not network and market her work adequately without it. Laverne also said that she could sell a lot more of her product if she only had transportation. She was unable to deliver her baked goods on a regular basis ("*I had to stop doing that because I had no drivers*"), so she cut back to baking only for holidays.

Several entrepreneurs had problems with employees. Javier went into debt when his salesperson stole from the business. Vera said that qualified help is difficult to find: "*people will tell you they know how to sew, when they can't thread a needle.*" Sara found that employees often do not have the skill or do not want to work hard: "*The most prominent obstacle is to find employees that can actually paint. Everybody says they can, until they are actually on the job. . . . I've probably gone through maybe ten other people. They can't paint. They show up for work and they don't really want to work.*"

Others had difficulties with their partners. Jennifer never really knew why her business partner "*stepped out*" six months into the business, but thought that the business required too much of her partner's time and profits were disappointing. Although the MDP provided counseling and support, Jennifer recognized that this crisis took a toll on her business. Fred's partners also left his business, causing him to downsize: "*After they all left, pursuing their own avenues, that's when I seen it necessary to downsize. . . . And I borrowed money to rebuild the house I'm in and after my help left, I decided I would just move all my business back here to a home-based business. . . .*"

Others lacked different forms of business infrastructure, including connections in the business community and to potential markets. Occasionally, the entrepreneurs developed business networks among each other (e.g., hiring each other, sending business their way, or exchanging business services), or with business owners they met in the MDP training or in their business work. For example,

Vera said that she remained in contact with, and exchanged business services with, one or two former members of her peer group. Unfortunately for most of the entrepreneurs, these relationships were rarely sustained. Gwen said she bartered with other business owners on occasion, including her chiropractor, with whom she exchanged picture-framing services. Another entrepreneur, Terri, traded haircuts a couple of times for work done in her shop. Lanette offered her training for free in exchange for someone helping her with typing and fund-raising. A friend of Juanita's helped her market her product in exchange for free merchandise. Although it is unclear if bartering helped her business, Sherri said she bartered with several people:

> *I do trades with different people. . . . The booth display that I'm going to do for the festival—that's being traded. At this point, people are paying me rent for my space upstairs. If they don't have $125.00 for the rent then I've said, "OK, let's just work it out."*

Some entrepreneurs developed other social networks that helped them to leverage support and resources for their businesses. Susan said that she developed good relationships with her lenders that resulted in help for her business: "*Then as time went on we were fortunate in not only technical assistance from lenders but one of the groups gave us a computer.*" Laurel's main customer lent her a computer—and later also lent her money that she paid back by publishing his materials at a reduced rate. In Doris's case, a friend who bought and sold used computer equipment gave her a computer. She also reported that she had received outdated business equipment from a local community center.

But most entrepreneurs did not establish reliable and steady relationships that reached wealthier customers and more resource-rich environments. As a result, most remained relatively socially isolated as they pursued their business goals. Several said they felt uncomfortable and unwelcome in the local business community and, as a result, believed they missed business opportunities. For instance, Lois felt confident about her business abilities. She had a bachelor's degree in fine arts, experience in art administration, and skills in business management. Nonetheless, she said, "*[I] still don't feel confident to go into high-profile*" places. Shawn said she had made an effort to get involved in the local Chamber of Commerce, but members never reached out to her or patronized her business. Jennifer tried to join a local businesswomen's association, but said she felt out of place. Although she did not tie her comment *directly* to business growth, this quote illustrates the difficulty of building connections to the business community:

> *They were women that had been in business for years. A lot more years than what I had. We went to that group meeting. They invited us, of*

*course, being in the community now. [But] they were not as supportive
as what I thought they would be. They were very—me, a low-to middle-
class person—they were very high class. I did not fit in whatsoever. I
just didn't feel comfortable. So I did not stay with that group.*

A few entrepreneurs gained access to substantial business opportunities
through their various social networks. For example, Thomas' business benefited from his connections to other business owners. His employer allowed him
to use the facility as a base of operations for some of his catering activity: *"If it
weren't for [my employer], I wouldn't be where I am today . . . [it] has been real
good to me. I have used what I want to use there. I have been a chef there for
many years. I come and go as I please. As long as the work gets done, and I get
out what needs to be done there, I don't have any problem."* Moreover, Thomas
constantly built connections to others in the community through volunteer work
and other joint activities. He said: *"I do a lot of things for my friends. Different
functions come up, and they'll call us and we do things for them, for different
churches, different organizations."* These relationships paid off. For instance,
Thomas said that he *"had a few doors open"* and he obtained some equipment
because he knew some influential people through his job.

Thomas' catering business also benefited from family support. His wife
kept the books and the whole family, including his grown children, helped on a
regular basis:

*All my family—all of them—work other jobs, and when they get off other
jobs, if we have something to do, they do it. My son now works . . . and
during the night, or afternoon when he gets out, he asks his dad, "Do
you need me to do so and so tonight?" or "Do you need me to do so
and so tomorrow for the catering business?" They all jump right in. I
have a church that I feed every Wednesday night, and when [my son]
gets off work . . . he will go and serve about 60 people at the church. I
have [another job] that I feed twice a day, and those boys eat at 10:00
at night, and he will leave the church and go over there tonight. On
Tuesdays and Thursdays, [my son] goes to school, and my brother's
sister, she'll go [work] one or two nights a week. My daughter, she'll
prepare stuff for tonight. I just took time off so I could talk to you,
today. So, like I said, it's just a family thing. We plan our lives and our
things around what we have to do. My wife has a little appointment
book here, and everything is printed there, and everything for the weekend, she prints it on a board, and everybody knows what has to be
done, and what time. Like my daughter—she just got married—and her
and her husband will figure out, "If we are going to have to do grocery
shopping, we will have to do it tomorrow night, or if I get my hair fixed,*

on Wednesday night—because they know Friday and Saturday we are going to have to feed . . . Everybody works around [the business].

These relationships were reciprocal. Thomas shared business profits with the family and included them in decision making: *"We know that after the function is done, we are rewarded. They know that I don't pocket all the money, or take all the proceeds. If there is something to be bought, we all sit down and discuss it. I don't go out and make a decision and say we are going to buy this, and that's it. It's not done that way. If I see a pattern of dishes I like, or my daughter sees one, we all come in and we all see if we can afford it, and we buy it."*

Compare Thomas' experience to Geneva's. Geneva's husband was supportive, emotionally and financially, and the children helped out on a regular basis. She had a job with benefits and never had to rely on social assistance programs of any kind. But when her husband lost his job, she had to close the business. The support she had from her husband did not extend very deep nor did she have any connections to the larger business community.

Or compare Thomas' experience to Doña Gloria's. She had support from a niece who helped her get into the business and assisted in purchasing low cost supplies, a daughter-in-law had a business and provided advice, and her children provided transportation (she did not have a car) and other assistance. But like Geneva, the support was shallow and it was not long term. Her niece quit the business after a year or so to take a job and other family members entered periods of instability. She reported: *"My niece looked for other work, my daughter-in-law closed her business. My uncle had an accident, and all of this disrupted my business. I had to go to my uncle's funeral. It was only four days, but I came back completely disheartened."* Without transportation, she could not continue to attend classes. An inveterate businesswoman, Doña Gloria continued to sell, but only to those in the immediate neighborhood and only with the merchandise she happened to have on hand. Her business stayed open, but it did not thrive.

Business Capital

Although microentrepreneurs generated or borrowed capital from the MDPs, banks, personal savings, family, friends, and credit cards, many reported that these sources were inadequate and resulted in lack of growth or poor business performance. Over two-fifths (35) of respondents explained that downturns in business profits were partially a result of insufficient capital (Table 6.8). The entrepreneurs said they especially needed more capital for equipment, supplies, advertising, and expansion.

Isabel said she needed more money for equipment to increase her productivity and product quality. Specifically, she needed a larger sewing machine: *"I*

Table 6.8
Explaining Decline: Business Capital (n = 35)

	Number of Entrepreneurs
Lack capital generally	18
For advertising	8
For business expansion	4
For equipment	2
For supplies	2
Timing of loans	1

think that I could have done better with more money. Well . . . I lacked the sewing machine . . . I tried to do alterations but I didn't have the machine. I had a little machine but it couldn't do the job. At that time they offered me an alterations job and I went to work."

Although the MDPs provided the most stable source of funding for the most businesses, the entrepreneurs pointed out that there were shortcomings to this form of borrowing. The most common problem was that the loans were too small. Clarise observed that the loan program was like *"dangling a bone in front of a hungry dog. When people got $1,500 they probably did not use it for what it was planned for because they had so many other needs to take care of."* Rosa María also thought the loan offered was insufficient: *"They could have loaned me more money. One thousand dollars is not much when you are running a business. They also changed directors at [the program] and the new director was really strict. . . . She would not lend as much money."* Thomas who succeeded in raising capital without much help from the MDP, observed, *"The main thing was, I think I got five thousand dollars from them one time, but . . . that was like pulling a needle out of a haystack, it was nothing to get your feet wet with."*

Peer group loans, in particular, were viewed as problematic.[3] While group members did not necessarily object to incremental lending (successively larger amounts lent as the loans are paid),[4] many did not like the idea of group liability. As Joanne said: *"If one person 'messed up' they punished everyone in the program for it through their loans. This is the reason I decided to go for my credit line instead of working with [the program]."* Brenda believed that the MDP misrepresented itself in the process:

We were in a group, and in the beginning, it started out really well. But then it got to where everything was oppressed, because of the meetings,

*because it would take a long time. Some of the members had applied for
loans and when they did the second level [applied for a larger second
loan] and got to the third level, they were denied and told that they
could not get that amount. It just made everybody a little upset. Because
to me, it was a little deceptive, you know.*

Loans that were too small meant that entrepreneurs often had to choose to
invest in one aspect of their business, leaving another waiting until there were
funds. Although business owners face many difficult choices, in some cases,
the businesses were below a basic threshold for survival. For example, Yolanda,
who operated a catering business out of her home, said that when the program
gave her $500, she invested in supplies she needed, but she did not have enough
for advertising. As a result, *"because I didn't have many ads, I couldn't make
any money. . . . the most I made was $250. I think if I had more funds I could
have made more."*

Several said they lacked capital for business expansion. Terri, a barber,
lamented, *"I had an opportunity to buy another beauty salon. I really wanted to
do it for an investment but the bank wouldn't loan me the money—because they
said I had too many bills and they couldn't see how I could swing it."* Cassandra said that the loans were only enough to keep the business going, but not
enough to make it profitable: *"You keep turning [the money] over, trying to get
your business started. [But] you don't make a profit."*

Others said they were led to believe that they would receive larger loans.
George, for example, felt misled when he only received $5,000 of the
$25,000 that he thought he was going to receive. Without adequate funds, he
said he could not buy the necessary supplies and equipment, which threatened his business viability. Angie also felt *"tricked"* by her case manager into
joining a peer-lending group where she was lent only $8,000 of the $20,000
that she needed to expand her business, despite having paid off two previous
loans successfully.

Others thought the interest on loans was too high and they were expected
to repay too quickly.[5] This was especially difficult when their businesses were
just getting under way. Because of high interest rates and short pay-back schedules, Juanita said she did not want to take out another loan: *"When I applied for
the first loan, the amount that we paid back was so high, and I had a difficult
time with trying to get the money because I was in school. . . ."* Shawn thought
that the financial pressure of high loan payments together with the costs she in-
curred when she hired an employee were responsible for her business closing.

Some entrepreneurs avoided loans—even when their business needed
them—for fear of incurring too much debt.[6] Ruth explained: *"The loans I received were never larger than $600. I didn't want to risk asking for more be-
cause the payments would be higher and if I couldn't earn that much it would*

be difficult." When asked if she thought the money she received was sufficient for her business plans, she continued: "*No, it wasn't enough (capital)
but I said to myself I can pay this even if something [unforeseen] happens. I
didn't want to tempt myself with $1,000 because if I couldn't pay it back, what
would I do?*" Too much debt might also give them a bad credit rating. Shelby
pointed out, for instance, that she did not want to risk taking out a large loan
because she was trying to build her credit rating in hopes of eventually purchasing a home. Many of the entrepreneurs talked about the difficult decisions they had to make about the amount they could borrow, weighing their
business needs against their financial obligations and the amount of time that
they could operate at low capacity.

Borrowing enough money to build a business without taking on too much
debt created tensions for many business owners. "*There is no business that
doesn't have debts,*" said Doña Chela. Many of the entrepreneurs had experience with debt and bad credit in the past and were understandably reluctant to
borrow large sums for their businesses, even when it might have been a good
business decision.

Life Events

Living at a financial edge, there was little money or time for dealing with
family problems or other crises that disrupted their businesses and directly impacted business performance (Table 6.9). Crises included illness and injury,
pregnancy, depression, divorce, and job loss. These crises caused interruptions
in business, forcing some to cut back on their hours or to close temporarily and
often drained resources from the businesses. These problems often led to major
business setbacks or permanent closure.

Health problems and disabilities among the entrepreneurs and their families included sickness, chronic health problems, hospitalization, and accidents.
Acute illnesses set back businesses because of health care costs, time away
from the business, and costs associated with paying someone to help. For example, Anita suffered an injury that forced her to stop working and to seek assistance from welfare. Her business did not survive. When Laurel got pregnant
and ran out of money before the baby was born, her employer advanced her
money and she paid it back later by doing publishing for him at a reduced rate.
Rosa María had to take money from her business to pay for her medical bills.
She did not have adequate time to invest in her business. After moving in with
her married son, she began a part-time job cleaning homes, although that too
had to be put on hold when she became ill. In the end, her illness caused her to
lose many customers.

Several suffered from chronic illnesses or disabilities that took a long-term
toll on business. Ironically, several of these entrepreneurs chose microenterprise

Table 6.9
Explaining Decline: Life Events (n = 22)

	Number of Entrepreneurs
Illness/accident	17
Pregnancy	2
Depression	1
Divorce	1
Spouse job loss	1

because it offered a way to make a living while accommodating a long-term disability or chronic illness (see chapter 3). Unfortunately, a disabling condition sometimes also made it difficult to operate a business. For example, Iris's business had grown slowly partly because her arthritis prevented her from working many hours at a time: "*It gets so bad that usually when I'm out and I get wet or something, I'm in bed for a few days after that.*" Her illness also prevented her from attending shows to sell her craft. She coped by making at least one item per day—a personal goal that kept her and her business going. Kathleen, a masseuse, said that her ability to work was markedly reduced by chronic pain. Business revenues fell because of the stress, her health worsened, and she then had to cut back on her hours. During some months she did not have any income at all from her business, although at the time of the interview she said, "*Now I'm stabilized and I feel pretty safe.*" Carol contended with several health conditions at the same time: she had arthritis, her husband was chronically ill, her adolescent daughter was pregnant, and her mother was sick. Her business, while moderately successful, did not bring in enough profit for them to survive financially. They patched together income, including odd jobs such as yard-work, but the stress was high as they tried to make ends meet and cope with personal troubles at the same time. As a result, their enthusiasm for the business was high but sporadic:

> We were trying to figure out our business plan in the class, what type of business to do, and we didn't want to live on welfare. My husband's always had health problems and I have rheumatoid arthritis. . . . It's hard to focus when your family life has gone to heck.

Other Personal Issues

Several other personal issues interfered with business as well, including lack of time, family interference, family responsibilities, and motivation (Table 6.10). Lack of time was an issue that many entrepreneurs simply could

Table 6.10
Explaining Decline: Personal Issues (n = 20)

	Number of Entrepreneurs
Motivation/time	9
Family responsibilities	7
Goals conflicts	2
Family interference	1
Confidence/anxiety	1

not overcome and it took a toll on business. Businesses often competed with the demands of child care, elder care, part-time or full-time jobs, or school. Although time is in short supply for everyone, patching together various sources of earned and unearned income (chapter 5) increases time pressures for low-income entrepreneurs.

Several entrepreneurs worked full-time jobs, several jobs, or attended school, in addition to taking care of their families. For example, although Clarise knew that the more time she spent on the business the better it performed, working full-time *"was an advantage because it was more money."* She continued, *"but it was a disadvantage because I would be at work five days a week, nine-to-five, and I couldn't get out to do my business."* Cora's tax preparation business suffered because she was also in school and worked a part-time job.

The difficulties of operating a business and making time and ends meet sometimes resulted in lack of motivation. As Diane, whose business had closed, observed: *". . . I had the energy to buy the supplies, but when it came to actually making the product I was burned out."*

Family matters sometimes interfered with business development. Ed's family, for example, was supportive and things went well for the first couple of years, but then *"All of a sudden my sister-in-law started creating all sorts of problems. That was when I had to move the business off the [family's] property to a separate location."* This conflict set his business back. Another participant, Allison, took in three foster children to help make ends meet. Not surprisingly, with the children to care for, her business slowed down. She had managed to keep the business open, however, and was working to rebuild it.

Multiple Challenges in Enhancing Business Performance

This chapter underscores the importance of ongoing support for microenterprise, especially for skill-building and financial capital. The entrepreneurs attributed good business performance to the skills they brought to their businesses, but they also attributed poor performance to lack of business skills. Generally, they had greater confidence in their business product, but less confidence in their ability to manage their business and to market their product. Some of the skill areas identified were particular to their specific business (e.g., specialty foods), and some were more general (e.g., financial management). These findings suggest the importance of assessing skill levels prior to opening a business and upgrading skill levels prior to opening a business. However, skill-building requisites continue well past start-up, suggesting the importance of ongoing training and individual guidance or coaching.

Many entrepreneurs also emphasized the importance and the difficulty of obtaining adequate financial capital at the right time for the business. In chapter 4, the entrepreneurs acknowledged the importance of microloans in helping them get their businesses off the ground. In this chapter, a few entrepreneurs said that the availability of loans, including microloans, contributed to business success over time. Others underscored the advantage of having some assets. For example, owning a home provided some entrepreneurs a stable business location that did not cost them additional rent. But many more said that they lacked adequate capital to develop their businesses. Relatively few were likely to qualify for traditional loans because credit-scoring techniques[7] used to determine creditworthiness, tend to disqualify low-income people, especially those with past credit problems. Moreover, many entrepreneurs continued to be torn between needing financial capital on the one hand, and trying to avoid too much debt on the other. This situation suggests the value of developing financial reserves (Schreiner & Morduch, 2002). Thus, saving strategies may be as important as credit.

The entrepreneurs said that their social support networks provided tangible and emotional support that helped business performance. This support was helpful in dealing with a variety of personal challenges, including illness and disability, lack of motivation, time pressures, and family troubles and responsibilities. Sometimes social support was not sufficient, particularly when it was not matched with other kinds of support. In other words, when entrepreneurs lacked health insurance or reliable child care, occasional baby-sitting or help with the business was not enough. A serious bout of illness, disability, or an accident exacted a toll on business performance. These findings suggest that MDPs should help entrepreneurs think through—in a very concrete way—the types and levels of support they will need.

Many of the entrepreneurs chose business at least in part because it offered multiple benefits, including the ability to earn income from a job and a business, and to care for family at the same time (see chapter 3). But data in this chapter suggest that, for some, multiple responsibilities led to time and stress management problems, making it difficult to work out a long-term investment strategy for the business. A few entrepreneurs admitted that, in the end, they realized they were unprepared for the time and stress involved in operating a business, especially given their family responsibility, job, and/or schooling, all of which competed for time and resources.

As chapter 4 indicates, MDPs facilitated entry into, and provided initial resources for, businesses. But over the longer term, these resources were not sufficient. The entrepreneurs highlighted a need for a visible, safe, and easy-to-reach location, appropriate transportation, effective ways to contact new customers, and ways to keep overhead expenses low.

They also mentioned lack of entrée and acceptance in business networks. Unlike the ethnic entrepreneurs described by Ivan Light and Steven Gold (2000), who benefited from the resources of coethnics, few in this study appeared to have benefited from such links. To some extent, this may be a function of selection, since these entrepreneurs turned to an MDP for capital and training, as opposed to alternative structures of support and opportunity within their co-ethnic group. In other words, low-income entrepreneurs with access to social networks with sufficient resources for enterprise formation may be less likely to turn to an MDP. Unfortunately, for the entrepreneurs in this study, their families, friends, and the MDPs lacked the ability to link the entrepreneurs to business networks. The MDPs attempted to build these bridges by bringing in speakers from the business community, and trying to establish mentoring relationships through programs like the Service Corps of Retired Executives (SCORE), but the entrepreneurs seldom pointed to these efforts when discussing business performance. In fact, the few times that these efforts were addressed (e.g., participants who attempted to join business groups) were negative. It is crucial that entrepreneurs build support and social networks beyond family and friends, and eventually, beyond the MDP.

Although a few entrepreneurs said that the economic and social context was strong and helped their businesses, many more described the challenge of operating a small business in an adverse climate. A closer look at the economic boom of the 1990s shows that while most Americans' income and wealth grew, many did not share in the economic prosperity (Porter & Dupree, 2001). They lived in communities where the opportunities for decent jobs with living wages were scarce, welfare reform had dealt a blow, businesses were leaving, education and social services were inadequate, and they continued to face discrimination. Passed over by economic growth, these "pockets of poverty" could not seem to grab hold of economic opportunity that was embracing other American communities. In the 1990s, as President Clinton promoted the New Markets and Community Renewal Initiative, he traveled to some of the most persistently poor areas of the country. On one of those trips, reporters talked to a man in Appalachia who said, "It seems like [Clinton's] big boom skipped this place." He added: "Now the welfare cutbacks in food stamps and all is hurting us bad. The only money around here is during the two weeks after the welfare checks come" (Clines, 1999).

Several entrepreneurs highlighted the difficulty of selling to very low-income consumers, especially during lean times. In such a situation, business owners do not easily prosper.

Similarly, the microentrepreneurs in this study said that local economies were hurt by currency devaluation in neighboring countries, business cutbacks and factory closings, and competition from large corporate enterprises. These economic factors are completely beyond the control of the entrepreneurs and the MDPs. We can only conclude that microenterprise cannot be highly successful everywhere, and unfortunately, it may be least successful where it is most needed.

Similarly, the microentrepreneurs said that changes in welfare policy impacted their businesses. Although social assistance policy provided support for self-employment to some of the participants (Plimpton & Greenberg, 2000), several participants pointed out that there was lack of coordination between microenterprise programs and the social welfare system that were disincentives to business formation and development. As Carol said: "*I never felt cooperation between the two departments [welfare and MDP]. . . . It requires money to start a business, and you're not going to get anywhere if they pull your food.*" Cooperation is needed so "*they don't pull the rug out from under you. . . . I'm not sure the waiver they did get in place really helped because it only waived you from certain things.*" Candy said that because of welfare regulations, she lost her benefits very soon after she began to earn some revenues in her business. She felt penalized, saying that she was dropped from welfare and food stamps and also lost her subsidized housing (her rent increased from $350 to $500 a month). Although she could be considered a success because her business was still open, she said she still was not making a profit when she was dropped from the welfare roles. This raises two questions: how are entrepreneurs reporting business revenues and profits, and how actively is the welfare department supporting microenterprise?

Loss of Medicaid coverage was particularly difficult for some microentrepreneurs. As we have seen, many of the entrepreneurs coped with disabilities, family illness, and other health issues. Requirements to work full-time and loss of medical benefits would challenge even the most enterprising business owners. Monica, for example, had to hire help to care for her chronically ill baby, but her business was going well. She had found a niche market where competition was low, but as a single mother on welfare, she was frustrated by new welfare-to-work rules that did not take her situation into account.[8] She talked to a welfare worker who "*literally treated me like . . . I was scamming welfare.*" Finally, they "*nailed me to the wall,*" and required her to accept a forty-hour-a-week job, in addition to trying to run her business and take care of her baby. "*I have never come to these state programs with my hand out. I don't know many women who would go back to work with . . .*

[such a sick] baby!" Finally *"I threw up my hands. . . . It was literally the turning point."* She was forced to close her business after her Medicaid was terminated because she could not afford the health insurance.

Race, ethnic, and gender discrimination also affected business performance. As highly motivated and resourceful people, the microentrepreneurs worked hard to overcome these barriers, and in some cases were successful. Despite their awareness of the challenges, in their own businesses they tried to develop a broad customer base, regardless of social class and racial or ethnic identity. However, the relatively better business performance of male and whites during the study period (see chapter 5) indicates that disadvantages of gender and race are not always overcome. Gender and race discrimination described by some of the entrepreneurs supports feminist theory and disadvantaged worker theory. The work history described in chapter 3 also provides evidence of employment barriers.

Results suggest the importance of human capital theory in explaining business performance. Business experience and the training provided by MDPs helped, but they needed more financial education and business training and a way to continue building their skills.

Resource constraints included lack of financial backup, business connections, and a geographic and social context conducive to business development. Loans from the MDP assisted with business capitalization, but were insufficient. The entrepreneurs' social capital provided emotional support and some instrumental assistance, but did not extend to business networks that might have helped them gain access to information and resources outside their immediate context. Furthermore, the entrepreneurks often lacked access to transportation and communication needed to operate successful businesses. Another type of resource, financial assets, including savings or a house, provided support for households and businesses. This suggests the important role of assets as a foundation for the risk taking required in business development (Sherraden, 1991).

The barriers that entrepreneurs encountered in microenterprise require a range of solutions at the individual or microlevel, at the intermediary or mezzolevel, and at the policy or macrolevel. At the microlevel, entrepreneurs need greater opportunities, especially over the longer-term, to build skills and generate capital. At the mezzo-level, entrepreneurs need an improved business infrastructure with more effective links to business networks. At the macrolevel, policy could be designed to provide health coverage, child care, supportive business policies, regulatory reform, and universal financial education that would provide a supportive context for microenterprise (as well as other development strategies). We discuss these in detail in chapter 8. Before that, however, chapter 7 explores why most of the entrepreneurs interviewed in this study say they preferred small business to other types of work.

Notes

1. Along with financial and human capital constraints, Bates writes that firms located in constrained markets are less likely to survive and prosper (1989).

2. There is increasing evidence that these small slights have a cumulative effect. According to Brush, being taken seriously was an issue especially for women in nontraditional sectors who "believed they had to work harder to achieve credibility than their male counterparts" (1997, 10). Although there is no empirical evidence, there is a perception that women's home-based businesses are less growth-oriented.

3. This is a common problem in MDPs (Taub, 1998; Schreiner & Morduch, 2002), and has led many programs to abandon this strategy.

4. Not everyone objected to the incremental approach. For example, Catarina described how she borrowed greater and greater amounts and built her business over time: "*I had some money and I had gone to Los Angeles to get clothes to sell. . . . Then I looked for a little place and began to sell [the clothes]. But I didn't have enough merchandise. Then someone told me about the loans and I couldn't believe it, but I went, and then I took out my first [loan] for $1,000. Later I took one for $2,000, another of $4,000, then $6,000. . . . I took out a loan of $15,000 because I didn't have a vehicle to buy merchandise. . . . I finished paying back each loan before getting the next one, and so it went well.*"

5. Despite a reluctance to take out business loans, many families used credit cards and other debt to meet household expenses. This included 35 (out of 79 reporting) who reported having credit card debt ranging from $100 to $23,000 (average, $3,624, median, $1,000). Others borrowed from other sources to get over the rough spots. Chester received a loan to help refinance his house. "*I have borrowed money from people who said when I got money I could pay them back. One helped me from having my house foreclosed.*" Laurel used her student loans to help make ends meet (and also to keep her business going). Kim's home equity loans helped her support her household. Angie said that she occasionally borrowed money from her son and then paid it right back.

6. Himes and Servon also found that entrepreneurs (some who were financially stable and some who were not) left the credit-led ACCIÓN program for the same reason (1998, 34–35).

7. Credit scoring predicts the chances that a borrower will default. It is based on bill-paying history, the number and type of accounts, late payments, collection actions, outstanding debt, and the age of accounts. Creditors compare the credit history to consumers with similar profiles to determine a credit score. The credit score is then used to predict creditworthiness and is used to grant or deny a loan application and determine rates of interest (FTC, 1998; Mester, 1997; Schreiner, 2003).

8. Servon (1999) found similar problems with the welfare bureaucracy, concluding that red tape, inappropriate programs, and lack of understanding among staff of entrepreneurs' efforts at self-employment were a constant problem.

CHAPTER 7

Beyond Profit:
Multiple Outcomes of Microenterprise

*I wouldn't work for someone else if they offered me $100,000, an-
other house and a car. No way, no how. I like being self-employed.
I like the meaning of it, the whole connotation. Being independent, not having someone else tell me what to do. . . . No, I
wouldn't change.*

—Lessie, hairstylist

It gives families hope.

—Laurel, desktop publishing

*It has made a big difference because it has allowed my children
to know that if you go to college to get a degree [it] does not
mean you have to work for [somebody else]. You work for yourself to become self-sufficient and independent and this way you
don't have to worry. It has allowed them to become conscious of
money, conscious of how important it is to value your money
and things you do.*

—Clarise, boutique

*I have changed a lot. I am not as easy going. I worry about
paychecks. . . . It is stressful. It creates problems.*

—Chester, textiles

155

After several years of operating their small business, we asked the entrepreneurs if they preferred self-employment or a "good job." Despite the
challenges, hard work, and, in some cases, business failure, the majority of
respondents (56 percent) said that they still had a definite preference for self-
employment, even if they could get a "good" job. Approximately one-third
(31 percent) said they were open to either operating a microenterprise or taking a job, depending on the relative benefits of each. Twelve percent said they
would definitely prefer a good job. Given the modest financial outcomes of
microenterprise reported in chapter 5, we must ask, why did most men and
women in this study remain enthusiastic about the idea of self-employment?
Despite warnings about the time, energy, money, and luck required for a successful business, it is not surprising to find high levels of enthusiasm at the outset given the high value placed on entrepreneurship in the United States.[1] But
high levels of enthusiasm for self-employment—even after many businesses
failed—is more perplexing. This chapter analyzes how the entrepreneurs
assessed their experiences in business.

Microenterprise Outcomes

In addition to whether they prefer self-employment or a "good" job, we
asked how self-employment affected them and their families. This was followed by other questions. Had business changed their standard of living or
quality of life? Did they believe that self-employment is a way for families to
"get ahead?" Who did they think might be successful in business? The discussion was open-ended and the entrepreneurs focused their comments on the outcomes that were most important to them.[2]

Given the range of goals for the businesses reported in chapter 3, it is not too
surprising that business outcomes also varied widely. We group their comments
into seven categories: (1) financial, (2) personal growth and learning, (3) autonomy and control, (4) children and family, (5) hours and stress, (6) new business
and vocational plans, (7) and civic and community involvement (Table 7.1 and
7.2). Although their emphasis was on the positive aspects of the experience, most
entrepreneurs also raised negative outcomes of business ownership.

Financial Outcomes

A total of forty-seven people (55 percent) said that their businesses made
a positive financial contribution to the household. Fifteen said that their business income made a significant financial contribution to their household. For
example, Paula, who owned a pawnshop, said *"Life's easy now; we can pay our
bills,"* and Toni said her business was *"very important"* and helped them reach
"middle income." John believed that his janitorial business provided good

income: *"The income has been good, given the relatively few hours I work. . . . The income has been solid and met all my needs. It has allowed me to pursue other interests. . . . I am able to afford more toys–that's good. There are some*

Table 7.1
Types of Microenterprise Outcomes,
According to Microentrepreneurs (n = 86)

1. FINANCIAL OUTCOMES

Major contribution to family finances
- Supported household
- Increased family assets
- Significantly improved credit ratings

Supplement family income
- Paid for some things
- Intermittent source of income
- Unstable source of income

No or negative contribution to family finances
- No financial improvement
- Not enough money
- Added to household debt
- Lowered standard of living

2. PERSONAL GROWTH AND LEARNING

Confidence
- Increased self confidence
- Built self confidence
- Increased self respect
- Felt happier
- Could envision a future

Skills
- Increased work and job skills
- Increased business skills
- Increased living skills

3. AUTONOMY AND CONTROL OUTCOMES

- Increased freedom
- Increased control over life
- Felt more self sufficient
- Made own decisions
- Had authority
- Was in charge

(continued)

Table 7.1 (*continued*)
Types of Microenterprise Outcomes,
According to Microentrepreneurs (n = 86)

4. CHILDREN AND FAMILY OUTCOMES

Role model for children
- Was role model for children
- Taught children business skills
- Taught children independence

Flexibility
- More time with family
- Flexible time
- Time to care for children
- Improved communication/relationships
- Home schooling

Negative influence
- Less time for children
- Less hours/quality time for family
- Space problems
- Marital tension

5. STRESS AND TIME OUTCOMES

- Do not have enough time
- Feel stress, worry and fear
- Feel depressed
- Feel tied down
- Work too hard
- Feel too much responsibility

6. NEW BUSINESS AND VOCATIONAL PLANS

- Business or non-profit
- Job or school

7. CIVIC/COMMUNITY INVOLVEMENT OUTCOMES

- Enhanced image in the community
- Conscious about role in community

---

things that are above the range of my finances but I keep a cool head about it. I don't feel like I'm doing without."

Some said their business income had surpassed their previous employment income. Compared to her past work, Leticia said the business had helped them get ahead: "*Well, now I'm doing pretty well. I worked for almost 15 years* *for other people doing the same work that I do now [in my business], and the most I earned was $350, and I think that now I earn more than that."* For Jackie, who owned a silk-screening business, self-employment was not the most *"secure"* way to make a living, but, according to her, it still was the best way to get ahead:

> *I am always telling people to go to their own business. I think it is the only way we can really get ahead. The system is set up (for you) to just be getting by. The way to get ahead is to include working for yourself.*

Of those who said the business contributed financially, thirty-two said it made small and irregular contributions to households. In most of these cases, business income was a supplement to other income sources. Doña Gloria said that in order to support a household, she would need a larger business. However,

Table 7.2
Microenterprise Outcomes, According to Entrepreneurs
(n = 86)

Financial Results	66 total
Very positive	15
Somewhat positive	32
None or negative	19
Personal Growth and Learning	54 total
Confidence	40
Skills	13
Autonomy and Control	45 total
Children and Family Well-being	44 total
Role model	22
Flexibility	13
Negative influence	9
Stress and Time Pressures	24 total
Stress	11
Time	6
Work	5
Responsibility	2
New Business and Vocational Plans	16 total
Business	11
Job or school	5
Civic/Community Involvement	11 total

she was only interested in supplementing her social security, not operating a large business. With the supplemental income from her business, Catarina said it was possible to "*survive with some small luxury.*" Jo's business covered the family's food expenses, but she added that they had to use her husband's savings sometimes to pay for other necessities. Cora said her business income supplemented household income and permitted her to buy insurance, although she was uncertain about the exact state of her finances: "*Yes, it helped pay for insurance, life and health. I think I took out more than I put back though. . . .*"

As a result of owning a business, several participants felt more secure financially. For example, Clarise said: "*. . . it is nice having that extra money.*" Despite relatively low business earnings, she nevertheless believed that business was the only way to get ahead. Marta believed that a business is more secure than a job: "*A job never is secure. If the boss leaves the business closes. . . .*" Similarly, Gwen said she made less money in business than she could in a job, but she would rather have a little less money than worry about losing a job. She felt she had more job security working for herself than for someone else.

Others did not agree that business income was secure. Although small income flows from the business were helpful, they were often uncertain. Charles, whose boutique was closed by the time of the interview, said that it provided some financial benefits for a while, but did not offer financial security. As he said, "*We enjoyed it and had a wonderful time . . . We're glad we did it, we just didn't make a lot of money.*" Similarly, Joanne said: "*The problem is that self-employment is not steady income. Yes. . . . Some months are good others are not. However, you can not depend on stable income.*" Asked how the business affected her and her family, Barbara said there were "*Good times and some bad times. It was up and down all the time.*"

There were other financial advantages to business. In addition to household income, some participants said their business resulted in an improved credit rating because of the financial education they received and the opportunity to borrow from the microenterprise development program (MDP). When Monica entered the program she had no credit established. In fact her ex-husband had left her with a large debt. The loans from the MDP helped her establish creditworthiness. In another example, Clarise slowly invested job income and personal savings into her business before taking a microloan from the MDP. She found that she could borrow increasingly large sums:

> *In terms of funds or capital, it helped me with my credit report and it gave a good rating for my credit report. It helped me with [the MDP] because if the loans I got I repaid back, then they would be willing to give me thousands and thousands of dollars next time. This really helped me because I just don't have $500 or $800 of cash on hand for my inventory.*

A few entrepreneurs earned enough to be able to take advantage of business tax deductions. For example, Ed said that his business allowed for tax-deductible travel: "*By having the business we were able to do a certain amount of travel—go to trade shows. And it gave us a chance to have a little vacation and be able to get more business knowledge at the same time.*"

Analyzing others' comments, the articulated sense of financial well-being may have been linked in part to an enhanced ability to accumulate assets, especially a house. Candy said that she believed her business changed her standard of living in large measure because she would not have her own house without it. Owning the business gave her the psychological and financial willingness to "*go out on a limb*" and take a risk such as buying a home. Sergio said that the business "*. . . changed our standard of living materialistically. We now own a house and several cars.*"

A home could be used as a place of business. For example, even though Leticia went into debt and did not show much profit the year after she bought her house, she believed it was worth it because she now had adequate space for her business to grow:

> *You might say that my business had a positive, not a negative, impact. I feel sure that we were able to buy a house because of the earnings from my work. Because if both my husband and I had been employees, I think we would not have had the opportunity to qualify for a house and we would not have been able to accumulate sufficient [funds] to be able to buy a house. And I think that the down payment money for the house—the major part came from what I saved from my work.*

A house also offered some security. For instance, George, who had run into bad times with his business, said that he and his family were living off of personal savings, their home equity, other credit, and his wife's earnings.

For others, business earnings afforded a way to increase their assets by repairing or rehabilitating their house. Marta could not remember exactly how much profit she realized, but it was enough to pay herself a salary of $2,000 a month, and to remodel and purchase new appliances for her home. Toni had costly house payments and utility bills when she started her business, but after a few years she was able to afford to buy new appliances and to renovate the house, thereby decreasing the household bills.

Others were accumulating assets in other ways. For instance, Thomas was building his family's savings through extra earnings from his business:

> *Extra money stays in the checking account, or personal savings. We have an account for my baby for her college, and that's an account by itself; it is separate. . . . Some months [my wife] puts $300 in and some*

*[months] $150, and some $1,000. The goal each year is $1,500 to
$1,800. The grandbaby, there's an automatic $50 put into her school
fund every month. And the wife and I try to put $100 into our savings.
And if we have an extra $200 or $100, it is put in [savings]. If I have
extra money, we work with it. I give my son $100, I give my daughter
$100, and [my wife] will take $100, and I will take $100.*

Linda also said her business helped her make more money to purchase
more and to save money, which she never thought she would be able to do. During the time his auto-reconditioning shop was open, Rich was building tax-free
trust funds for his children using the income that he "*paid*" them for working in
the business. Although her original business closed, Theresa had opened a new
one and was saving for her son's college tuition. Eventually she said she hoped
to invest her savings in a profitable venture, perhaps land. She said her business
". . . *gives me more options, it increases my possibilities of things happening on
a positive scale, financially.*"

Almost one-quarter of the entrepreneurs (19), however, believed their economic situation stagnated or even worsened as a result of their business venture. For example, saying there was too much financial uncertainty in small
business ownership, Anne, who operated a bakery shop, said, "*There wasn't
any future in it. There was too much worry for me and my family. Everything
was too uncertain.*" Others reported that business earnings were too small to
help much.

Some were worried about money they lost in the business, debt accumulated during their time their businesses were open, or ruined credit records.
Chester said he was now seriously "*in the hole.*" Eileen said that after putting
up her personal property for collateral, her outstanding business loans "*ruined
her credit.*" Overall, she said that the business depleted her household money.
And Carol observed that even though her business was beginning to make a
small contribution to her household and she believed that business ownership
"*gives people hope,*" she also saw "*a lot of despair too*" among the entrepreneurs in the program. She thought that small business might be a way to help a
family live, but too often it did not support a family because cash flow is uncertain and families accumulate too much debt. For example, Chester thought
the business had a negative impact on his family. Although the situation had improved by the time of the interview, he still felt guilty about placing so much
financial strain on his family.

As a result, some closed their businesses. Others, despite some disap-
pointments, still preferred business ownership and adjusted their lifestyles to
accommodate this choice. For example, Lanette said that she no longer
shopped at Neiman Marcus. Instead she shopped at thrift stores and bought sec-
ondhand but high quality clothes. Her car was not a luxury vehicle, but a more

practical small car "*one step above [the subway]. The changes don't bother me. I would rather have the business. I'm surviving.*" For Lois being self-employed allowed her to do what she loved despite giving up some creature comforts: "*It would be nice to have a steady paycheck, but this is not really possible [in this field]. Being self-employed has improved the quality of my life. I am earning money as an artist and supporting myself and my daughter.*"

Personal Growth and Learning Outcomes

Money was not the only outcome that mattered to the entrepreneurs. In retrospect, Shawn believed that her business was a "*bad financial investment,*" but a "*good non-financial investment.*" What did she mean? Two-thirds of the respondents (54) believed their businesses contributed to personal growth and learning. For example, Catarina's boutique business offered income, satisfaction, and a way to avoid farm labor: "*I work to survive and I like it, and I don't want to work in the fields.*" But she also said: "*I make friends. For me that counts. . . . That gives me a better morale.*" Before she had to close her business for financial reasons, Eleanor said, that although the business only provided a small financial benefit, she persisted for personal reasons: "*I did it for me. It made me feel like I could keep going and going. The money part would have to come.*" These examples suggest that financial contributions were important, but so was the opportunity to learn and grow.

Many said that their business increased their self-confidence and self-esteem. Meeting the challenge of business ownership made Lanette feel stronger: "*I like the way my personality is going. It is much stronger and I know how to endure now . . . I have to succeed because I can't turn back now.*" Sara, too, felt a sense of accomplishment and pride from her house-painting business:

> *The sense of accomplishment—once you accomplish one thing, it makes you want to accomplish just a little bit more. . . . That's what keeps me going. . . . It really feels good to spend a week, a day, an hour, and look back when you're finished with a product, and [be able to say], "That's a damn good job." It just makes me want to go do more. I give myself a lot of pride.*

Brenda also felt this keen sense of accomplishment:

> *I feel I have accomplished something in life that I wanted to do. It was a challenge and I went out and tried it. So, I feel like if it fails, at least I gave it a try. And if it does well, I can look back and say it worked for me. A lot of times, we have ideas and we just sit down and don't ever try to see it through.*

Similarly, Allison believed that her future would be brighter as a result of owning her sewing business:

> *I think I am a little bit more positive in my outlook. I remember back, working for someone else, and the fact of the daily grind, of always living from paycheck to paycheck, and never seeming to get ahead. . . . It seemed to me more like a heavy cloud of gloom and now, in a way, I am not much better off than I was, but my outlook is better. Somehow, I think it is all going to work out.*

She later said that by believing in her own abilities, she was more motivated to work hard. She observed: "*you have to put forth the effort and work hard at it . . . I think it made me know I can do something, and [that] makes me work harder to see it through.*"

Owning assets, especially important ones like a business, made some people feel good about themselves. For example, Thomas said: "*. . . Anybody that has anything of their own, it makes you feel good about yourself.*" This sense of pride in owning a business is evident in Kim's assertion that she liked being her own boss and even though it was hard work, it was worth it: "*It's great to have something that you can call your own.*" Echoing her remarks, Heather said she does not regret starting her own business: "*I'm not getting rich, but I'm not complaining. My business is still something that I can call my own. I feel proud. My children feel proud.*"

Some believed there was a link between self-confidence, skill, and quality work. For example, Shelby thought that her ability to provide quality child care led to an increase in skills and self-esteem: "*It taught me organizational skills. It taught me how to have a budget. It taught me self-esteem.*" Similarly, Rich thought there was a connection:

> *It gives you an advantage of actually seeing who you are and what you are really made of. With lack of confidence it's because you are not sure you can do things, without having some[body] else being there to tell you. Or you are always wondering if it is good enough. Once you get into the position of doing things for yourself, then you realize that you become a perfectionist. And then you know it's right. I put that guarantee behind every car I ever did or anything I ever did. If the vehicle that I do don't sell itself, then you don't pay. And I never had one dissatisfied customer.*

Being a businessperson producing a quality product, made him feel like he was somebody: "*It just made me emotionally and mentally feel better. What I did then, I probably could have done . . . earlier, but I just didn't realize that.*"

It didn't make me feel as good, until I felt like I was somebody. I guess like The Jerk on TV, who didn't feel like he was somebody until he put his name in the phone book, and then he felt like he was somebody."

Others talked about gaining new skills. Renée said that she learned she could do other things beside sewing and alterations. In the process of setting up her sewing business, she started doing workshops and learned that she was a good teacher. She believed this opened other vocational possibilities for her.

John seemed slightly embarrassed about his janitorial business. Although his comments did not display the same level of pride and inspiration as others, he nonetheless said he had learned many skills in his business and believed it boosted his self-esteem and taught him how to engage professionally with others:

> *There are people which I know who have worked in a number of jobs—and some in a capacity which is more than I can fathom—who seem to be dumbfounded that I own my own business. It's not as though it's an unachievable goal. It's just a matter of self-discipline. It has been extremely helpful in my development, as well as for the business, to deal with people and negotiate contracts . . .*

Autonomy and Control Outcomes

For some, the drive for autonomy was intense, as Sara observed: *"I'll probably work for myself until the day I die. I hope that I will never have to go to work for someone else."* Over half (45) of the entrepreneurs said their businesses gave them greater autonomy and control over their lives. The appeal of microenterprise for Stacy was *"not the money, but the freedom it brings."* Likewise, Charles said, *"We're glad we did it. We just didn't make a lot of money. It gave us a little independence."* And Jackie said: *"My freedom is very important to me. It accomplished that for me. . . ."* Kathleen, the masseuse, said, *"I like the independence, pace, schedule, picking my own space. I can't do these things if I'm working for someone else."* However, she pointed out that business was *"Not for everybody [and] some people must have stability and can't operate in unpredictability."*

When we asked Charles if he would prefer a job, he said he would not mind a second, steady job with good hours (*"I really don't have nothing against doin' another job as long as it's something I like to do."*). But giving it more thought, he said less income was a price he was willing to pay for his autonomy:

> *I couldn't just work a nine-to-five job for the rest of my life. I do not care how much money I have. . . . It helps the mind frame. We do not have to go out and work for somebody. We found that it's not always how much money you make but it's a peace of mind with the little that*

*you make. . . . There've been times when we don't have much and I
don't complain.*

Others felt a sense of relief being out from underneath "the boss" and
other workplace constraints. "*When I look around,*" John said, "*and I realize
that there are so many people around making . . . [a lot of] money, or riding the
government dole, I really feel privileged to be able to write my own ticket and
not have to answer directly to a boss.*" Sharon preferred to have her own business because she hated having to work in the "*day-to-day crap of petty office
gossip*" in a company. She also disliked the feeling of being "*lost in the shuffle
of corporate America*" and she liked to control her own schedule.

Control over work schedules and hours was repeated in many conversations. Ed liked to arrange his own schedule: "*I don't like punching a time card.
I like the freedom to be able to come and go as I please. That [is] one reason I
got involved in another business and I'll probably get involved in another business.*" Brenda said that control over her working hours made self-employment
much better than working in a job:

> *I like working for other people. But having my own business, I am able
> to make my own hours. If I want to work late, it's my choice. I put a lot
> of time in, but I don't mind doing that. The experiences I have had
> working for other people have been bad, as far as the hours are con-
> cerned . . . I just got paid for 45 hours even if I put 60 or 80 hours in
> . . . I don't mind working. I like working and I like a challenging job,
> but what I have experienced has not been that great.*

Self reliance is what many of the entrepreneurs sought as they opened up
their own business—even if it was unsuccessful. As Eleanor said: "*I would
rather work for myself because there is so much out there going on. You have
to put up with so much. If I work for myself, I just have to put up with myself. If
I make it, good. It's good. And if I mess up, I've messed up. . . .*" Clarise believed
self-employment "*helps people become independent, not be lazy, it makes them
know that they have to do this because they have to feed themselves.*" Theresa
thought that her whole family would gain a sense of self-reliance:

> *I think I would still like to work for myself. I still like to be in control
> and in charge. I still like to call the shots. . . . In getting older, you
> kind of mellow in a way. I just realize that everything is not going to
> come overnight. It's going to take more sweat than I realized and
> more money that I budgeted for, but I have a more of a "hang-in-
> there" attitude. A do-not-give-up attitude. Eventually I'll have that
> "right" situation. . . . Depending on the type of business, I think it*

can help the family become closer, but I also think it can help them be
less dependent on other people, other situations.

Children and Family Outcomes

Like Theresa, many entrepreneurs (44) talked about impact of their business on their family. In most cases the effect was positive. Many entrepreneurs started their businesses because of the potential for flexibility (chapter 3), however, when discussing outcomes, they talked more about opportunity. Specifically, they said their children learned how to set goals and how to operate a business. Marta said her microenterprise taught "*my children how to work.*" Candy said that her son learned to manage money. Catarina believed she provided a good role model for her daughter, who occasionally set up a stand of her own little business in front of her mother's store. Thomas, who had been in business for a long time, noted a cumulative effect on his children: "*my kids were brought up working [with me]. My daughter is 20 years old, and she does a lot of things that she watched me do. My son is the same way.*" Rich was building tax-free trust funds for the kids with money they "earned" helping him with the business.

Clara said that owning a business changed her children, but also changed the way she thought about their futures. Expressing a distrust of the labor market and traditional career planning, she had more faith in business:

[My business] changed the way I think about the future for my daugh-
ter. . . . Do you want a philosophical answer? I am 50 and I do not be-
lieve that there is as much economic stability in this country as people
keep their blinders to. The ability to be flexible in perceiving who we
are is incredibly important. And not raising our children in the tradi-
tional fashion is a good survival technique. For example, you will go to
college and get all "A's" and you will be rewarded for your "A's." [But]
it is never a valid assumption about life. Learning any kind of survival
skills, which may in fact sound "retro" to some people, are in fact
world-honored survival skills, such as working, bartering, creative
flexibility, re-tooling—whatever lingo you want to use.

Marta said she believed the business made her family more cohesive, saying that the business "*has made my relationship with my daughters stronger and has made us communicate better.*" This was due, in part, to more flexibility to arrange her day to accommodate the children: "*I am able to program my day around the girls. I also am able to attend school activities or take them to the doctor's without a problem. I get to spend more time with my girls. When I used to work I would leave at 6:30 a.m. and then pick them up at school around 3:30 p.m. I did not see them all day long.*"

Others explained that a more flexible time schedule reduced the stress of arranging child care and permitted more time with their children. For instance, Ed said that operating his own upholstery business facilitated child care: "*It was a very handy situation 'cause it made my work hours flexible.*" According to Leticia, her business allowed her to care for her children the way she wanted:

> *Whenever, I can spend time with my daughters, I can check that they are doing their homework, see that they eat at the right times, [and] watch a little television with them. I think that it is very, very important to share these times with my daughters because they won't be young for long. And also so that they feel their home has the care, attention, and love that they need, . . . I'm afraid that if I don't watch after them, they will come to no good. I prefer to work for myself, what I earn with my business I don't think I could earn in any factory or store doing the kind of work I do and with the flexibility it gives me.*

Similarly, self-employment permitted Brenda to take care of family responsibilities. "*If I need to leave early or if I have an emergency, I don't have to get permission [from a boss] . . . having my own business, I am able to make my own hours. If I want to work late, it's my choice.*"

But for nine entrepreneurs, business created strain in the family. For some, operating a business out of their homes was stressful on the family. Shelby said that the business "*was hard on my kids,*" mostly because her day care children were always in the house. Diane, who also operated her business out of her home, said: "*I was able to spend more time at home, [but] it hurt us in a way because it wasn't good quality time.*"

Time with the family was also an issue. Carol recalled that they were putting so much of themselves into their business to "*keep from drowning,*" that their children did not get the attention or financial support they needed. Stacy pointed out that sometimes businesses "*make some people lose sight of their priorities. You can spend 10 to 20 hours per day at your business, but then you don't have a family.*" She predicted that—partly because of the pressures of her business—she would be divorced in the next five years. Lessie finally decided to rely more on her husband's income, when she realized the business was taking a toll on the family: "*When I tried to make a lot of money once, for three years, I was losing both [my husband] and the kids. So I said 'okay, this is not what I set out to do. This is supposed to be a help, not a hindrance.' [So] I found money some other way.*"

Despite the challenge of operating a business while caring for a family, some still saw a "silver lining." Isabel, for example, thought that the lack of support that her husband offered the first years of her business would no longer be a problem. "*I think that my husband could give me a little more support this time than the last time, because now he's older and he sees that I have talent for these things [business]."*

Stress and Time Outcomes

With self-employment, come long hours, hard work, and, often, considerable stress (24).[3] Some entrepreneurs said that the benefits outweighed the stress, but many believed that it was not worth the headache. For example, Jeff remarked that the long hours and responsibilities of operating his business made him *"cantankerous,"* and that he had had to learn how to balance work and home life. Chester talked about the profound responsibilities of business ownership. He said that when working for a big corporation, *"There were always problems, but of a different type. I didn't have to worry about employees, light bills, rent insurance. [Now] I have to worry about my employees' well-being too. They are working for you. They need a check. It has been a nightmare. I have spent a lot of nights worrying about how to meet payroll. It's a stressful thing."* Diane pointed out that there were too many financial worries in self-employment compared to a job: *"Working for someone else you don't have to worry as much. [You] still have to worry about the bills, but you don't have to worry as much because you know you are going to have a check to spend. Working for yourself you have to worry about the bills and whether you are going to have any income."* Shelby said, despite the benefits of self-employment, it is risky and makes the future uncertain: *"When you work for someone else you have a reliable income. I like working for someone else, well, I don't have to worry about insurance, health insurance, benefits and that kind of thing."* She said that when she was running her own business, she felt she was living for the moment instead of building a future.

For some, the flexible work hours they sought went unrealized. As Dan explained: *"I always thought that working for myself was nice because I set my own hours, but the way the car wash went, my hours weren't flexible because I was there all the time."* Allison said her sewing business offered flexibility, but it never permitted the luxury of *"being able to take that hat off."* In contrast, in a job, *"you can shut [your] door after 5:00 and leave that part of your life behind, and totally emotionally be available for your family."* For Javier, instead of one boss, being in business meant he now had *"many bosses"*: *"Every customer who walks through the door is your boss. . . . [It's] hard to have a lot of time for yourself when you're in business for yourself."*

For some, the responsibility, work, and worry was overwhelming. For example, Shawn said, *"I did not want to live like this any longer. . . . [I'm] spending time, but not seeing the profit . . . I didn't want to spend the rest of my life living like this. I didn't want to suffer like this."* When she remarried, she decided to close the business and return to school for more training. Eileen said her business drained her so she closed it and only recently had started to get her "*old energy back.*" Terri said that although she preferred owning her own business, a job "*wouldn't have all that stress and that pressure.*" She went on to explain: "*It's hard 'cause you put in a lot of hours, and if there's no money you don't get to pay yourself,*" suggesting that the stress and time might be manageable if there were greater economic rewards.

New Business and Other Plans

Sixteen entrepreneurs said that the experience of owning a microenterprise helped create future opportunities, including eleven who said they were thinking seriously about a new business. Several talked about how they would "*do it different the next time.*" Most said that their new skills and increased self-confidence led them to consider new ones. John was planning a new business, but believed he was more prepared because of his experience in the first one: "*I have gotten a better sense of self esteem . . . because I am the king of my own domain. I think that I could start a company with more grandiose prospects now.*" Sara valued her business, but, because of her advancing age, planned to start a new one that would be a little less strenuous.

Four others believed that their microenterprise experience led to other economic prospects. For example, Peggy, who was working at a steady and relatively well-paying factory job with benefits, implied that the connections she made in her business helped her obtain the job: "*If the business had not happened, I would not be who I am or where I am today. I wouldn't have the connections that I have now. Everything happens for a reason. Everything you do builds on itself.*" Monica thought that her business skills helped her in her job: "*I think that I'm a more valuable employee because I owned my own business and know the bottom line.*" Shelby said that the skills she learned, including organizational and budgeting skills, helped her to compete successfully in the job market. She had recently been offered a full-time position that would double her income: "*I felt like I had enough self-esteem built up from owning my own business that when I interviewed they were impressed with my initiative. . . .*"

Civic and Community Involvement Outcomes

Finally, eleven respondents suggested that business ownership increased their civic participation and social status. Carla mentioned that owning a business made her more likely to purchase products from local businesses. Others volunteered in the community. Stacy was proud that she had been able to help four community people start businesses of their own. Jackie reported that her silk-screen business allowed her the flexibility to become even more involved in her ministry. Thomas, the caterer, fed the homeless every

Thanksgiving. He understood the public relations benefits of such work, but also was compassionate about the less fortunate: "*For the last five years we have fed the homeless on Thanksgiving . . . and deliver plates to people who are shut in. . . . The Lord has been good to me. We feed about 270 in the restaurant and carry about 350 plates [to homes]. We had a lot of volunteers.*" Fred believed that his family business showed others that African Americans do not always have to work for someone else: "*Being . . . Black . . . we had a mind set that we would always have to work for someone else. Through our family history, it has shown that we can work for ourselves.*" Susan said that she really was trying to operate her adult day care business in a way that would really help the elderly: "*It gives me a real good sense of community to be able to help families that are in need. There's too many times when organizations have great intent, but they don't actually follow through in the real world of helping people.*"

A few entrepreneurs had decided that they wanted to apply their business skills to endeavors that would improve other people's lives. Geneva wanted to move from clothing production to operating a women's shelter, and Lanette, whose vignette was presented in chapter 6, said that she wanted to open an institute to teach women how to start businesses of their own. Cassandra wanted to shift her focus from selling nice clothing to girls who have trouble finding clothes that fit, to counseling young women with various problems: "*I would like to counsel young women. They don't know what to do with their children. They let their children go crazy. And they don't know how to deal with them. . . . They need so much help. They're children raising children, it's sad . . . they need counseling [to show] . . . them how to shop with their little money.*"

For others, business ownership had not increased civic and community involvement. However, they experienced a heightened sense of social status, and their comments suggest that it might eventually lead to greater civic engagement. For instance, many said that owning a business made them more aware of their image as a business owner in town. Heather believed that she was better known about town since she opened her video sales and rental business. Terri said that people began to treat her differently. After being involved in an abusive relationship, a divorce, and having to seek welfare assistance, the business "*boosts my self esteem. It makes me feel good to be a business owner. A lot of people have a lot of respect for me.*" In Rich's case, the business (which did not survive) had significant impact on his and his children's social standing:

> *. . . you go from driving an old beat up VW bus, to driving a Cadillac, that was pretty much how it felt—going from walking to riding a beautiful new bike. It changed the way we live. We got a little nicer clothes, and felt better about ourselves. My kids didn't have to go to school and say, "Hey, we are welfare kids." [Instead they could say]*

"My dad owns his own business." Which made me get a swollen head and work harder.

Multiple Outcomes of Microenterprise

Most entrepreneurs were decidedly upbeat about microenterprise, despite generally modest economic rewards, long hours, and hard work. The question must be asked, why did so many of the entrepreneurs remain enthusiastic?

Positive Outcomes

Despite relatively modest financial benefits, microenterprise helped many entrepreneurs support their families or supplement household income. In these cases the extra income from self-employment was viewed as an important part of the families' income portfolio. Another perceived economic benefit of participating in the MDP and operating a microenterprise was improvement in their creditworthiness. Another financial outcome of participating in the MDP and owning a microenterprise was an increase in business and household assets. Several participants mentioned the importance of owning a business and purchasing or improving their house. Moreover, qualifying for home or business loans compelled several to pay off accumulated debt and to get their financial lives in order. This made them feel more secure financially.

But for most, the financial benefits were only part of the story. As this chapter points out, microenterprise made multiple non-economic contributions to well-being. For example, Jackie observed that families gain far more than financial benefits from business ownership:

> *Every family should own something, even if it is a home-based business. I believe that the . . . jobs we get are stepping-stones. We learn skills there, how to interact with the public. The small business will unify the family. It unifies people when they have a common goal or vision. It teaches public relations, how to talk, public speaking, how to make requests. . . . So it's time for people to be encouraged to be entrepreneurs. Not for the finances. That's just part of it . . . it gives a lot of hope, gives young people a lot of hope . . . when they see their parents in business.*

In this example, Jackie suggests that business ownership teaches skills and helps people to envision a better future. Again, compensating differential theory, which suggests that there are non-monetary factors that affect economic decision making, is supported. But what are these non-monetary factors and how can theory capture the experiences of low-income microentrepreneurs, whose behavior appears to be unreasonable from an economic point of view?

First, the entrepreneurs seem to be seeking a work environment where they can develop their skills and potential. Compared to low-wage jobs that are often boring, repetitive, and lack opportunities for personal growth, and social status, a microenterprise offers a real alternative. Even though some experts view these as substandard jobs (Ehlers & Main, 1998), the business owners themselves believed they learned new skills and developed a greater sense of self-confidence. Many also believed that the skills they learned in business were transferable and would be helpful in obtaining or doing well on a job in the labor market. They also enjoyed greater day-to-day autonomy and control over their work lives. They no longer worked for bosses who made unreasonable demands, treated them with disrespect, or subjected them to harassment or bullying. Others said that although the money may not have been great, that their business offered security that jobs often lacked. Furthermore, a few said that entrepreneurship gave them an opportunity to hold their heads high in the community. As Ivan Light and Carolyn Rosenstein have suggested:

> Entrepreneurship is superior to destitution for both economic and so-cial reasons. First, even marginal entrepreneurs produce goods and services that enhance the community's wealth, whereas the destitute unemployed consume without producing. Second, as producers, even marginal entrepreneurs participate in the policy and the culture, help-ing in the process to tame the crime, apathy, hopelessness, and sub-stance abuse that accompany destitution and racism. Here we are addressing noneconomic benefits of entrepreneurship. We do not know what or how big they are, but think that cost-effective programs of entrepreneurship enhancement will have noneconomic benefits as well as economic benefits. (1995, 215)

Interviews with the microentrepreneurs suggest another benefit of business ownership—a chance to expose children to the value of work and to the benefits of working for oneself. From their viewpoint, working long hours in self-employment compared favorably to having their children watch them don a uniform to work a minimum wage job as custodians or fast-food employees. Some entrepreneurs said that increased flexibility to spend time with family members and opportunities to model good work behavior were accompanied by increased family cohesiveness. Microenterprise frequently became a family project. Microenterprise also offered greater flexibility to care for a young child or a sick relative, and in some cases, even compensated for low earnings.

Overall, multiple positive outcomes appear to be an important part of the microenterprise story. Some of these outcomes are economic (e.g., income and assets); some are not immediately economic (e.g., new skills or future business plans); and some are not economic at all (e.g., self-esteem or civic involvement). It is apparent from these results that compensating differential theory is onto something important in explaining microenterprise. However, this "theory" does not say what the "compensating" factors are, and, in this sense, it is not a theory but only a broad statement. The findings of this study begin to specify what the compensating factors are. These too remain far from a well-specified theory, but they are steps toward this goal.

Negative Outcomes

For a minority, however, microenterprise was a limited, and unrewarding, or even painful, experience. Most often, poor economic performance and insecurity, compounded by the stress and long hours of business ownership, contributed to the feeling that jobs are better than owning a business. For example, while Glenn's business was open, it "*took care of us totally and comfortably*"; however, he was glad he had closed it and taken a job: "*It was perfect for the time, but I don't miss it [now]. [It was] time for it to go.*" Some found the stress of having a home-based business and the long hours placed too much strain on the family. As Gerald Mars and Robin Ward say, entrepreneurs must "work long and unsocial hours" (1984, 17). A few entrepreneurs joked that the benefit of flexible hours was eclipsed by the fact that they really had no time off because of the heavy responsibilities associated with business ownership. A few of these entrepreneurs were still in business and were trying to get out. Others had closed their businesses and taken jobs in the labor market. A few had married, giving them an opportunity to close the business and have someone else to share in the responsibility of supporting their family.

What are the theoretical implications of negative outcomes? Certainly microentrepreneurs do not seek these outcomes, so compensating differential thinking, and its specification do not apply. Overall, the messages of negative outcomes repeat the lessons in chapter 6, regarding business context, infrastructure, resources, and human capital constraints. The sour fruits of these constraints appear as failed businesses and other negative personal outcomes.

Given the strong evidence of limitations on performance in chapter 6, we find it noteworthy that reported negative outcomes are so modestly represented in the data. What could explain this? Are the microentrepreneurs putting a "happy face" on their struggles? Or do positive outcomes somehow emerge from these challenges? Our interviews suggest the latter, but there is a great deal that we do not yet know about these complexities.

Research and Policy Directions

There is evidence to suggest that when entrepreneurs are more serious about making money in business, that their businesses are more successful. Several factors that point to this level of seriousness are correlated with higher business earnings. A goal to earn an income that would sustain a family, keeping business accounts separate from household accounts, working out of a shop instead of a home, and a perception that the business was doing well financially are all associated with higher business earnings.[4] Although the results in this study require testing with a large controlled study, these relationships suggest that people who aim for financially successful businesses and treat them more as formal businesses are more likely to realize this aim. There are two potential problems with this conclusion that must be tested in future studies. One, entrepreneurs may adjust their expectations, perceptions, and behaviors to the level of resources they have to invest in their business. In other words, people with greater skills, financial backing, and connections believe they are more likely to do better in business, and adjust their behaviors and perceptions accordingly. Second, and related to the first, participants interviewed after five years may report business goals that correspond to the outcomes. Looking back at open-ended questions in 1991, however, when researchers asked, "Why did you start this business?" the data suggest more agreement than disagreement across the years. Using a rough measure of those who reported economic goals versus non-economic goals, there is a convergence of 37 participants who said economic and 34 reported non-economic goals in both waves, while 13 said economic in one wave and a non-economic goal in the other. (However, there is no way to distinguish between those who were aiming for supplementary "patching" income and those who sought full income, a distinction that the current research suggests is significant.) Nonetheless, these findings suggest that it is important to fully explore participants' goals and resource levels as they embark on microenterprise.

From a policy point of view, this chapter raises several questions. First, the financial contributions of the microenterprises are helpful to households. However, the contribution is usually modest. Without a doubt, financial goals should be clarified at the outset. For entrepreneurs who seek only supplemental income, minimal intervention may be needed. However, for those who aim to earn enough income to sustain their families (or better), there should be appropriate support that enables these businesses to grow.

Second, our findings suggest that it is important to evaluate if microenterprise is the most efficient and effective way for people to achieve the range of outcomes described in this chapter. In other words, are there better ways for entrepreneurs to achieve financial stability, gain control, build a sense of self-efficacy, be a role model for their children, build assets, contribute to their community, and so forth? Clearly, we must identify other approaches for people whose goals and circumstances are not compatible with microenterprise. Therefore, this chapter suggests that MDP staff discuss at length potential participants' goals before they open a business. Before investing time, energy, and capital, prospective entrepreneurs should think about the range of ways they might enable them to reach their goals, including a business or a job or other activity.

Notes

1. In an analysis of self-employment, Messenger and Stettner (2000) argue that Americans have a positive view of self-employment and choose it for a variety of financial and non-pecuniary reasons.

2. Interviewers asked a general question and followed up with specific queries when the response seemed incomplete or when the respondent needed additional encouragement to talk. Most participants tended to focus on one or two outcomes. If they had been prompted about each outcome discussed in this chapter, more may have responded to the full range of possibilities. The benefit of this approach is that the entrepreneurs spoke about the outcomes that were foremost in their minds, but might not have given expression to a full range of outcomes.

3. Erickcek (1997) found that the stress of running a small business exceeded expectations in their survey of small business owners in Kalamazoo and Cleveland.

4. Statistical analysis suggests that business income was higher among more formal businesses and among those viewed by their owners as moneymakers. Income from the business (in 1995) was significantly greater for those with a primary goal of making a full income for their family ($10,144) compared to those reporting that they had aimed to earn partial income or to achieve other goals ($3,280) (t = 3.03, df = 50, p ≤ .05) (chapter 3). Those with separate financial boundaries between household and business had significantly higher income from the business in 1995 ($10,980) than those with likely mingled ($4,299) and mingled ($4,004) finances (chapter 5). Those with shop-based businesses had a greater change in percent of income from the business between 1991 and 1995 (14 percent) compared to home-based business (less than 1 percent) (chapter 3). Finally, regarding income from the business in 1995, those reporting a lot of financial gain from the business ($16,080) varied significantly from both those entrepreneurs reporting some gain ($4,160), and from those who did not mention financial gain as an outcome ($3,711) (chapter 7).

CHAPTER 8

Fighting Poverty or
Promoting Development?

Is business ownership for low-income families a good idea? As we have seen, from the point of view of most of the entrepreneurs in this study, the answer is an enthusiastic "yes." Most said that they preferred owning their own business to working in the labor market and believed that they and their families gained from the experience. Even after five years during which many had closed their businesses, the majority still preferred microenterprise to a "good" job. Most entrepreneurs expressed enthusiasm for business ownership and believed that their businesses made important economic and non-economic contributions.

At the same time, the anti-poverty effects of microenterprise are less apparent. Although most of the businesses earned at least some income—and in a few cases, substantial income—for the entrepreneurs' households, most entrepreneurs remained low-income. The analysis suggests that the majority of entrepreneurs were realizing only modest financial returns from their businesses. The average business contributed about one-third of household income. A little less than one-half of the households' incomes rose above poverty (defined in this study as 150 percent of the official poverty line), while more than half remained below, including about one-third whose household incomes declined between 1991 and 1995. Most of the entrepreneurs probably could have earned as much or more in labor market jobs.

These findings suggest a dilemma. Microenterprise does not consistently raise household incomes, but it appears to enrich and help in other important ways. Modest income gains raise serious questions about the direct anti-poverty benefits of microenterprise. But the financial success of some of the businesses, combined with enthusiastic endorsement by the entrepreneurs, make the microenterprise strategy difficult to dismiss. This dilemma poses public policy choices. We first turn to theory and evidence for help in evaluating and charting

177

a future course for microenterprise. After that, we tap the findings of this study for program and policy directions.

Beyond Profits Alone

Why did these individuals choose microenterprise, and what were the outcomes? Microenterprise looked attractive to many because they had been unable to find decent jobs. Many of the entrepreneurs said that the available jobs were characterized by low wages, insecurity, poor working conditions, poor benefits, and little mobility. In addition to factors that limited their access to better jobs (e.g., low levels of education and training and geographic location), some pointed out that that their access to jobs and mobility were blocked by gender or racial discrimination (Bates, 1997). This suggests that many of the entrepreneurs were indeed "disadvantaged workers" (Tomaskovic-Devey, 1993). Did they choose microenterprise for the "wrong reason," that is, because they were pushed out of the wage labor market? Some undoubtedly did.

Many of the entrepreneurs reported choosing business because they thought they had the skills, experience, creativity, and motivation to operate successful microbusinesses. Most were confident about the quality of their product. In many cases they also believed they could earn a better return on these skills in self-employment than they could in the labor market. They believed their product skills were in large part responsible for the times when their businesses performed well. The ideas behind theories of human capital resonated among the entrepreneurs who were highly motivated, worked long hours, and had a range of business skills. They also understood that they needed start-up and expansion capital. For some, the availability of microenterprise loans was a key factor in the decision to open a business, but many pointed out that their businesses would have performed better if they had better access to capital, in the appropriate amounts, and at the right times. Access to formal loans and more education were associated with higher income from the business, supporting the idea that access to human and financial capital are critical factors for success (Bates, 1997).

The interviews also suggest that asset accumulation was a factor in the choice of microenterprise and in their business success. Some entrepreneurs began their businesses with an eye toward earning enough money to purchase a house. Others said they started businesses because they wanted *to own* their own business, have more control over their work lives, and have financial assets to pass on to their children. The empirical evidence, while not overwhelming, indicates that household assets increased for most entrepreneurs. Many of the entrepreneurs helped to finance their businesses from small savings and home equity. Although the mechanisms are not entirely clear, a desire to own something, usually a business or a home, was a marker for success for many of the entrepreneurs and an important factor in the attractiveness of self-employment. Entrepreneurs also said that their credit rating had improved as a result of more careful financial management learned from participating in microenterprise training and owning their business.

While the research suggests that most wanted to "make a decent living," they also made it clear that they also chose self-employment for non-monetary reasons (Hamilton, 2000). As compensating differential theory suggests, the entrepreneurs offered ample evidence that they sought "value" when they chose self-employment (Light & Rosenstein, 1995). Whether that value had to do with a desire for autonomy, the flexibility to care for children or elders, or an opportunity to learn and grow in their work, most of the entrepreneurs sought more than income. The qualitative evidence suggests that these other goals were significant and enduring. Thus, the decision to open a business was the result of an assessment of their opportunities in the labor market, but also of their individual capacity and preparation, business resources (e.g., access to a microenterprise program), family responsibilities, and personal goals.

To some extent, the large numbers of women, especially poor women, in this study drive the results. Concern about how to be involved in their children's lives, feel in control of their own lives, and learn and grow, goes a long way to explain their willingness to work hard earning only modest incomes. Few could hope to find a job that would offer these benefits. This is not simply a gender issue, however, because many men mentioned some of the same issues.

Despite relatively modest economic gains, microenterprise, according to the entrepreneurs, offered an opportunity to earn some income, be a good role model, develop as individuals, work in a positive environment, have control over their lives, be able to envision a future business or job, and see themselves as productive citizens. Jobs in the labor market often do not provide these opportunities, so even though most of the microentrepreneurs earned relatively little in their businesses, these enterprises may have provided greater options than the available jobs. At least in microenterprise, for example, entrepreneurs could safely care for their children, accommodate a disability, or achieve work satisfaction. The fact that most entrepreneurs continued to prefer owning a business, even when they earned little and some had even closed their businesses, underscores the importance of these non-monetary features.

From a theoretical perspective, how do we specify these non-monetary contributions? Although compensating differential theory suggests that these factors compensate for lower earnings, it tells us little about what these factors are and why they are important. First, it may be helpful to think about microenterprise from a human or social development perspective (Beverly & Sherraden, 1995). Interviews indicated that the "learning curve" in operating a business is steep. The entrepreneurs, even those whose businesses failed, gained skills useful in a variety of settings, including how to set goals, work efficiently ("*self-discipline*"), plan and make decisions, communicate, negotiate, and finance a business. They articulated a sense of accomplishment (a feeling of "*getting ahead*") resulting from business ownership that they did not realize through prior jobs. Moreover, they felt an increase in self-esteem ("*I'm somebody*"). They gained autonomy ("*independence*") and control over their lives, including their work hours. As some suggested, new skills and greater self-confidence helped them develop their businesses. And some women, in particular, said that the skills and confidence they learned in business helped them obtain jobs.

Women often chose self-employment over labor market employment because of child care, eldercare, and other family responsibilities. While perhaps at a financial price, most women could not find this kind of flexibility in wage employment. Operating a business proved to be time-consuming (for some "*stressful*"), and the promise of flexibility was not always realized. But other benefits for the family, noted by several entrepreneurs (including men), included increased cohesion and communication within the family through shared goals and work. Significantly, microenterprise also provided a way for parents to model dignified work and productive behaviors for their children. They liked, in Lessie's words, the "*whole connotation*" of owning their own businesses.

Taking these outcomes into consideration, it becomes more understandable why the entrepreneurs maintained a positive view of microenterprise even in the face of modest economic rewards. Furthermore, this suggests that it may be more fruitful to view microenterprise as a development strategy, rather than as an anti-poverty strategy. As Sandra pointed out, the poor deserve an opportunity to do something "*good in life*":

> *Small business is something that if you can deal with it you should go for it. As a matter of fact, I think we should stress more of it. . . . I've always felt that there are a lot of people . . . that are on welfare that have talent. And, they can do things. . . . And I've always said that I feel that we could probably cut the welfare force into half if we can take each individual, sit down and talk with that person, find out what this person can do good in life to create a business or go on a job. And just give that person that opportunity.*

Even though the evidence suggests that relatively few of those on welfare can use a microenterprise strategy (Schreiner, 1999a), this quote suggests that people want greater opportunity. They want to generate income, but they are also looking for work that offers a future for themselves and their children. An anti-poverty strategy means "not poverty," but development suggests broader goals that take into account people's capabilities (Sen, 1999), hopes, and aspirations.

It may be more fruitful, therefore, to think about microenterprise from a personal and household development perspective. Many of the entrepreneurs (although not all) talked about their venture into business as a transformative experience. The interviews suggest that the sense of transformation comes from the unique opportunity to develop their own and their families' capabilities (Sen, 1999) and futures. Some entrepreneurs pursued business primarily for its potential learning and future growth opportunities. These broad and multifaceted effects of microenterprise may be as important, perhaps sometimes even more important, than increases in short-term income.

Microenterprise Policy

Despite positive outcomes for microenterprise, the entrepreneurs encountered many problems. This section addresses some of the key policy issues raised by the entrepreneurs. The entrepreneurs believed that skills, experience, motivation, creativity, and health mattered in their business performance. But so did factors such as good business contacts, good local markets, and supportive welfare policies. Unfortunately, interviews indicate that many faced the opposite: poor business contacts, poor local markets, and punitive and inflexible welfare policies. Resource disadvantage persisted despite concerted efforts of microenterprise development programs (MDPs). As Ivan Light and Steven Gold suggest, "resource disadvantage is worse than labor market disadvantage in that those resource-deprived lack the resources to undertake formal sector self-employment in response to labor market disadvantage" (2000, 202). In other words, those who experience severe disadvantages in the labor market can, and often do, opt for self-employment, but if they also lack access to resources, they are limited to the informal self-employment sector. Many of the entrepreneurs appear to have encountered this situation, and many of the businesses stagnated or closed as a result.

Discrimination or disadvantages associated with gender, race, age, and disability compounded problems associated with lack of access to resources for business. Despite the considerable efforts of MDPs, statistical analysis shows that women, African Americans, and Latinos were less successful in their businesses, suggesting that some forms of discrimination may have negatively impacted their businesses. This suggests the continuing importance of facilitating greater access to markets for minority and women business owners and guidance toward more promising businesses.

Social capital, including extensive social networks, could serve to mitigate some resource deficiencies, but were not in much evidence. Light and Gold (2000) document a variety of business supports (e.g., training, financial capital, labor, consumer demand, and political resources) that support ethnic enterprise.

Although MDPs attempt to provide such resources, limited funding and an individually focused service delivery model impede their capacity to provide support. With the exception of occasionally successful efforts to build peer group support, the focus is on training, mentoring, and technical assistance for individual entrepreneurs. There was little evidence of efforts to build intermediary support structures aimed at creating bridging social capital that could increase access to human, social, and financial resources outside the immediate environment. One MDP planned a new building for microenterprises but it failed. Some MDPs tried to promote connections to existing business networks, usually by inviting business owners to address the microentrepreneurs in training sessions, or by encouraging mentoring relationships. However, examples of these attempts did not emerge in the interviews very often, and when they did, there was little evidence that they provided lasting access to business contacts and networks. The entrepreneurs reported few efforts to bring microentrepreneurs into such organizations as the Rotary or the chamber of commerce, and the entrepreneurs who tried to participate felt out of place.

The decision to open a business does not necessarily mean that the individual foregoes wage employment. In fact, the more common strategy among entrepreneurs in this study is to combine self-employment and wage employment. Families, and even individuals, often have multiple income sources. Some are formal, some informal. Some are earned, some unearned. The entrepreneurs reported an average of three sources of cash income at one time, and about one-third of households also received some form of in-kind support. This study suggests that a decision to diversify income sources is aimed at enhancing income security while operating a business, maximizing income, and in a few cases, contributing to quality of life. In support of existing theoretical work in this area, these diversifying strategies are mostly aimed at financial survival, not at future investment (Chen & Dunn, 1996). Poor households struggle to survive financially by combining earned income, unearned income, and in-kind support.

Microenterprise may offer a way for some low-income Americans to supplement their income through "minimalist" businesses. For example, Doña Gloria was not interested in a larger business. She wanted to keep her business small *"I'm not going to rent a place to put my merchandise. I can't pay for it. [A large business] would need to have a lot of merchandise, and I want to have only a little."* But her small enterprise permitted Doña Gloria to supplement her disability payments and, at the same time, gave her something rewarding to do.[1] For minimalist enterprises like Doña Gloria's, MDPs offer basic training, small loans, and other minimal support. Although this kind of microenterprise support costs money, there are many potential benefits. The effects of minimalist microenterprise might include increased household income, formation of future businesses, small increases in tax revenues, greater work satisfaction for owners, improved skills that owners can use in business or in jobs, and business experience and positive influences on children. This study suggests that access to small loans and low levels of training and technical assistance helps some minimalist businesses survive for many years.

For others, microenterprise may be a way for people to launch innovative and fast growing small "gazelle" firms (Birch, 1987). In this study, the more successful businesses tended to do better from the start and had more resources than those that were less successful. This suggests that it may be possible to identify businesses with greater potential fairly early. But they require assistance beyond start-up training and loans. As Carol, the owner of a books-on-tape business, asserted: *"If the government wants to help things . . . you've got to build a bridge for people to walk out on. . . . Halfway through the river you don't pull the bridge out from under them."* Bruce Kirchoff has argued that the smallest firms constitute 18 to 20 percent of total employment and that they are the driving force behind what he calls "dynamic capitalism" (1994). Microenterprises could help feed this dynamism. The next section discusses some of the ways in which policy can promote the creation and development of both minimalist and growth businesses.

Policy and Programs

This section addresses the central issues raised in this study and draws on a wide range of research and policy strategies discussed in microenterprise circles and in research over the last ten years. We divide policy and program ideas into those that focus on individual firms at the micro-level, on intermediary structures at the mezzo-level, and on policies at the macrolevel (Table 8.1; Sherraden & Sanders, 1997). At the level of the firm, strategies focus on maximizing entrepreneurial ability to operate successful businesses. At the intermediary level, strategies focus on improving access to information, support, and resources. At the policy level, strategies aim to reduce or remove barriers and increase levels of support for microenterprise in low-income households. This section highlights some strategies that have been adopted in recent years.

Micro-level Strategies: A Developmental Approach to Microenterprise

At the level of the firm, the goal is to maximize entrepreneurial potential and increase the "margin for error" as business start-ups gain experience. Here we adopt a developmental approach (Midgley, 1995), viewing business ownership as a process that different people should start at different points, and aimed at reaching a range of goals. Instead of starting everyone at the same point (e.g., a feasibility study), program support would depend on the entrepreneur's level of human, financial, and social resources. In other words, participants could

Table 8.1
Micro-, Mezzo-, and Macro-level Strategies for
Microenterprise Development

Micro-level Strategies	Mezzo-Level Strategies	Macro-level Strategies
Participant goals, resources, and selection	Microbusiness incubators	Social policy
Internships and apprenticeships	Open-air marketing	Financial education in schools
Market research	Sectors and flexible network development	Regulatory and tax reform
Infrastructure assessment and assistance	Information and e-communication	"Cross training" in social and economic development for staff
Credit, savings, and grants	Microenterprise associations	
Financial services and financial education Training, coaching, and mentoring		
Personal and family support		

enter MDPs at any point along the way, depending on their readiness. More-over, entrepreneur goals would guide the types of support that programs would make available.

PARTICIPANT GOALS, RESOURCES, AND SELECTION. Programs should be clear about program goals when choosing participants. If the emphasis is on poverty alleviation, it is important to provide access to a variety of forms of income gen-eration—not just microenterprise. For example, Judy concluded (after a failed attempt to run a textile business): "*I like a regular income. For me a good job means a lot of freedom and flexibility, and good pay, relatively. Like knowing I can count on a certain amount of money. I feel more creative when I can rely on having money to pay the bills. I feel a lot happier.*" In Judy's case, education and training for a good job would likely have generated more income than would business ownership. In such cases it would be more productive to assist people in seeking appropriate labor market alternatives, especially given research find-ings suggesting only a very small percentage of the poorest will benefit from business ownership (Schreiner, 1999a). At the very least, self-employment is not the best choice for individuals who are not fully committed to owning a business (Edgcomb, 2002).[2] As Angie warned, someone thinking about opening a micro business should *"think long and hard"* about what she wants: *"Find out as much information as possible. Get some skills in bookkeeping. It's no joke . . . owning a business is not for everybody. A lot of people don't have that drive. Until you wake up at three or four a.m. with thoughts about the business in your head, you aren't in the business."* Therefore, programs should recruit appropriate participants, and conduct thorough assessments of entrepreneur goals (Boshara, et al., 1997; Bhatt, 2001; Klein, 2002; Robichaud, et al., 2001).

Entrepreneurs also should have some basic resources in order to build a successful business, even one that provides supplementary household income. The entrepreneurs in this study understood this. Most had other sources of household income. Although many in the field of microenterprise believe that anyone, regardless of income, who is committed to small business and has the will to work at it should have access to the opportunity. The reality of business operation suggests that readiness, potential, and resources should be carefully assessed prior to delivering microenterprise support services.

INTERNSHIPS AND APPRENTICESHIPS. Successful businesspeople often have experience and/or training in the types of businesses they later own. It is unrealistic to expect that poor people with little or no prior business experience, and little background in a particular type of business, will be successful without similar opportunities. This study suggests that it might have been helpful for participants to "get their feet wet" before opening a business. Some programs have adopted this developmental approach, particularly for women, by providing training, supporting a transition to self-employment, and helping participants clarify their goals along the way (Straatmann & Sherraden, 2001). A developmental approach could help to build women's comparative advantage and also facilitate the learning curve for business. Promoting entry into businesses that are not traditionally seen as "women's businesses" might also result in more successful businesses with higher individual earnings (Loscocco & Robinson, 1991; Otero, 1994).

This study indicates that while some entrepreneurs had prior business experience, the majority had little or none. Many mentioned the need for more exposure and training. It may be helpful to offer "in-business training" in the form of internships and apprenticeships prior to (or simultaneously with) regular business training for the least experienced. Additional funding would be needed to provide stipends during this training phase. Welfare rules would also have to count internships and apprenticeships as approved "work activities."

MARKET RESEARCH. In most cases, the MDPs in this study left decisions about choice of business up to the individual microentrepreneur. Unfortunately, without formal business education and access to business networks, entrepreneurs typically lacked information about good business choices, including niche markets and sectors of the economy that are conducive to successful microenterprise (Ehlers & Main, 1998). They chose businesses based on their skills and ideas, often without exploring other business possibilities that might have greater growth potential.

As Timothy Bates (1997) and others argue, businesses in "emerging" sectors, rather than traditional ones, have more growth potential. The successful clothing design firm FUBU ("For Us, By Us"), for example, began in 1992 as a microenterprise by a twenty-two-year-old restaurant waiter and three friends who discovered opportunity in a growing urban clothing industry (*CNN Money*, 1998).

Others recommend developing businesses in niche markets in non-traditional fields, alliances with other successful firms, non-physical retail businesses (e.g., e-commerce, catalog sales, catering, and exhibits for fairs); and semimanufacturing rather than retail (Bendick & Egan, 1991); and in "industry clusters" that have growth potential (Bhatt, 2001). The economy provides many such opportunities for small business, but the poor are unlikely to be in a position to know which directions are feasible and most promising (Rubin & Zorn, 1985).

Although programs should not dictate to entrepreneurs what type of business to open (that approach was unsuccessful in the few cases where it occurred in this study), information could help guide their decisions. Many of the entrepreneurs were attempting to compete in impossible situations (e.g., selling floral arrangements in competition with low-price imports available in a local discount house), when a different business approach could have been more promising. It makes sense for program staff to provide tools to evaluate business ideas and ways for future entrepreneurs to gain skills and competence in business. This will usually take time—as the entrepreneur researches, interns, receives training, and so forth—but it is more likely to result in a successful business endeavor.

INFRASTRUCTURE ASSESSMENT AND ASSISTANCE. Many of the business owners in this study said that lack of key business infrastructure elements, such as transportation, a decent location, parking, adequate space, and dependable employees, affected their business performance. A thorough assessment of infrastructure should be part of the feasibility study and business plan. Lack of key infrastructure components might appropriately delay business start-up or lead to a change in business focus. This would be far better than opening a business that is destined to fail.

CREDIT, SAVINGS, AND GRANTS. A few entrepreneurs had inheritances, savings, or grants to help with the business, but in most cases, the amount of money available for the businesses was small. Loans were helpful, but insufficient. Some worried about debt and admitted that their reluctance to borrow may have diminished business performance. Nitin Bhatt (2001) suggests that loan sizes and terms be more carefully matched with market demand. But if people with low incomes are to build successful businesses, it is important to consider more than credit. Two additional sources of capital, savings and grants, are worth considering.

Savings, which are increasingly emphasized in international microenterprise programs, could provide evidence of discipline, working capital, a cushion against income shocks, and a way to improve entrepreneurs' ability to borrow at lower rates (Edgcomb & Barton, 1998). Mark Schreiner and Jonathan Morduch (2002) argue that, for generating working capital for businesses, helping entrepreneurs become creditworthy and helping them increase their personal savings is better than a pure loan strategy. With savings, entrepreneurs could invest in their businesses with greater confidence that they would be able to repay loans without draining household income. Recognizing the importance of savings, more microenterprise programs in recent years have started Individual Development Accounts (IDAs) that match participants' savings and can be used for long-term investments, including small business (Sherraden, 1991). Research on IDAs suggests that even the very poor are able to save (Schreiner, et al., 2001). IDAs may serve several purposes for entrepreneurs, including financial awareness, initial business capital, collateral, and capital for business expansion (Ssewamala, 2003). A period of accumulating savings may also provide time to acquire more training and to think critically about plans for a business.

Grant programs and in-kind contributions for microenterprises could also provide key assistance to low-income entrepreneurs.[3] A grant program might help pay for equipment purchases that are essential for a business but beyond an entrepreneur's means. For example, a grant program could provide access to computer technology. Few entrepreneurs have the start-up capital necessary to purchase a computer with access to the Internet. In addition to serving the daily needs of the business, computers could also be used for continued training and contact between MDPs and low-income entrepreneurs.

FINANCIAL SERVICES AND FINANCIAL EDUCATION. Effective access to, and use of, financial capital requires access to formal financial services, sometimes called "microfinance," which includes a variety of services such as savings, insurance, and credit (Littlefield, et al., 2003). Regarding education, most microenterprise programs already address problems of debt, credit records, and basic financial planning. However, training tends to be limited to the period of business start-up and takes the form of classes. As we have seen in this study, even after years of doing business, many of the entrepreneurs still did not separate their business accounts from household accounts, and some did not use a bank at all. Effective financial education could further assist entrepreneurs to make levelheaded financial decisions and, combined with more financial options (Caskey, 1997), could help them make the most of business growth opportunities. Many of the entrepreneurs wanted more assistance with financial management, but in part because of time constraints, were skeptical about formal classroom approaches. Many of the most promising educational tools are computer-based, underscoring the importance of computer training and access to computer technology (Dumas, 2001).

BUSINESS TRAINING, COACHING, AND MENTORING. The entrepreneurs stressed the need for appropriate training, ongoing assistance, mentoring, and technical support. They emphasized the importance of training for their specific venture, particularly after the start-up phase. As others have suggested (Servon & Bates, 1998; Bhatt, 2001), entrepreneur preparation should be assessed and the appropriate kinds of training provided (Nelson, 2002), in a manner suited to adult learners (Edgcomb, 2002). In this study, although entrepreneurs were grateful for the training and assistance at the outset, many said they needed more in-depth guidance in the form of coaching or mentoring, especially focused on marketing their particular product (see also Boshara, et al., 1997; Microenterprise FIELD, 2000d; Kantor, 2000; Zinger, et al., 2001). Edgcomb and Malm suggest three forms: one-on-one *consulting* by a business advisor, guiding and motivational *coaching*, and counseling or *mentoring* (2002). Bhatt (2001) suggests that training should be separated from lending. Other organizations, such as Small Business Development Centers and community colleges, may be more appropriate venues for continuing business education. Opportunities for mentoring and coaching could help entrepreneurs when they face specific choices and problems in their businesses and could help them assess when they should close a failing business or when they should invest more time or resources in a promising business.[4] Schreiner (1999b) suggests that it may be less costly and more effective to provide on-call advice over a longer period of time than intensive training at the outset. Providing sophisticated technical assistance to entrepreneurs is most challenging and costly if the program serves a wide variety of microbusinesses, especially those that are geographically dispersed. Programs like the Service Corps of Retired Executives (SCORE) may be of some assistance, but volunteers should be appropriately motivated and trained to be able to relate to low-income entrepreneurs. It may be most effective for MDPs to focus on particular business sectors (see the next section). Potentially high costs of monitoring and coaching could be offset through creative use of telephone, teleconferencing, Internet, list serves, and E-mail. An example includes MicroMentor project of the Aspen Institute that links mentors with protégés via the Internet (Microenterprise FIELD, 2003a). Nonetheless, training remains expensive and difficult.

PERSONAL AND FAMILY SUPPORT. Health problems and personal crises inevitably occur. As this study suggests, for families with few backup resources, an emergency or chronic illness can drag a business down. In such cases, short- or long-term support may be needed. Respite care and day care for elderly and sick family members could prevent entrepreneurs from having to close their businesses. Other mechanisms to support entrepreneurs through periods of crisis are emergency grant funds or short-term loans for temporary assistance and tax credits for long-term support. In other cases, child care may be needed as a business takes more time than an entrepreneur imagined. Several of the entrepreneurs chose a home-based business so they could spend more time with their children, but as a result, some said they were unable to devote attention to their business. Half-day child care or some other arrangement could free them to focus on their businesses while still allowing them to care for their children. MDPs do not have to provide these services directly, but can partner with other agencies to ensure that support is available.

Mezzo-Level Strategies: Building Intermediary Structures to Support Microenterprise

While MDPs focus on training, capital, and social support for individual entrepreneurs, these approaches are unlikely to overcome many of the serious obstacles discussed by the entrepreneurs in this study. While these individual-level strategies provide critical assistance, they do not address lack of access to markets, depressed local economies with sagging consumer spending, and competition from large retailers (Everett & Watson, 1998). These problems cannot be remedied on an individual level; they require different methods (Piore & Sabel, 1984).

At least two alternatives could be considered. One approach is to link low-income entrepreneurs with existing business structures (Edgcomb & Barton, 1998).[5] Business organizations, such as the chamber of commerce and the Rotary, as well as social institutions where businesspeople meet, such as country clubs and athletic associations are powerful groups that help their constituents gain access to economic power, resources, and political decision making. However, people with low incomes have not been embraced in such organizations and it may be difficult for them to find "a place at the table." For example, as Brian Uzzi and James Gillespie (1999) suggest, personal relationships are taken into account that make it particularly difficult for those outside the social networks of bankers (e.g., women, minorities, and, especially, the poor) to qualify for loans. The few participants who said they attended local meetings of business groups felt out of place.

The other approach is to create alternative structures that address specific obstacles facing low-income, minority, and women entrepreneurs (Edgcomb & Barton, 1998). These structures provide access to information, research, supplies, technical assistance, coaching, and markets. In the long run, these structures should provide mechanisms for participation in existing business organizations and in policy (see the next section), but in the meantime they would begin to address differential access to resources in existing structures (Kantor, 2000). In addition to supply-side strategies that increase entrepreneurial capacity (discussed earlier), Karen Doyle Grossman and her colleagues (2002) identify demand-side strategies used by MDPs to create venues for market access and sales support to microentrepreneurs. The following are examples of intermediary structures that could operate as either linking or sales support mechanisms.

MICROBUSINESS INCUBATORS. Although business incubators have not been used much with low-income microentrepreneurs (Balkin, 1989), they have been successful in helping jump-start small businesses in technology, service, light industrial, or specific niches or sectors (Allen & Rahman, 1985; NBIA, 2001). Incubators provide access to physical space and other resources for business start-up, including overhead and operational costs, usually for a period of two to three years (e.g., photocopying, secretarial services, and janitorial services), access to equipment, expandable space, managerial support, and access to markets (NBIA, 2001). Incubators minimize costs by centralization of services for multiple users. Three-quarters are non-profit, although the numbers of for-profit incubators is growing. The Appalachian Center for Economic Networks (ACEnet) in Athens, Ohio, has pioneered the use of a kitchen incubator for microenterprise (Holley, 1995; Kantor, 2000).

OPEN-AIR MARKETING. Another, perhaps more realistic, intermediary strategy is to protect what might be called "natural incubators" where low-income entrepreneurs can get a start with low overhead and ready access to consumers. As previously mentioned, some programs have built mini-malls to help launch small storefront businesses. A less-expensive option is protection of existing open-air markets and street vending, which can provide marketing venues for low-income microentrepreneurs (Balkin, 1989; Openair-Market Net, 2001). Urban development projects often include open-air marketing, but too often do not protect existing low-income markets. The near-demise of Chicago's largest outdoor market, Maxwell Street, is but one example of what can occur with urban redevelopment (Morales, et. al., 1995). The Maxwell Street market was moved to another location, saving some of the open-air businesses, but in other cities even this has not been attempted (Sutin, 2000). Another low overhead marketing option is street vending. Immigrants historically have used street vending as a way to get started in business. Unfortunately, many cities restrict or prohibit street vending, rules that fall especially hard on low-income operators (Openair-Market Net, 2001). Another model are the hawker's stands in Singapore, where former food venders were brought together in a mini-mall setting with access to sanitary facilities. Public financing is needed to protect low-overhead open-air markets for microentrepreneurs, ones that incidentally often serve low-income consumers.

DEVELOPMENT OF SECTORS AND FLEXIBLE NETWORKS. A strategy that has been attempted on a small scale by MDPs is to identify and develop ideas for more lucrative businesses (Holley & Wadia, 2001). Most MDPs provide assistance to disparate businesses, while a sectoral approach focuses on identifying and developing opportunities within a market sector or subsector, promoting linkages for marketing, networking, and training entrepreneurs (Kantor, 2000; Grossman, et al., 2002). ACEnet has promoted this approach by working to identify and develop certain promising markets in specialty foods and furniture. According to ACEnet founder June Holley (1996), the rewards are high using this strategy because specialty products provide a higher return than commodities. However, this approach is challenging because successes in specialty markets ". . . demand a continual stream of new products, impeccable quality, quick response to demands that cannot be predicted ahead of time, and a capacity to deal with the rigorous business procedures of the buyers" (Holley, 1995, 19). Else and Clay-Thompson (1998) concur, pointing out, for example, that assisting establishment of import-export markets, for example, is complex, long term, and requires specialized knowledge on the part of staff. By focusing on a specific product or service, trainers could gain enough knowledge and skills to be useful to the microentrepreneurs.

A related idea is the development of flexible business networks (Piore & Sabel, 1994). Of European origin, flexible networks are clusters of related firms that aim to improve competitiveness and market share for small firms. They do this through cooperation, shared costs of research and development, joint production, economies of scale through bulk purchasing and marketing, cooperative purchase of technology, and customized and flexible response to changing market conditions (Hatch, 1988, 1991; Hirst & Zeitlin, 1991). The idea of flexible networks—that balance cooperation and competition among firms—emerged in response to the growth of international markets that make cooperation, innovation, and quick response to consumer demand essential to survival of firms (Hirst & Zeitlin, 1991). This model has not been adopted extensively with microenterprise, although the idea may have applicability. MDPs could work with clusters of firms to provide market "intelligence," develop and maintain relationships with key purchasers, help firms network with each other, and offer sector-based training (Holley, 1998). Alliances could be formal joint ventures or informal arrangements to share equipment and information and purchase supplies (Holley, 1998). However, like the sector-based approach, nurturing flexible business networks requires considerable skills and resources on the part of MDPs. Roger Wilkens and June Holley (1992) also suggest that networks of firms engaged in collaborative projects and joint ventures would require secure and advanced computer technology.

INFORMATION AND E-COMMUNICATION. Kantor (2000), in an assessment of information resources for women entrepreneurs, points out that programs that provide information to start-up and expanding businesses, such as Small Business Development Centers, women's business centers, and on-line business information services, offer great potential for reaching entrepreneurs. Generally, the entrepreneurs in this study were limited to community-based support services. They may have benefited from access to broader information through expanded electronic communication. Access to information, training, and mentoring could be facilitated by these methods, not only for rural entrepreneurs who find it expensive and time-consuming to drive to a central location, but also for urban entrepreneurs who may find it difficult to attend training sessions. Karen Doyle Grossman and her colleagues recommend more attention to appropriate use of technology in microenterprise development, including use of business software, distance online learning, and web-based research, communication and marketing (2003). Moreover, business development programs, incubators, and networks could be facilitated through e-communication. Unfortunately, microenterprises often lack access to adequate computer technology and computer skills. Investment in computer skills training and access to equipment for microentrepreneurs could begin to address a "digital divide" in the business world.

MICROENTERPRISE ASSOCIATIONS. A growing number of regional, state, and national associations seek to improve the environment for microenterprise by providing opportunities to network, engage in continuing education, influence public policy, and educate the public (CFED, 1997; Stone, 1997). They are encouraging greater attention to microenterprise by state and local departments of development, which have traditionally focused on large-scale business development. The Corporation for Enterprise Development convenes state microenterprise associations to promote policy development. The Association for Enterprise Opportunity is a trade association that promotes microenterprise development.[6] Some states, such as Nebraska, have organized state associations of MDPs that have achieved notable success in funding and generating new programs.[7] The National Association for the Self-Employed (NASE) also provides a range of benefits and supports to businesses with up to ten employees.[8] The Microenterprise Fund for Innovation, Effectiveness, Learning, and Dissemination (FIELD), a program of the Aspen Institute, conducts research and development dedicated to expansion and sustainability of microenterprise, especially for the poor (Microenterprise FIELD, 1998).[9] Following on the heels of the Self-Employment Learning Project (SELP), FIELD funds projects and identifies "best practices." Moreover, FIELD is involved in research and public education in support of microenterprise. Such efforts may be useful in generating effective and cost-efficient microenterprise development (AEO, 2002b).

Intermediary structures are a missing link in microenterprise development in the United States. Without a quality product and solid business skills, no business will succeed. But without access to intermediary institutions, especially for market research, purchasing, and marketing, microenterprises are also likely to fail. MDPs currently provide training and capital to help people get their businesses off the ground, but they tend to lack resources to link microenterprises to larger structures that can facilitate business growth and success. MDPs could help businesses or groups of businesses identify trends and new markets, organize collaborative and joint ventures, establish outdoor markets or malls, build incubators, educate the public about microenterprise, and facilitate the use of new technologies in production and communications. Advances such as these would begin to change the business context and facilitate success for microenterprise.

Intermediary structures also might be vehicles for social development that U.S. programs have sought to generate through largely unsuccessful peer-lending programs. The Grameen Bank in Bangladesh, which brings women together in peer-lending groups (Hossain, 1986), also strengthens women's place in the community and provides opportunities to establish an individual identity and exchange scarce resources. As Lisa Larance points out in her study of women entrepreneurs in the Grameen Bank program: "Sustainable prosperity—both economic and social—seems to be cultivated by regular and frequent interaction at a sanctioned gathering place" (2001, 30). For women whose social and economic lives had been severely restricted, there is evidence that such activities generate social capital and are transformative (Schuler & Hashemi, 1994; Larance, 2001). However, in the United States, such activities may not have the same impact. In this study, we found little evidence that peer-lending or group interaction offered the same advantages. It may be more appropriate in the U.S. context to build social capital through the use of intermediary structures that provide opportunities for low-income entrepreneurs to gain a place at the table through linkages to business networks. Although the entrepreneurs reported increased confidence and stature in the community, there was little evidence that this was enough to increase business success. Therefore, increases in bonding social capital did not address barriers to business success, such as sagging local economies, competition with large franchises, and access to adequate business infrastructure. Development of intermediary structures may provide the bridging social capital that would better meet the demands of U.S. microenterprise.

Macrolevel Strategies: Removing Barriers and Facilitating Success of Microenterprise

Policy changes are also needed to support microenterprise development strategies. Some policy reforms could remove barriers to microenterprise. As one successful microentrepreneur, Joanne, pointed out: "*It would be easier if the government would help small business get going and on their feet through taxes, regulations, and helping them stay alive.*" Currently, as Schreiner and

Morduch point out, various policies (e.g., welfare rules, licensing, and taxation) that "work for the majority turn out to hinder attempts to spread microenterprise in the United States" (2002, 31). Other policy changes could support new and expanded micro- and mezzo-level strategies (or opportunity structures) and support for microentrepreneurs and their families.

SOCIAL POLICY SUPPORTS. As the entrepreneurs noted, lack of public assistance and health benefits threaten business viability. According to one entrepreneur, who was encouraged to open a business as part of a welfare-to-work program, welfare workers seemed to have an attitude of "*how dare you attempt to start your own business and survive on state assistance?*" With an emphasis on 'work first,' pressure is on public welfare officials to terminate public benefits as quickly as possible. But strict limits on public assistance benefits, medical insurance, housing subsidies, and Food Stamps discourages business growth and development because recipients would lose benefits long before their businesses are sufficiently established. As noted in chapter 7, Monica said Medicaid provided "*bridge*" support at first, but when it ran out, she had to close the business because she could not afford private health insurance. She called losing Medicaid a "*counter-incentive*." Currently, microenterprise can be used to fulfill Temporary Assistance for Needy Families (TANF) work requirements, and, as long as participants remain income-eligible, they may receive Medicaid and child-care stipends temporarily (Greenberg, 1999). Some MDPs are working with welfare departments to help women in self-employment (Bonavoglia & Wadia, 2001). Unfortunately, such programs are threatened by rising state budget deficits. While only some states do so, they should consider microenterprise training, internships, and business start-up as legitimate job training and work activities (Alisultanov, et al., 2002). Moreover, too often if family earnings move above income-eligibility, benefits are reduced or cut. And while Medicaid now covers many low- and moderate- income children, in most states only the poorest adults are covered, and only if they have children. Clearly, withdrawal of support (especially health and child care) could be devastating for a start-up business. The large numbers of entrepreneurs in this study who encountered health problems that affected their businesses suggest consideration of some form of state-based subsidized group coverage for microentrepreneurs. State and national microenterprise associations may be helpful in securing funding and policy initiatives (CFED, n.d.).

FINANCIAL EDUCATION IN SCHOOLS. Currently, microenterprise programs are spending a great deal of time helping participants clean credit records, open bank accounts, and use checking accounts, instead of focusing on teaching business accounting and financial planning. Training in finance and financial management should begin in elementary and secondary school. Although economic education is expanding, more state and federal support is necessary (NEFE, 2001). This type of training can help young people learn how to manage their personal finances, but could also form a foundation for more advanced financial training for business.

REGULATORY AND TAX REFORM. Entrepreneurs in this study emphasized the challenges they encountered finding attractive and secure locations they could afford with access to supplies and customers. William Dennis (1998) argues that although we do not know the full impact of zoning and regulation on new very small firms (including prohibition of home-based businesses, licensing or permit costs, fees, and regulatory hassles), they were designed with little thought to the impact on microenterprise. These should be reexamined with an eye toward removing regulations that thwart legitimate home-based, vendor-based, open-air, or storefront microbusinesses (Balkin, 1989). For example, communities that limit or prohibit home-based businesses might modify those rules to permit types of microbusinesses that are congruent with the type of permitted land use (Solomon, 1992), and licensing procedures should be streamlined (Staley, et al., 2001). Arbitrary regulations, unnecessary paperwork, and rules that protect larger businesses (Mellor, 1996) should be eliminated and access to legal services increased (Dean, 2001).

There may also be ways to make the tax system more favorable for microentrepreneurs. Speaking about the tax system, a microentrepreneur in a focus group said, "*it's like putting a seed in the ground and [they] try to pick off the leaves when it is germinating.*" For instance, low-income entrepreneurs could benefit from tax breaks for a certain number of years. Over the longer term, some have suggested expanding tax credits to set up pension plans through tax-deferred savings accounts because the low-income self-employed are not building up adequate retirement savings (Messenger & Stettner, 2000). Refundable tax credits would encourage microentrepreneurs to formalize their businesses, keep separate accounts, and, eventually, pay taxes.

"CROSS-TRAINING" IN SOCIAL AND ECONOMIC DEVELOPMENT FOR STAFF. Talking with the microentrepreneurs, it was clear that staff in microenterprise programs should possess what is currently an unusual mix of skills. Transcending typical professional training, staff should possess both business development and human relations skills, but they also should have organizing, management, and advocacy skills, and be able to work in interdisciplinary teams across private and public sectors. For example, few people have skills in effectively involving members of the community in design and implementation of development programs (Bhatt, 1997), and, among those who do, there may be only a few who are also skilled in accounting. Currently, there are relatively few educational programs that offer training across this social and economic development "divide" that prepares professionals to work in interdisciplinary teams in microenterprise development (Rubin & Sherraden, forthcoming). New models, including interdisciplinary degree programs, are necessary to meet this growing demand.[10]

Future Research

As this study provides insight into the experiences and outcomes of microenterprise in low-income households, it also raises new questions. Ongoing research is needed to expand knowledge about microenterprise participants and programs. Controlled experimental studies that provide long-term data (including those that assess postbusiness outcomes and intergenerational effects) are required to assess more fully the explanatory power of competing theories and to identify outcomes. Studies using experimental design maximize internal validity and can help specify whether the outcomes found among program participants are a direct or indirect result of program interventions. To date, there has been no true experimental study of microenterprise, and indeed, few studies that include any comparison groups (Sanders, 2002, is one of the few). The lack of experimental or at least quasi-experimental studies creates a risk of overestimating the impacts of microenterprise and the effects of MDPs. Second, there should be more microenterprise program comparisons, including cost studies (Schreiner, 2002), that identify truly successful policy and program strategies.

Turning to particular areas of inquiry, this study raises serious concerns about the reliability of business and household financial data in studies of low-income households and businesses. We found that the financial boundary between business and household was often fuzzy and highly permeable. It was difficult to sort out financial data due to absent or inadequate accounting, and perhaps sometimes due to a reluctance to report financial data accurately. Better methods for collection of business and household financial data will be required. One approach is to use a combination of quantitative and qualitative methods. Qualitative in-depth interviewing can help in two ways. First, more trust is developed with participants, helping them to understand the reasons for the study, and this aids in collecting more accurate data. Second, participants often do not clearly understand how to calculate revenue and profits, and a less structured approach to interviewing can help the interviewer clarify terms and generate more reliable data (Edin, 1993). Another possible approach is to create software that keeps track of financial transactions. Although this approach would likely require substantial effort on the part of the programs and participants, it could generate more reliable data. It would also likely change participant behavior. If participants were trained to use business accounting software, and if their loans and savings were being "tracked" by the software, they would be more likely to keep records. Programs using software to monitor business activities could also use the data to research program effects. A study of Individual Development Accounts has successfully created and used software for management and research purposes, suggesting that this might be a viable strategy (Johnson, et al., 2001).

Studies are needed in a variety of settings and programs. What types of innovations impact the business bottom line? For example, research on different approaches to training and mentoring could point to effective practices. Research, including thorough case studies, on the use of such innovations as incubators and business sector approaches for low-income entrepreneurs can assess intermediary interventions. While experimental studies are difficult in these circumstances, well-designed pre- and poststudies can contribute to understanding what innovations may make a substantial difference in business outcomes. Additionally, in-depth interviews and case studies can assess, from the perspective of microenterprise participants, whether experiences and outcomes change as a result of different policy and practice models. Research should also examine more explicitly the experiences and challenges imposed by gender, race, and ethnicity (Woller et al., 1999; Schreiner, 1999c; Sanders, 2000). Specifically, it is important to understand what types of microbusinesses do well, including traditionally female versus traditionally male businesses.

The multiple outcomes of microenterprise that have emerged in this study suggest that the benefits of microenterprise are complex and that many are not easy to measure. More academic attention especially should be paid to the following outcomes: skill development, sense of control, integration of work with family responsibilities, asset accumulation, and personal satisfaction. In addition, long-term impacts should be studied, especially impacts on future labor market and/or business performance and impacts on children. Some entrepreneurs in this study said that they believed that the skills learned in business would help with future businesses and would also help them acquire and perform better in wage employment. But what kinds of business skills translate into job skills? Many entrepreneurs believed that their businesses also had a positive impact on their children. But what effects on children result from owning a business, and what particular aspects of microenterprise lead to these effects? Is it ownership per se, or parental enthusiasm, or exposure to business processes, or actual skill development that makes a difference? Comparative studies of child welfare and development in families that are employed in the labor market versus in microenterprise could provide valuable insights.

More attention should also be given to diversification of income streams in low-income households. The trend in advanced economies is toward less stable labor markets and perhaps toward greater diversification of income. Is diversification of income a conscious decision to maximize income security, or is it simply a mode of survival and making ends meet? Does diversification of income streams in fact provide more stability for the poor? If so, how much diversification is desirable in different circumstances? Is there a "tipping point" beyond which the costs of diversification costs outweigh the protective effects? Is it possible that engaging in multiple activities to increase income security in the short run can compromise household economic growth development in the long run? Do some kinds of jobs lend themselves to diversification and others not?

Likewise, research should examine the impact of owning business assets on household welfare. Support for microenterprise is one of the few public policies that promotes asset ownership among the poor. Are there important effects of assets or net worth not captured by focusing primarily on income generated from the business (Sherraden, 1991)? What are these in the case of microenterprise? If assets matter, is microenterprise an effective way for public policy to build assets (compared, e.g., to home ownership or education)?

Although very difficult to assess, it is possible that microenterprise has positive impacts on communities (Servon, 1999). This study provides little insight into this question, although a few of the microentrepreneurs believed that their business increased their involvement in civic affairs. If microenterprise is shown to provide important products and services in under-served communities, generate other businesses, create new associations, increase community revenues through taxation, and/or provide positive role models, then a case for additional investment could be made. In other words, is the "social utility" of these ventures "multifold," as Lewis Solomon (1992) suggests? Does such an approach epitomize "strong policy" (Sherraden, 2001)?

Conclusion

Helping individuals and families build a future requires more than providing a safety net. It requires significant public and private investments in increasing opportunity for building capability among the poor (Sen, 1999). Providing opportunities for microenterprise may be one way to accomplish this goal. This study, however, documents the challenges in this undertaking. Considerable resources can be invested in training, financing, and supporting low-income entrepreneurs in their efforts to build small businesses, but success in terms of financial gain often remains elusive.

At the same time, most of the entrepreneurs in this study evaluated their microenterprise experience in a positive light and their enthusiasm suggests that business ownership has strong appeal. According to the entrepreneurs, microenterprise offers an opportunity for them to develop skills and knowledge, to make decisions and have control over work conditions, to build their household assets, to care for loved ones, and to fulfill personal goals. In many cases, entrepreneurs perceive that these benefits overcome limited income (and sometimes losses) and long hours and stress associated with business operation.

The availability of microenterprise loans is unlikely to overcome the significant challenges to business success in the United States. At the same time, a full array of interventions, such as those outlined in this chapter, may not be politically and/or economically feasible. Implementing all of these strategies, while they make sense based on what we have learned from the entrepreneurs, would be very expensive (Schreiner & Woller, 2003). Indeed, studies suggest that existing MDPs are far from sustainable from the standpoint of cost and subsidy (Servon, et al., 2000; Schreiner & Morduch, 2002).

Given the policies that have historically supported business among the better-off, and a history of discrimination against women and repression of entrepreneurship among Blacks in America, a case can be made that extraordinary efforts to increase business opportunities for women and in low-income and minority communities are justified. Moreover, there is some evidence that microenterprise survival rates are not much different than other small businesses (as discussed in chapter 2), and that rates for exiting poverty are not much different among microentrepreneurs and those in jobs in the labor market (Sanders, 2002). In other words, there is little evidence to suggest that microenterprise is a bad idea, and at the same time, there is also a larger and long-term agenda of democratic capitalism that together may justify significant investments in microenterprise.

But how to do this? The answer is not simply to expand operating subsidies and other financial supports based on existing models of microenterprise. This study suggests strategies and innovations that would increase the likelihood of positive business performance in both minimalist and high-potential businesses. Some of these strategies would cost quite a lot more money, but others less. Some of the more cost-effective strategies might be in targeting entrepreneurs and their businesses for specialized support. Some of the least cost-effective approaches are broad recruitment of poverty populations for business ownership when it is clear that only a very small percentage will likely succeed. Future research should sort out which approaches to microenterprise development have the greatest effects on business success, compared to costs.

MDPs should be clear about their goals. On one hand, if the goal is to create high-potential and growth-oriented businesses, then programs should expect to make a large and long-term investment in microenterprise. The expectation should be high future returns in the form of economic and social benefits for the family, and possibly greater economic and social vitality of low-income neighborhoods. In these situations, programs could assist entrepreneurs with a range of training, capital, and business network development over a five-year start-up period. These individual-level strategies also could be accompanied by developing intermediary business supports and reforming public policy.

On the other hand, MDPs aimed at helping families to diversify their incomes should help with a variety of income-generating opportunities. These might include job training and access to better jobs with better working conditions, securing appropriate income and other supports (such as the Earned Income Tax Credit and Medicaid), and *possibly* support for a business. This study suggests that it is quite unlikely that minimalist businesses will bring in more than a small part of total household income. In other words, self-employment is one of a number of possible approaches, but should not be the primary focus of an anti-poverty program.

As demonstrated in this study, microenterprise is a strategy for broad and multifaceted *development* of individuals and households. Outcomes in skills, satisfaction, self-esteem, flexibility in caring for children, and other areas, appear to be strong. In the long run, these may be very important. That is the message from the entrepreneurs in this study.

Some observers, trained to equate income and consumption with well-being, will be tempted to dismiss these findings on multiple positive outcomes as of secondary importance. Some will continue to think that only income really matters. This viewpoint, we believe, would miss important effects of microenterprise. We prefer the capabilities perspective of Amartya Sen (1999). Clearly, because of their microenterprises, these respondents are more able to undertake activities and achieve conditions that they have reason to value. There is general evidence, and evidence in this study, that small entrepreneurs are willing to sacrifice income for these valued activities and conditions. The proper reasoning should be that these activities and conditions are, to these individuals, at least as important as income.

In closing, we turn to the words of Doug who summarized his thinking about the role of microenterprise and microenterprise development programs:

> *A lot of people have dreams. It is probably good for them to be able to live out their dreams. Some of them probably are going to succeed, and most of them aren't. I think that if the program is going to be viable, [MDPs] need to start from square one, and follow [the entrepreneurs] at least three to four years out, and really stay close with them so that they do succeed.*

If they choose, poor people also deserve a shot at capitalism. As Doug says, some will do well financially, but most probably will not. We have learned in this study, however, that for most microentrepreneurs, rewards go beyond financial gain. In other words, capitalism is about more than income. It would be inadequate public policy and community development that did not recognize these multiple effects of microenterprise.

At the same time, public and community resources should not be wasted in making thousands of loans to thousands of unsuccessful businesses. The challenge will be to identify strategic investments and supports that meet particular goals. We have learned in this study that economic goals of microentrepreneurs differ markedly. To oversimplify, some are interested in growing a business, some are trying to supplement household income, and some are self-employed because it suits other circumstances in their lives. Public policy and microenterprise development programs should recognize these differences and make targeted investments and program decisions accordingly.

Notes

1. This characterization is similar to what Guarnizo calls "subsistence" firms (1998) and what Light and Rosenstein call "income self-employment" (1995, 175).

2. For example, evidence that some women turn to self-employment because wage jobs do not offer flexibility to care for children, suggests that "employers should be 'more friendly' to women with young children" (Boden, 1999, 81).

3. The Consultative Group to Assist the Poorest (CGAP) recommends making one-time microgrants available in developing countries which are monitored and accompanied by training in situations where a grant could help a person move from "vulnerability to economic self-sufficiency" and avoid piling on debt (Parker & Pearce, 2001). They recommend that the recipients contribute 5 to 10 percent.

4. Although a few entrepreneurs mentioned SCORE business counselors, who are retired or working business owner volunteers who are available on call (Kantor, 2000), they made little use of them. An MDP program director pointed out that the social class and cultural differences between SCORE volunteers and MDP participants frequently inhibited successful relationships. Success often depended on a good match of volunteer and participant.

5. Edgcomb and Barton (1998) distinguish between "linking" systems of social intermediation (social capital-building) with financial institutions and "parallel" systems that are alternative financial systems (e.g., solidarity groups and village banking). The level of analysis is on the firm, but applies to the intermediary structures under discussion.

6. *http://www.microenterpriseworks.org.*

7. *http://www.neon.neded.org.*

8. *http://www.nase.org.*

9. *http://www.fieldus.org.*

10. Programs that are attempting to breach this divide include Southern New Hampshire University's School of Community Economic Development, which also sponsors an annual Microenterprise Institute.

Appendix A
Glossary

Assets are the stock of wealth of a person, association, corporation, or estate applicable or subject to the payment of debts (SBA, 2002).

Business assets are the assets owned by the business.

Business liabilities are how much the business owes.

A *business plan* is a comprehensive planning document that describes the business objective of an existing or proposed business, including what, how, and from where resources will be obtained and utilized (SBA, 2002).

Business revenues are the gross earnings or sales from the business.

Capital is (1) assets less liabilities, representing ownership interest in a business; (2) a stock of accumulated goods, especially at a specified time and in contrast to income received during a specified time period; (3) accumulated goods devoted to the production of goods; and (4) accumulated possessions calculated to bring income (SBA, 2002).

Collateral is property offered to secure a loan or other credit and that is subject to seizure on default (Federal Reserve of Chicago, 2003).

Credit is the promise to pay in the future in order to buy or borrow in the present and the right to defer payment of debt (Federal Reserve of Chicago, 2003).

Credit history is a record of how a person has borrowed and paid debts.

Earned income is money taken from the business, or wages and salary earned from a job working for someone else.

An *entrepreneur* is "a person who assumes the financial risk of the initiation, operation and management of a given business or undertaking" (SBA, 2002).

Financing is "new funds provided to a business, by either loans or purchase of debt securities or capital stock" (SBA, 2002).

A *grant* is money given to a business that does not require repayment (SBA, 2002).

Household assets are assets owned by a family or household unit.

Household liabilities are how much a family or household unit owes.

Household net worth is the household assets minus the household liabilities.

An *incubator* is a "facility designed to encourage entrepreneurship and minimize obstacles to new business formation and growth . . . by housing a number of fledgling enterprises that share an array of services" (SBA, 2002). They typically share secretarial, telephone, copying, and other office-related services and are charged on an as-used basis. Some provide technical assistance, training, and financing (CFED, 1997).

An *innovation* is an "introduction of a new idea into the marketplace in the form of a new product or service, or an improvement in organization or process" (SBA, 2002).

An *intermediary organization* plays "a fundamental role in encouraging, promoting, and facilitating business-to-business linkages and mentor-protégé partnerships. These can include both nonprofit and for-profit organizations: chambers of commerce; trade associations; local, civic, and community groups; state and local governments; academic institutions; and private corporations" (SBA, 2002).

A *lending institution* is "any institution, including a commercial bank, savings and loan association, commercial finance company, or other lender" that makes loans (SBA, 2002).

Liability is debt owed, including bank loans or accounts payable (SBA, 2002).

Line of credit is "a short-term loan, usually less than one year" (SBA, 2002).

Market research targets a specific community or neighborhood and seeks to improve the chance of survival for start-up businesses by identifying what types of businesses offer the highest chance for success (CFED, 1997).

A *microenterprise* is a sole proprietorship that has fewer than five employees (usually a sole proprietor and no employees), has not had access to loans, and typically uses an initial loan of less than $15,000, usually much less. Most microenterprises are operated by the owner alone and have annual sales of $250,000 or less (Langer, et al., 1999; Walker & Blair, 2002).

A *microenterprise development program* (MDP) is a program operated by a non-profit or public entity that provides any combination of loans, technical assistance, training, and other business or personal assistance services to microentrepreneurs.

A *microloan* is a very small loan made to a microenterprise. Loan amounts vary considerably by program, from a few hundred dollars up to $35,000 in the SBA program.

Net worth or owner equity is assets minus debts and obligations (liabilities).

Peer group lending circles are small groups of borrowers who are organized in micro-enterprise programs that make decisions about who should be granted a loan and how much and monitor the repayment of loans.

Profit is net income from a business (gross income minus expenses).

A *proprietorship* is "the most common legal form of business ownership; about 85 percent of all small businesses are proprietorships. The liability of the owner is unlimited in this form of ownership" (SBA, 2002). A *sole proprietorship* is a business owned by one person, the most typical form found in microenterprise.

Return on investment is the amount of profit based on the amount of resources used to produce it. Also, the ability of a given investment to earn a return for its use (SBA, 2002).

Sectoral business development selects an industry or sector—such as grocery stores, day care, or home health care—that has potential to grow and assists in forming related microenterprises linked through a cooperative or networking structure (CFED, 1997).

Service Corps of Retired Executives (SCORE) is a 12,400-member volunteer association sponsored by the SBA that matches volunteer business counselors with small business owners in need of expert advice (SCORE, *http://www.score.org*).

A *swap meet* is a flea market that meets on a regular basis.

Unearned income is income not earned by someone in the household, including alimony, child support and non-means-tested sources of income (e.g., including pensions, social security, unemployment insurance benefits), and means-tested sources of income (e.g., public assistance, Food Stamps, and other governmental poverty programs).

Appendix B
Research Methods

The low-income microentrepreneurs in this study participated in the Aspen Institute's Self-Employment Learning Project (SELP), a five-year study of entrepreneurs from microenterprise development programs around the United States.[1] When the Aspen Institute initiated this study, little was known about microenterprise in the United States. Today, SELP remains one of the few and one of the largest studies of its kind. After conducting case studies and program profiles of the seven microenterprise programs and surveying 405 randomly selected microentrepreneurs from the programs, researchers at SELP and their collaborators in microenterprise programs and funding agencies, decided to learn more about the low-income participants in the sample. Because the field of microenterprise was concerned about the anti-poverty potential of microenterprise, only those with incomes below 150 percent of poverty were selected for inclusion in the study's fourth wave of data collection. At the same time, it was decided to approach data collection through in-depth interviewing, which would generate a qualitative portrait of the low-income microenterprise experience that was not captured by the annual surveys.

SELP evaluators asked researchers at the Center for Social Development (CSD) at Washington University to design and implement the in-depth interview study for Wave Four. Using a mixed methods approach (Hulme, 1997), this book is derived in large measure from the qualitative findings from Wave Four, but also relies on other data sources from SELP. These include reanalysis of respondent survey data, including close-ended and open-ended responses from the Wave One survey. Although entrepreneurs were selected randomly, it is important to note that this study, like the larger SELP study, does not employ a control group. Thus, results are suggestive and require future testing with a larger sample in a case-controlled design.

Annual Survey Interviews with Entrepreneurs

Demographic information and measures of microenterprise outcomes come from survey data collected by SELP between 1991 and 1996. Additionally data are drawn from published and unpublished baseline results from the first three waves and the fifth wave of the study, in addition to program case studies (Clark & Huston, 1993; Clark & Kays, 1995; Edgcomb, et al., 1996; Clark & Kays, et al., 1999).[2] Wave One (1991–92) and Wave Two (1992–93) of the survey were designed and collected by James Bell Associates in collaboration with SELP staff. Wave Three (1994–95) was designed and managed by SELP staff partnering with Abt Associates who were responsible for data verification, survey design, and data processing. Wave Five (1996) was managed by SELP and data were processed by Abt Associates, although some of the data were collected by CSD at the end of the qualitative interview.[3] Annual survey interviews were conducted by telephone and lasted approximately one hour each, although the first two survey interviews were longer than the last two.

Generally, surveys addressed the following topics: (1) basic demographic and household information about the entrepreneur and family; (2) primary and secondary sources of earnings and household income; (3) household economic characteristics, including details about each source of earned and unearned income (e.g., jobs, business, and government assistance), as well as household expenses, household liabilities, and assets; (4) business characteristics, including description, hours devoted to business, employees, revenues, expenses, assets, liabilities, and significant annual changes; (5) an assessment of how the business is prospering, including barriers and supports; (6) a description of program participation, including training, peer group, loan history, technical assistance, and other activities, and an assessment of impact; and (7) access to workplace or business benefits, including health insurance.

Despite similarities, the survey interviews differed in significant ways. While Waves One and Two established baseline information and incorporated many open-ended questions on the development and impact of the business, Wave Five data collection focused narrowly on household and business data. To illustrate, the Wave One survey asked about entrepreneur's previous full-time job and experience related to the business, and business start-up characteristics (e.g., sources of capital and other supports, customers, suppliers, markets, and financial records) and open-ended questions about business barriers and program evaluation. By Wave Five, the survey basically covered sources of income and earnings, business status, and household and business expenses, revenues, assets, and liabilities. Answers to open-ended questions had not been analyzed and reported previously; therefore, we include some of these data here.

In-Depth Interviews with Low-Income Entrepreneurs

The first step in developing in-depth interviews was to discuss findings from the first three waves of data collection with SELP evaluators and to obtain their ideas about key issues and questions that should be addressed qualitatively. Their main question concerned whether microenterprise is an effective anti-poverty strategy. In other words, what role did the microenterprise play in helping low-income participants and their families to become more economically viable and to move out of poverty? They also had other questions, if households were still poor after opening a business, why? Who was successful in business and why? What were the obstacles to business development?

Would those with unsuccessful businesses rather be working in a job? What role did the microenterprise play in launching the business and helping people move out of poverty? What additional services did microentrepreneurs want or require? From the questions posed by SELP evaluators and by others, we derived a set of research questions and preliminary hypotheses that guided the qualitative research.

The second step was to hold two focus groups to help prepare the interview instrument. We talked with fifteen low-income microentrepreneurs (none were participants in SELP program sites) from two microenterprise programs in St. Louis. Participants, who were paid $25 for their time, operated a variety of microbusinesses. The discussions lasted over two hours and covered six topics: background and business goals, barriers and facilitators to microbusiness development, patterns of household income, role of microenterprise earnings in savings and investment, boundaries between household and business, and outcomes.

The third step was to prepare the in-depth interview guide, which would provide direction to the conversation with respondents, without inhibiting them from bringing up other topics of interest and concern. The interview itself was informal and relaxed, and designed to build trust and collaboration, to help entrepreneurs feel in control, and to elicit forthright and clear responses about sometimes sensitive topics (Sherraden & Barrera, 1995). In-depth interviewers, trained to be interested and sympathetic listeners, tried to understand the business experience from participants' perspectives. Interviewers also helped participants clarify their recollections, and explore apparent contradictions (that emerged within the interview or with prior surveys). Clarification of this kind is particularly important because of the limited amount of social science research and understanding of low-income families in business.

The instrument was pre-tested with seven participants in the SELP study whose incomes were just above the cut off for inclusion in the poverty subsample. Modifications in the interview guide were made. In the meantime, the research plan received approval from the institutional review board at Washington University, and we began to recruit and train interviewers. In-depth interviews require highly skilled interviewers. The interviewer has responsibility for guiding wide-ranging and potentially unpredictable discussions. This means that the interviewer has to be able to engage the respondent, ask good questions, be a good listener, be able to interpret answers, follow up, be flexible, have a thorough understanding of the research questions, be responsive to sensitive issues, and keep the interview on track. The nine interviewers were master's and doctoral social work students at the George Warren Brown School of Social Work. Fortunately, the interviewers had prior training as interviewers (i.e., they knew how to ask questions, convey empathy, clarify, follow up, deal with digression, and get feedback). Training focused on the particular application and demands of research interviews (as opposed to therapeutic interviews), including understanding the specific research objectives, confidentiality and consent issues, and the research protocol details. A total of nine interviewers were trained, however, a core group of six—including Cynthia K. Sanders, one of the authors of this study—conducted most of the interviews. Additionally, as initial interviews took place, we listened to them and provided suggestions for improvements in interviewing techniques.

Letters were sent to all 138 entrepreneurs interviewed in 1991 (89 had been reinterviewed in the third wave survey). Interviewers contacted each potential respondent to explain the purpose and type of interview and to inquire about entrepreneurs' willingness to participate in this part of the study. Of those who we were unable to contact, many had moved or we could not locate them. Some would not return our calls, even after several tries. Three refused to be interviewed. One was incarcerated, and although he was willing to be interviewed, we could not arrange a sufficiently long time when he would be allowed to use the telephone.

Ultimately, 86 agreed to be interviewed and appointments were set up (an 87th interview was conducted but was judged unreliable because of the psychological state of the respondent).[4] Formal consent was requested at the outset of the interview, including permission to tape-record. We know little about the 52 microentrepreneurs we could not reach. The program with the highest proportion of people who could not be reached was the program that had closed its doors (CWED, the Coalition for Women's Economic Development). Nonetheless, we can hypothesize that the sample underestimates to an unknown extent the negative financial impacts and overestimates positive financial impacts of microenterprise because those doing well in business are likely to have remained in the same location compared to those who were doing poorly (Hulme, 1997).

Interviews were conducted between 1996 and 1997. They were held in one to two sessions, totaling between 1 and 2.5 hours. For their time and willingness to be interviewed, respondents were paid $25. Interviewers taped the interviews and also took notes during the interview. Of the 17 Hispanic microentrepreneurs, 12 elected to be interviewed in Spanish or a combination of English and Spanish. After completing the interview, each interviewer listened to the tape and completed an instrument that covered the basic points, a summary sheet for quick examination of results, and a short case profile. Interviewers completed an interview form with data and verbatim quotes from participants. After this initial recording, each interview was reviewed for accuracy one to two more times by another person as a check on reliability and as an opportunity to extract additional data.

We designed the in-depth interviews to provide description, explanation, and also interpretation of data collected in other years of the project (Merton, et al., 1990; Rubin & Rubin, 1995). Following a natural chronology, the interview began by asking what motivated the entrepreneur to think about and start a business, how they proceeded, what were their business goals, how well the business was going, an assessment of business resources, issues that hindered or facilitated business success, how much business earnings and profits were generated and how they were used, the household economic situation (formal and informal sources of earned and unearned income and in-kind support), the relationship and financial boundaries between household and business, and the entrepreneurs' assessment of outcomes. Within the interview, prompts and follow-up questions were used to help entrepreneurs understand the intent of the questions and to generate deeper exploration of topics. The interview itself was semi-structured with all open-ended questions.

Qualitative interviewing generates large amounts of data that must be systematically reduced during the analysis phase. The process of data reduction occurred after the interview (instead of prior to data collection as in survey interviews). Data were entered into the qualitative software program, Folio Views, to facilitate organization and coding of the data and development of concepts and theory (Li-Ron, 1995; Miles & Huberman, 1994). This method maintained the integrity of the original data and kept it readily accessible (Lewis, 1998). Additionally, some qualitative data were enumerated, entered into Statistical Package for The Social Sciences (SPSS), and used for descriptive and analytic purposes.

Systematic and reproducible techniques were utilized throughout analysis of the data in order to guard against bias and validate findings, including attention to descriptive, interpretive, theoretical, and evaluative validity, as well as generalizability (Maxwell, 1992). We developed an initial coding scheme based on theoretical and empirical analyses. Next, two of the authors of this study, along with one of the student interviewers, "open coded" the interviews line-by-line, examining each sentence and phrase within the interviews in order to develop a list of "codes" or "themes" (Charmaz, 1988; Strauss & Corbin, 1990). We based these codes on the content of interviews, rather than on common usage or accepted definitions. All three coded the same five initial interviews until we achieved substantially similar coding patterns (MacQueen, et al., 1998). Then two people coded each of ten interviews until we consistently used the same root code. The rest were coded separately, occasionally checking codes or excerpts that raised questions. Root codes were often followed by several "sub-codes," or more refined ideas. These often differed among coders, so we relied on root codes for the initial analysis and used sub-codes to provide insight into specific situations and to help generate more theoretical ideas. In this way, the original code list was transformed as it was built by the three coders. Based on the results of this process, we defined a sub-set of analytic categories that form the core of the analysis.

In addition to this coding process described, each interviewer had created a profile of each respondent's interview. The content of the profile was organized according to key demographic variables and the basic research questions. As we coded the interviews we added information to the profiles. The profiles enabled us to check emerging codes and categories against the coherence of respondent's actual life stories and experiences—to prevent us from forgetting whose experiences we were analyzing. Using coded interviews and profiles, we examined relationships among different coded categories and generated inferences. In this way, emerging patterns helped us develop the concepts that are reported in this book. Periodically, we examined cases and situations that did not fit the patterns and explored potential alternative hypotheses. These sometimes led us to ask other questions of the data. For example, we noticed early on that many entrepreneurs emphasized non-economic business goals.

Folio Views' simple search mechanism allowed us to extract, in Boolean fashion, parts of interviews by code. Once the first round of coding was done, we identified the key themes (e.g., business goals, business facilitators and barriers, and outcomes), paying attention to new ideas that emerged in the course of the interview (e.g., labor market experiences, role of discrimination, impact of aging, and disability). Additional codes were added to interviews as analysis proceeded. Some qualitative variables were identified and quantified at this time. For example, in analyzing goals and motivation for beginning a business, we extracted all excerpts from the interviews where the codes motivation, goals, or origins appeared. We created three files by importing all relevant excerpts (about 100 pages) of interviews into a word-processing program. Extractions such as these formed the basis of the research report (Sherraden, et al., 1998). The second part of analysis in preparation for research papers and this book was conducted in a similar way, although the analysis was more detailed.

Notes

1. SELP evaluators contacted a random sample of 517 participants from the seven programs. Active participants—those who had taken out a loan after January 1, 1990 or those considered by staff to be "likely to take out a loan" because they had completed training or other program requirements—were eligible for the study. This selection method means that people who decided not to pursue a business were not included in the sample. After 112 were excluded because they did not fit the selection criteria, the study included a total of 405 participants (Clark & Kays, 1995, 15). Among those included in the study, 133 were close to or below 150 percent of poverty in the first year of the survey.

2. Our findings do not entirely match those of SELP (Clark & Kays, et al., 1999). Our access to SELP's data for the four survey waves included photocopies of original survey instruments. We extracted information from the original instruments for descriptive tables for business characteristics (employees, assets, liabilities, net worth, revenues, expenses, profits, and losses) and household characteristics (income, income sources, assets, liabilities, and net worth) for each survey wave. We recalculated the values and in the process, corrected some values and extrapolated other values that resulted in differences in findings, especially with respect to dependent variables (outcomes).

3. The in-depth interviews included a section at the very end that updated basic details about each household and business. Respondents and interviewers were tired at this point in the interview and details were incomplete; therefore, SELP staff recontacted many of these respondents.

4. Later as we carefully reviewed copies of the original survey instruments, we found eight participants whose incomes were over slightly over 150 percent of poverty. They were retained in the qualitative analysis because they were dealing with poverty issues, but we excluded three of them from the quantitative analysis because of large amounts of missing data. The others were retained because they were only slightly over 150 percent of poverty and were all receiving at least one source of public assistance, indicating significant economic hardship.

Appendix C

Entrepreneurs, Demographic Characteristics, and Their Businesses*

Entrepreneur	Age	Race and ethnicity	Business	Type of business	Home or Shop based	Open or closed
Allison	46	White	Sewing	Product	Home	Open
Amy	41	White	Ceramics	Product	Home	Open
Angie	44	African American	Car products	Retail	Shop	Open
Anita	46	Latina	Floral	Retail	Shop	Closed
Anne	38	White	Bakery	Product	Shop	Closed
Barbara	40	White	Hauling and yard work	Service	Home	Open
Brenda	46	African American	Clothing	Retail	Home	Open
Candy	45	White	Communication seminars	Semi-professional	Home	Open
Carl	33	White	Accounting	Professional	Home	Open
Carla	32	White	Novelties and comic books	Retail	Shop	Open
Carlos	28	Latino	Used appliances	Retail	Home	Closed
Carol	45	White	Stories on tape	Product	Home	Open
Cassandra	75	African American	Clothing	Product	Home	Closed
Catarina	48	Latina	General merchandise and novelties	Retail	Shop	Open
Charles	48	African American	Boutique	Retail	Shop	Closed
Chester	47	White	Textiles	Product	Shop	Open
Clara	50	White	Publishing	Product	Home	Closed
Clarise	37	African American	Boutique	Retail	Home	Open
Cora	44	African American	Tax preparation	Semi-professional	Home	Open
Dan	31	White	Car detailing and cleaning	Service	Shop	Closed
Diane	38	White	Crafts	Product	Home	Closed
Doña Chela	66	Latina	Clothing	Retail	Home	Open

Name	Age	Ethnicity	Business	Type	Location	Status
Doña Gloria	67	Latina	Baby things, blankets, candy	Retail	Home	Open
Doris	44	African American	Grant writing and consultation	Semi-professional	Home	Closed
Doug	52	White	Clothing	Retail	Vending	Closed
Ed	47	White	Upholstery	Product	Home	Closed
Eileen	37	White	Toys	Product	Home	Closed
Eleanor	41	African American	Figurines, perfume, wallets	Retail	Home	Closed
Fred	47	African American	Upholstery	Product	Home	Open
Geneva	38	African American	Clothes	Retail	Home	Closed
George	46	White	Marketing	Semi-professional	Shop	Closed
Glenn	45	White	Jewelry	Product	Home	Open
Gwen	34	White	Framing and art gallery	Product	Shop	Open
Heather	34	White	Video sales and rentals	Retail	Shop	Open
Iris	56	African American	Arts and crafts	Retail	Home	Open
Isabel	49	Latina	Sewing	Product	Home	Closed
Jackie	40	African American	Silkscreening	Product	Shop	Open
Jamie	34	White	Party supplies	Retail	Shop	Closed
Javier	62	Latino	Electronics	Semi-professional	Shop	Open
Jeannette	70	African American	Jewelry	Product	Home	Open
Jeff	37	White	Phones and installation	Semi-professional	Home	Open
Jennifer	44	White	Specialty and natural foods	Retail	Shop	Closed
Jo	53	African American	Beauty salon	Service	Shop	Open
Joanne	62	White	Embroidery	Product	Home	Open
John	27	White	Janitorial	Service	Home	Open
Juanita	38	African American	Cosmetics	Retail	Home	Open
Judy	34	White	Textiles	Product	Shop	Open
Kathleen	57	White	Massage	Professional	Home	Open

(continued)

Entrepreneurs, Demographic Characteristics, and Their Businesses* (*continued*)

Entrepreneur	Age	Race and ethnicity	Business	Type of business	Home or Shop based	Open or closed
Kim	39	White	Concession stand	Retail	Vending	Open
Lanette	48	African American	Wellness training and career planning	Semi-professional	Home	Open
Laurel	44	White	Desktop publishing	Semi-professional	Home	Open
Laverne	70	African American	Bakery and catering	Product	Home	Open
Lessie	44	African American	Beauty salon	Service	Shop	Open
Leticia	39	Latina	Sewing and bridal	Product	Home	Open
Linda	26	White	Crafts	Retail	Home	Closed
Lois	45	White	Illustrator and artist	Semi-professional	Home	Open
Loretta	43	African American	Cosmetology	Service	Home	(never opened)
Marta	38	Latina	Clothing	Retail	Home	Open
Mary	44	White	Liquor	Retail	Shop	Open
Monica	42	White	Child safety and products installation	Service	Home	Open
Paula	44	White	Pawn shop	Retail	Shop	Open
Peggy	33	White	Jewelry and pottery	Product	Shop	Open
Renée	43	African American	Sewing	Product	Home	Open
Rich	33	White	Auto reconditioning	Service	Shop	Open
Robert	48	White	Tool sharpening	Service	Home	Closed
Roberto	58	Latino	Janitorial	Service	Home	Closed
Rosa María	52	Latina	Floral	Retail	Home	Closed
Ruth	49	Latina	Clothing	Retail	Home	Closed
Sandra	50	African American	Fashion design and sewing	Product	Home	Open
Sara	43	White	House painting	Service	Home	Open

Name	Age	Race/Ethnicity	Business	Category	Location	Status
Sergio	54	Latino	Janitorial	Service	Home	Open
Sharon	39	White	Wedding consultant	Service	Home	Closed
Shawn	26	White	Floral and party	Retail	Shop	Closed
Shelby	31	White	Childcare	Service	Home	Closed
Sherri	33	White	Clothing	Product	Shop	Open
Stacy	29	African American	Music	Retail	Shop	Open
Steven	60	Other	Desktop publishing and fax service	Professional	Home	Open
Susan	39	White	Elder daycare	Semi-professional	Shop	Open
Terri	37	White	Barber	Service	Shop	Open
Theresa	41	African American	Scholarship and educational consult	Semi-professional	Home	Closed
Thomas	46	African American	Catering	Service	Home	Open
Toni	65	African American	Childcare	Service	Home	Open
Vera	51	African American	Sewing	Product	Home	Open
Vilma	45	Latina	General merchandise and accessories	Retail	Home	Closed
Yolanda	55	Latina	Catering	Service	Home	Closed
Yvonne	57	African American	Cosmetics	Retail	Home	Closed

*All names are pseudonyms and minor details about their businesses have been altered to protect anonymity.

Appendix D
Business and Household
Financial Outcomes

Table 5.2
Business Revenue, Expenses, and Profits

	Mean	Median	Std. Deviation	Range	Significance
Business Revenue 1991 (n = 71)	$25,425	$ 6,517	$46,082	$0–$195,524	
Whites	$29,780	$10,428	$50,112	$0–$195,524	
Non-whites	$20,687	$ 5,866	$41,479	$0–$195,524	
Men	$70,245	$34,875	$79,306	$912–$195,524	***
Women	$14,417	$ 5,214	$23,850	$0–$156,419	
Married	$47,921	$15,642	$67,350	$0–$195,524	***
Non-married	$11,622	$ 5,214	$14,195	$912–$71,692	
Children < 5	$52,110	$19,552	$68,196	$2,607–$195,524	***
No children < 5	$13,445	$ 5,214	$24,274	$0–$156,419	
Business still open in 1995	$28,618	$ 9,450	$48,792	$0–$195,524	
Business closed in 1995	$18,762	$ 5,214	$40,025	$912–$195,524	
Business Revenue 1995 (n = 49)	$30,075	$11,840	$38,302	$0–$141,000	
Whites	$40,117	$22,660	$39,683	$0–$120,000	*
Non-whites	$20,241	$ 5,000	$35,284	$0–$141,000	
Men	$70,037	$70,548	$48,676	$15,200–$141,000	***
Women	$23,277	$ 8,540	$31,522	$0–$120,000	

Married	$ 53,577	$ 48,380	$46,359	$600–$141,000	***
Non-married	$ 18,576	$ 8,270	$27,024	$0–$120,000	
Children < 5	$ 50,852	$ 40,362	$48,247	$600–$120,000	**
No children < 5	$ 22,914	$ 11,840	$31,086	$0–$141,000	
Change in Business Revenue (n = 43)	$ −1,867	$ −1,347	$30,917	$−$100,524–$76,951	
Whites	$ 3,817	$ 3,611	$33,864	$−95,523–$76,950	***
Non-whites	$ 7,822	$ 2,350	$27,026	$−100,524–$48,380	
Men	$−33,187	$ −13,003	$51,995	$−100,524–$23,371	***
Women	$ 3,212	$ −955	$23,445	$−56,419–$76,950	
Married	$ −6,016	$ −810	$46,797	$−100,524–76,950	***
Non-married	$ 591	$ −1,347	$16,242	$−41,139–$47,393	
Children < 5	$−25,061	$ −5,917	$40,679	$−100,524–$18,219	***
No children < 5	$ 6,106	$ 163	$22,466	$−41,140–$76,950	
Business Expenses 1991 (n = 69)	$ 22,617	$ 9,646	$29,769	$521–$129,359	
Whites	$ 27,389	$ 16,815	$30,398	$521–$126,439	
Non-whites	$ 17,099	$ 6,439	$28,500	$978–$129,359	
Men	$ 43,202	$ 24,395	$42,801	$521–$129,359	***
Women	$ 17,377	$ 7,039	$23,176	$978–$126,439	

(continued)

Table 5.2 (*continued*)
Business Revenue, Expenses, and Profits

	Mean	Median	Std. Deviation	Range	Significance
Married	$37,902	$23,900	$39,851	$2,398–$129,359	***
Non-married	$13,375	$ 7,039	$16,045	$521–$69,411	
Children < 5	$38,081	$40,102	$20,999	$2,607–$129,359	***
No children < 5	$15,851	$21,078	$ 6,798	$521–$103,732	
Business still open in 1995	$25,146	$10,037	$32,909	$521–$129,359	
Business closed in 1995	$17,550	$ 7,560	$21,998	$1,134–$95,129	
Business Expenses 1995 (n = 48)	$24,600	$ 7,704	$35,985	$0–$140,972	
Whites	$32,295	$19,444	$36,177	$600–$114,400	
Non-whites	$17,625	$ 4,260	$35,982	$0–$140,972	
Men	$63,057	$55,600	$52,371	$7,440–$140,972	***
Women	$17,712	$ 6,170	$27,000	$0–$100,000	
Married	$45,630	$33,600	$46,013	$600–$140,972	***
Non-married	$13,855	$ 5,000	$23,195	$0–$100,000	
Children < 5	$45,777	$27,238	$46,621	$1,000–$114,400	**
No children < 5	$16,769	$ 7,854	$27,421	$0–$140,972	
Change in Business Expenses (n = 40)	$ 376	$ –390	$18,383	$ –42,419–$48,926	

Whites	$ 4,430	$ 2,861	$17,407	$-26,439-$48,926	
Non-whites	$-4,104	$-4,669	$18,846	$-42,418-$37,240	**
Men	$ 13,848	$ 17,970	$29,918	$-29,359-$48,926	
Women	$-2,001	$ -925	$14,999	$-42,419-$35,532	
Married	$ 3,959	$ 479	$24,133	$-29,359-$48,926	
Non-married	$-1,774	$ -873	$14,021	$-42,419-$29,022	
Children < 5	$-2,959	$-7,068	$22,631	$-29,359-$48,926	
No children < 5	$ 1,488	$ 286	$17,042	$-42,419-$37,240	
Business Profits 1991 (n = 69)	$ 3,130	$ 209	$26,185	$-70,806-$130,049	
Whites	$ 2,390	$-52.00	$32,451	$-70,806-$130,049	
Non-whites	$ 3,985	$ 280	$16,722	$-21,025-$66,165	***
Men	$ 27,042	$ 9,626	$44,237	$-26,878-$130,049	
Women	$-2,957	$ -313	$14,363	$-70,806-$29,980	***
Married	$ 10,859	$ (-)398	$40,002	$-70,806-$130,049	
Non-married	$-1,544	$ 235	$ 9,911	$-29,107-$17,141	**
Children < 5	$ 15,269	$ 2,477	$38,229	$-21,768-$130,049	
No children < 5	$-2,181	$ 0	$16,596	$-70,806-$52,687	***
Business still open in 1995	$ 4,092	$ 489	$27,333	$-70,806-$130,049	
Business closed in 1995	$ 1,204	$-482	$24,193	$-29,107-$100,395	

(continued)

Table 5.2 (continued)
Business Revenue, Expenses, and Profits

	Mean	Median	Std. Deviation	Range	Significance
Business Profits 1995 (n = 48)	$ 5,061	$ 1,066	$10,352	$−14,400–$46,400	
Whites	$ 7,426	$ 3,052	$13,344	$−14,400–$46,400	*
Non-whites	$ 2,616	$ 700	$ 4,820	$−5,000–$15,600	
Men	$ 6,980	$ 3,894	$16,776	$−14,400–$34,800	
Women	$ 4,862	$ 1,066	$ 9,008	$−5,000–$46,400	
Married	$ 7,947	$ 2,500	$14,788	$−14,400–$46,400	
Non-married	$ 3,637	$ 740	$ 6,825	$−5,000–$26,651	
Children < 5	$ 5,074	$ 1,750	$11,968	$−14,400–$34,800	
No children < 5	$ 5,298	$ 698	$10,064	$−5,000–$46,400	
Change in Business Profits 1991–1995 (n = 40)	$ −3,449	$ 800	$29,977	$−144,449–$47,599	
Whites	$ −2,688	$ 913	$36,323	$−144,449–$47,569	
Non-whites	$ −4,290	$ 687	$21,901	$−71,165–$18,175	
Men	$−47,035	$−30,010	$55,706	$−144,449–$−927	***
Women	$ 4,243	$ 2,358	$13,618	$−29,980–$47,569	
Married	$−10,199	$ 3,057	$48,306	$−144,449–$47,569	
Non-married	$ 601	$ −82.00	$ 7,316	$−16,400–$12,604	
Children < 5	$−24,341	$ −2,246	$48,702	$−144,449–$10,494	***
No children < 5	$ 3,516	$ 1,096	$16,483	$−52,659–$47,569	

*p ≤ .10, **p ≤ .05, ***p ≤ .01

Table 3.3
Business Assets, Liabilities, and Net Worth

	Mean	Median	Std. Deviation	Range	Significance
Business Assets 1991 (n = 76)	$12,250	$ 3,250	$24,878	$0–$152,617	
Whites	$18,201	$ 5,974	$30,761	$0–$152,617	**
Non-whites	$ 4,495	$ 1,305	$ 9,954	$0–$44,862	
Men	$28,696	$ 7,061	$44,697	$297–$152,617	***
Women	$ 8,206	$ 2,390	$14,942	$0–$76,037	
Married	$23,608	$ 7,367	$36,846	$0–$152,617	***
Non-married	$ 5,624	$ 2,335	$ 9,276	$0–$54,421	
Children < 5	$16,694	$ 3,833	$35,068	$0–$152,617	
No children < 5	$ 9,801	$ 2,716	$16,845	$0–$76,037	
Business still open in 1995	$12,921	$ 3,462	$24,571	$0–$110,580	
Business closed in 1995	$10,797	$ 1,608	$25,228	$0–$152,617	
	$18,163	$ 5,342	$30,616	$0–145,698	
Whites	$22,310	$10,490	$30,111	$641–$145,698	
Non-whites	$	$ 1,944	$31,249	$0–$111,701	
Men	3,791	$44,103	$2,914–$111,701	*	
Women	895	$26,583	$0–$145,698		

(continued)

Table 1 (continued)
Business Assets, Liabilities, and Net Worth

	Mean	Median	Std. Deviation	Range	Significance
Married	$ 26,584	$ 4,570	$31,699	$600–$111,702	
Non-married	$ 12,657	$ 3,691	$29,187	$0–$145,698	
Children < 5	$ 24,073	$ 5,134	$40,861	$0–$145,698	
No children < 5	$ 14,997	$ 4,895	$23,718	$0–$111,702	
Change in Business Assets (n = 43)	$ 3,391	$ 600	$31,893	$−132,117–$120,388	
Whites	$ 1,247	$ 1,866	$39,275	$−132,117–$120,388	
Non-whites	$ 6,098	$ 0	$19,710	$−3,236–$73,683	
Men	$ −16.00	$ 912	$64,601	$−132,117–$73,683	
Women	$ 4,053	$ 300	$22,414	$−30,195–$120,388	
Married	$ −2,010	$ 1,943	$41,184	$−132,117–$73,683	
Non-married	$ 6,922	$ −244	$24,300	$−4,729–$120,388	
Children < 5	$ 4,376	$ 600	$49,553	$−132,117–$120,388	
No children < 5	$ 2,863	$ 371	$17,555	$−30,195–$73,683	
Business Liabilities 1991 (n = 80)	$ 6,040	$ 953	$17,502	$0–$145,231	
Whites	$ 9,540	$ 957	$22,373	$0–$145,231	**
Non-whites	$ 1,763	$ 203	$ 6,495	$0–$39,105	

Men	$12,743	$1,578	$34,400	$0–$145,231	*
Women	$4,090	$ 953	$ 7,056	$0–$41,277	
Married	$11,208	$2,068	$27,427	$0–$145,231	**
Non-married	$2,339	$ 285	$ 4,739	$0–$20,096	
Children < 5	$11,445	$1,847	$28,226	$0–$145,231	
No children < 5	$ 3,287	$ 543	$ 6,641	$0–$41,277	
Business still open in 1995	$ 4,875	$ 285	$ 8,985	$0–$41,277	
Business closed in 1995	$ 8,204	$1,416	$27,134	$0–$145,231	
Business Liabilities 1995 (n = 43)	$ 6,827	$ 0	$13,510	$0–$54,394	
Whites	$ 9,903	$ 389	$16,632	$0–$54,394	*
Non-whites	$ 2,555	$ 0	$ 5,212	$0–$15,153	
Men	$15,428	$7,285	$21,448	$0–$54,394	*
Women	$ 5,433	$ 0	$11,607	$0–$52,661	
Married	$12,781	$1,436	$18,782	$0–$54,394	**
Non-married	$ 3,299	$ 0	$ 7,522	$0–$27,197	
Children < 5	$10,744	$1,100	$16,953	$0–$54,394	
No children < 5	$ 4,936	$ 0	$11,357	$0–$52,661	

(continued)

Table 5.3 (*continued*)
Business Assets, Liabilities, and Net Worth

	Mean	Median	Std. Deviation	Range	Significance
Change in Business Liabilities (n = 43)	$ 2,040	$ 0	$11,673	$−16,674–$54,394	
Whites	$ 2,175	$ −446	$14,991	$−16,674–$54,394	
Non-whites	$ 1,851	$ 0	$ 4,392	$−1,037–$14,898	
Men	$11,925	$5,112	$24,679	$−16,674–$54,394	**
Women	$ 436	$ 0	$ 7,446	$−16,237–$28,580	
Married	$ 5,605	$ 100	$16,740	$−16,674–$54,394	
Non-married	$−73.00	$ 0	$ 6,780	$−16,237–$23,603	
Children < 5	$ 4,413	$ 0	$18,385	$−16,674–$54,394	
No children < 5	$ 894	$ 0	$ 6,578	$−8,690–$23,603	
Business Net Worth 1991 (n = 76)	$ 5,935	$1,608	$20,027	$−34,651–$135,943	
Whites	$ 8,440	$2,064	$25,904	$−34,651–$33,943	
Non-whites	$ 2,670	$ 923	$ 6,315	$−1,847–$33,674	
Men	$13,622	$5,757	$36,889	$−34,651–$135,943	*
Women	$ 4,044	$1,120	$12,861	$−23,246–$55,398	
Married	$11,599	$2,368	$30,881	$−34,651–$135,943	*
Non-married	$ 2,630	$1,255	$ 7,866	$−5,866–$45,731	
Children < 5	$ 5,249	$1,032	$27,455	$−34,651–$135,943	
No children < 5	$ 6,313	$1,988	$14,763	$−23,246–$55,398	

Business still open in 1995	$ 8,045	$ 2,132	$22,193	$-23,246–$135,943
Business closed in 1995	$ 1,361	$ 14	$13,555	$-34,651–$45,731
Business Net Worth 1995 (n = 41)	$ 9,657	$ 2,914	$30,187	$-40,601–$145,698
Whites	$ 12,003	$ 7,305	$34,255	$-40,601–$145,698
Non-whites	$ 6,344	$ 486	$23,904	$-9,810–$97,132
Men	$ 12,887	$ 10,490	$47,234	$-40,601–$97,132
Women	$ 9,103	$ 2,428	$27,236	$-22,135–$145,698
Married	$ 9,898	$ 3,400	$31,698	$-40,601–$97,132
Non-married	$ 9,503	$ 2,914	$29,845	$-20,689–$145,698
Children < 5	$ 8,686	$ 200	$42,098	$-4,061–$145,698
No children < 5	$ 10,160	$ 4,515	$22,694	$-22,135–$97,132
Change in Business Net Worth (n = 41)	$ 359	$ 400	$32,446	$-115,443–$136,626
Whites	$ -1,019	$ 1,786	$40,276	$-115,443–$136,626
Non-whites	$ 2,303	$ -463	$17,122	$-23,134–$63,458
Men	$-19,311	$-14,304	$59,865	$-115,443–$63,458 *
Women	$ 3,731	$ 440	$25,130	$-27,817–$136,626
Married	$ 10,504	$ -2,087	$36,442	$-115,443–$63,458 *
Non-married	$ 7,311	$ 741	$28,206	$-27,750–$136,626
Children < 5	$ -2,883	$ -505	$51,926	$-115,443–$136,626
No children < 5	$ 2,040	$ 920	$16,212	$-27,817–$63,458

*p ≤ .10, **p ≤ .05, ***p ≤ .01

Table 5.4
Household Income from the Business

	Mean	Median	Std. Deviation	Range	Significance
HH Income from the Business in 1991 (n = 83)	$ 4,257	$ 895	$ 5,513	$0–$21,948	
Whites	$ 3,276	$ 0	$ 5,161	$0–$21,948	*
Non-whites	$ 5,362	$ 2,685	$ 5,750	$0–$21,948	
Men	$ 4,694	$ 990	$ 6,314	$0–$21,948	
Women	$ 4,135	$ 895	$ 5,318	$0–$21,948	
Married	$ 4,696	$ 806	$ 6,098	$0–$21,948	
Non-married	$ 3,967	$ 1,425	$ 5,134	$0–$21,948	
Children < 5	$ 4,722	$ 895	$ 6,233	$0–$21,948	
No children < 5	$ 4,032	$ 1,030	$ 5,176	$0–$21,948	
Business still open in 1995	$ 5,236	$ 1,893	$ 6,264	$0–$21,948	**
Business closed in 1995	$ 2,614	$ 565	$ 3,453	$0–$11,413	
HH Income from the Business in 1995 (n = 52)	$ 6,712	$ 3,000	$ 8,791	$0–$40,000	+***
Whites	$ 8,895	$ 5,000	$10,322	$0–$40,000	**
Non-whites	$ 3,959	$ 1,000	$ 5,418	$0–$18,000	
Men	$14,110	$12,000	$13,253	$0–$40,000	**
Women	$ 4,951	$ 2,100	$ 6,407	$0–$24,000	

Married	$ 9,958	$8,580	$10,551	$0–$40,000	**
Non-married	$ 4,683	$2,140	$ 6,919	$0–$27,500	
Children < 5	$ 8,749	$3,000	$10,898	$0–$40,000	
No children < 5	$ 5,723	$2,200	$ 7,547	$0–$27,500	
Change in HH Income from Business (n = 52)	$ 1,477	$57.00	$ 8,831	$–21,948–$24,000	
Whites	$ 5,079	$2,708	$ 8,637	$–5,819–$24,000	***
Non-whites	$–3,066	$–426	$ 6,869	$–21,948–$6,500	
Men	$ 7,143	$2,586	$ 9,656	$–3,714–$23,948	**
Women	$ 127	$ 0	$ 8,176	$–21,948–$24,000	
Married	$ 3,704	$ 444	$10,537	$–16,856–$24,000	
Non-married	$ 84	$ 0	$ 7,420	$–21,948–$20,000	
Children < 5	$ 2,434	$ 560	$11,041	$–16,856–$23,194	
No children < 5	$ 1,011	$ 0	$ 7,676	$–21,948–$24,000	
Whites	26%	0%	36%	0–100%	
Non-whites	35%	21%	37%	0–100%	
Men	37%	.5%	43%	0–100%	
Women	28%	.7%	35%	0–100%	
Married	29%	.3%	39%	0–100%	
Non-married	31%	.8%	36%	0–100%	
Children < 5	28%	.3%	35%	0–100%	
No children < 5	31%	.7%	38%	0–100%	

(continued)

Table 5.4 (*continued*)
Household Income from the Business

	Mean	Median	Std. Deviation	Range	Significance
Business still open in 1995	35%	18%	38%	0–100%	*
Business closed in 1995	21%	0%	32%	0–100%	
Percent HH Income from the Business 1995 (n = 52)	34%	18%	37%	0–100%	
Whites	40%	30%	37%	0–100%	
Non-whites	26%	.6%	37%	0–100%	
Men	53%	49%	39%	0–100%	*
Women	29%	1%	35%	0–100%	
Married	36%	32%	36%	0–100%	
Non-married	32%	14%	38%	0–100%	
Children < 5	36%	25%	36%	0–100%	
No children < 5	33%	.6%	38%	0–100%	

+1995 figure varies significantly from 1991

*p ≤ .10, **p ≤ .05, ***≤ .01

Table 5.5
Household Income

	Mean	Median	Std. Deviation	Range	Significance
1991 Household Income	$14,915	$12,395	$ 7,857	$2,546–$38,035	
Whites	$13,372	$11,414	$ 6,748	$3,026–$33,691	**
Non-whites	$16,655	$15,141	$ 8,708	$2,546–$38,035	
Men	$15,518	$14,793	$ 6,851	$6,714–$26,856	
Women	$14,748	$11,839	$ 8,154	$2,546–$38,035	
Married	$18,958	$20,366	$ 8,659	$3,026–$38,035	***
Non-married	$12,246	$11,212	$ 6,005	$2,546–$30,839	
Children < 5	$18,525	$19,521	$ 7,081	$7,833–$33,691	***
No children < 5	$13,174	$11,638	$ 7,671	$2,546–$38,035	
Business still open in 1995	$13,881	$11,738	$ 7,290	$2,546–$30,839	
Business closed in 1995	$16,648	$13,988	$ 8,569	$3,693–$38,035	
1995 Household Income	$20,893	$18,793	$11,974	$3,000–$52,800	+***
Whites	$22,143	$21,286	$12,809	$3,000–$52,800	
Non-whites	$19,482	$15,408	$10,949	$3,000–$46,483	
Men	$23,279	$19,687	$14,382	$3,000–$50,000	
Women	$20,232	$18,793	$11,257	$3,000–$52,800	

(continued)

Table 5.5
Household Income

	Mean	Median	Std. Deviation	Range	Significance
Married	$26,498	$24,837	$11,495	$7,320–$50,000	***
Non-married	$17,194	$14,922	$10,887	$3,000–$52,800	
Children < 5	$23,152	$21,600	$13,595	$3,000–$50,000	
No children < 5	$19,804	$17,139	$11,076	$3,000–$52,800	
Business still open in 1995	$20,637	$19,397	$12,097	$3,000–$52,000	
Business closed in 1995	$21,340	$17,774	$11,950	$5,504–$52,800	
Change in HH Income 1991–1995	$ 5,978	$ 4,471	$12,523	$ –20,349–$49,107	
Whites	$ 8,771	$ 5,884	$12,713	$ –6,983–$49,107	**
Non-whites	$ 2,827	$ 2,869	$11,676	$ –20,349–$29,077	
Men	$ 7,760	$ 5,781	$11,074	$ –5,063–$26,607	
Women	$ 5,485	$ 3,862	$12,932	$ –20,349–$49,107	
Married	$ 7,540	$ 7,145	$13,273	$ –20,349–$29,077	
Non-married	$ 4,948	$ 3,076	$12,028	$ –16,521–$49,107	
Children < 5	$ 4,627	$ 6,699	$12,719	$ –20,349–$26,607	
No children < 5	$ 6,630	$ 3,778	$12,491	$ –14,700–$49107	
Business still open in 1995	$ 6,745	$ 6,535	$11,748	$ –20,349–$45,685	
Business closed in 1995	$ 4,692	$ 1,499	$13,833	$ –14,700–$49,107	

+1995 figure varies significantly from 1991

*p ≤ .10, **p ≤ .05, ***p ≤ .01

Table 5.6
Poverty Status

	Percentage Above	Percentage Below
Poverty Status in 1995 (n = 83)	47%	53%
Whites	57%	43%
Non-whites	36%	64%
Men	56%	44%
Women	45%	55%
Married	55%	45%
Non-married	42%	58%
Children < 5	41%	59%
No children < 5	41%	59%
Business still open in 1995	48%	52%
Business closed in 1995	45%	55%

Table 5.7
Income-to-Needs Ratio

	Mean	Median	Std. Deviation	Range	Significance
Income-to-Needs Ratio 1991 (n = 83)	.69	.71	.25	.14–1.24	
Whites	.67	.66	.23	.17–1.18	
Non-whites	.72	.78	.27	.14–1.24	
Men	.72	.69	.28	.30–1.20	
Women	.69	.73	.24	.14–1.24	
Married	.70	.81	.25	.17–1.24	
Non-married	.69	.68	.25	.14–1.20	
Children < 5	.71	.71	.21	.34–1.24	
No children < 5	.69	.71	.27	.14–1.20	
Business still open in 1995	.68	.64	.25	.14–1.24	+***
Business closed in 1995	.72	.79	.26	.20–1.20	
Income-to-Needs Ratio 1995	1.05	.96	.66	.13–4.47	+***
Whites	1.15	1.14	.74	.24–4.47	
Non-whites	.93	.83	.54	.13–2.59	
Men	1.03	1.07	.53	.24–2.04	
Women	1.05	.90	.70	.13–4.47	

Married	1.06	1.13	.52	.23–2.59
Non-married	1.04	.84	.75	.13–4.47
Children < 5	.89	.78	.49	.13–1.88
No children < 5	1.12	.99	.72	.24–4.47
Business still open in 1995	1.07	.99	.67	.13–4.47
Business closed in 1995	1.01	.86	.63	.24–2.90
Change in Income-to-Needs Ratio 1991–95	.35	.25	.71	−.87–3.92
Whites	.48	.32	.78	−.43–3.92 *
Non-whites	.21	.20	.59	−.87–1.95
Men	.31	.30	.45	−.32–1.02
Women	.36	.25	.77	−.87–3.92
Married	.36	.28	.58	−.87–1.95
Non-married	.35	.24	.79	−.71–3.92
Children < 5	.18	.26	.51	−.87–.96
No children < 5	.43	.25	.78	−.63–3.92
Business still open in 1995	.39	.29	.73	−.87–3.92
Business closed in 1995	.29	.007	.68	−.63–2.69

+1995 figure varies significantly from 1991

*p ≤ .10, **p ≤ .05, ***p ≤ .01

Table 5.8
Household Assets, Liabilities, and Net Worth

	Mean	Median	Std. Deviation	Range	Significance
Household Assets 1991 (n = 78)	$26,350	$ 4,407	$38,718	$0–$165,000	
Whites	$17,461	$ 3,150	$30,587	$0–$126,873	**
Non-whites	$37,271	$29,437	$44,906	$0–$165,000	
Men	$38,710	$10,400	$46,941	$549–$157,505	
Women	$22,905	$ 3,259	$35,789	$0–$165,000	
Married	$43,721	$36,063	$46,074	$0–$165,000	***
Non-married	$14,893	$ 1,629	$28,061	$0–$114,056	
Children < 5	$26,090	$ 6,137	$34,918	$0–$126,873	
No children < 5	$26,466	$ 4,367	$40,605	$0–$165,000	
Business still open in 1995	$25,333	$ 4,657	$36,504	$0–$157,505	+***
Business closed in 1995	$27,978	$ 4,367	$42,617	$85–$165,000	
Household Assets 1995 (n = 70)	$39,495	$21,256	$43,979	$0–$177,266	+***
Whites	$32,635	$ 9,427	$37,996	$0–$120,444	
Non-whites	$48,126	$41,495	$49,818	$0–$177,266	
Men	$43,453	$24,234	$52,265	$0–$177,266	
Women	$38,506	$21,256	$42,141	$0–$159,500	

Married	$ 63,252	$60,200	$46,407	$0–$177,266	***
Non-married	$ 24,578	$ 4,954	$35,409	$0–$118,501	
Children < 5	$ 31,503	$ 4,929	$44,205	$0–$159,500	
No children < 5	$ 43,159	$38,598	$43,850	$0–$177,266	
Business still open in 1995	$ 42,967	$37,979	$45,373	$0–$177,266	
Business closed in 1995	$ 33,247	$10,490	$41,512	$0–$118,025	
Change in HH Assets 1991–1995 (n = 68)	$ 10,796	$ 2,897	$3,2871	$–94,953–$113,637	
Whites	$ 13,768	$ 3,552	$29,646	$–67,945–$113,637	
Non-whites	$ 6,798	$ 72.00	$36,930	$–94,953–$94,218	
Men	$ 1,190	$ 882	$15,886	$–35,023–$34,828	*
Women	$ 13,286	$ 3,346	$35,684	$–94,953–$113,637	
Married	$ 12,567	$ 7,645	$35,132	$–67,945–$94,218	
Non-married	$ 9,699	$ 2,283	$31,779	$–94,953–$113,637	
Children < 5	$ –2,601	$ 34.00	$32,905	$–94,953–$57,480	**
No children < 5	$ 16,377	$ 3,953	$31,534	$–52,813–$113,637	
Business still open in 1995	$ 15,925	$ 3,079	$25,434	$–13,778–$94,218	*
Business closed in 1995	$ 1,974	$ 667	$41,907	$–94,953–$113,637	

(continued)

Table 5.8 (continued)
Household Assets, Liabilities, and Net Worth

	Mean	Median	Std. Deviation	Range	Significance
Household Liabilities 1991 (n = 81)	$10,734	$ 4,345	$14,248	$0–$58,114	
Whites	$10,201	$ 5,621	$12,240	$0–$51,814	
Non-whites	$11,337	$ 3,802	$16,376	$0–$58,114	
Men	$13,721	$ 8,147	$16,166	$0–$54,312	
Women	$ 9,940	$ 4,209	$13,725	$0–$58,114	
Married	$16,269	$10,862	$18,077	$0–$58,114	***
Non-married	$ 6,928	$ 3,150	$ 9,315	$0–$45,079	
Children < 5	$11,253	$ 4,236	$14,634	$0–$58,114	
No children < 5	$10,474	$ 4,888	$14,184	$0–$54,312	
Business still open in 1995	$10,675	$ 5,431	$14,150	$0–$54,312	+**
Business closed in 1995	$10,829	$ 4,073	$14,640	$0–$58,114	
Household Liabilities 1995 (n = 72)	$16,302	$11,073	$19,579	$0–$76,346	+**
Whites	$17,361	$12,336	$20,247	$0–$74,792	
Non-whites	$15,050	$ 8,742	$18,993	$0–$76,346	
Men	$10,876	$ 5,300	$12,572	$0–$40,504	
Women	$17,730	$12,002	$20,894	$0–$76,346	

Married	$ 18,550	$ 13,866	$21,795	$0–$76,346	
Non-married	$ 14,786	$ 10,587	$18,042	$0–$74,792	
Children < 5	$ 8,652	$ 3,060	$11,548	$0–$40,504	***
No children < 5	$ 20,127	$ 12,481	$21,657	$0–$76,346	
Business still open in 1995	$ 17,226	$ 10,490	$20,812	$0–$74,792	
Business closed in 1995	$ 14,849	$ 12,093	$17,739	$0–$76,346	
Change in HH Liabilities 1991–1995 (n = 71)	$ 5,156	$ 320	$21,138	$−57,531–$74,792	
Whites	$ 6,286	$ −539	$19,637	$−20,452–$74,792	
Non-whites	$ 3,854	$ 946	$22,983	$−57,531–$72,000	
Men	$ −5,737	$ −3,874	$14,503	$−49,012–$13,891	**
Women	$ 7,831	$ 1,360	$21,742	$−57,531–$74,792	
Married	$ 1,284	$ −821	$24,860	$−57,531–$72,000	
Non-married	$ 7,829	$ 2,132	$17,967	$−20,452–$74,792	
Children < 5	$ −4,004	$ −950	$14,784	$−57,531–$16,512	***
No children < 5	$ 9,833	$ 3,418	$22,461	$−49,012–$74,792	
Business still open in 1995	$ 6,404	$ 1,138	$20,727	$−49,012–$74,792	
Business closed in 1995	$ 3,239	$ −736	$21,995	$−57,531–$72,000	

(continued)

Table 5.8 (continued)
Household Assets, Liabilities, and Net Worth

	Mean	Median	Std. Deviation	Range	Significance
Household Net Worth 1991 (n = 79)	$14,938	$ 1,086	$31,403	$−26,830−$126,982	
Whites	$ 7,095	$ 320	$24,782	$−26,830−102,976	**
Non-whites	$24,797	$ 8,733	$36,138	$−5,241−126,982	
Men	$23,601	$ 8,567	$37,985	$−11,114−103,193	
Women	$12,381	$ 557	$29,052	$−26,830−126,982	
Married	$27,478	$12,981	$36,687	$−4,291−126,982	***
Non-married	$ 6,400	$ 174	$24,109	$−26,830−106,452	
Children < 5	$15,357	$ 2,715	$29,121	$−22,221−102,976	
No children < 5	$14,744	$ 382	$32,668	$−26,830−126,982	
Business still open in 1995	$12,619	$ 1,168	$27,375	$−22,221−106,452	+**
Business closed in 1995	$18,725	$ 750	$37,257	$−26,830−126,982	
Household Net Worth 1995 (n = 66)	$20,365	$ 4,859	$36,336	$−27,197−171,966	
Whites	$15,218	$ 3,599	$29,865	$−19,032−96,452	
Non-whites	$26,932	$ 8,305	$42,879	$−27,197−171,966	
Men	$34,653	$ 8,305	$51,245	$−4,371−171,966	
Women	$16,861	$ 3,497	$31,319	$−27,197−103,737	

Married	$ 40,242	$32,491	$41,534	$ −13,866–171,966	***
Non-married	$ 8,245	$ 13.00	$26,702	$ −27,197–103,737	
Children < 5	$ 16,080	$ 2,482	$29,415	$ −15,531–96,452	
No children < 5	$ 22,228	$ 4,908	$39,117	$ −27,197–171,966	
Business still open in 1995	$ 21,818	$ 4,954	$37,721	$ −15,531–171,966	
Business closed in 1995	$ 17,983	$ 3,400	$34,567	$ −27,197–96,452	
Change in HH Net Worth 1991–1995 (n = 65)	$ 4,377	$ 2,987	$29,335	$ −89,898–$94,218	
Whites	$ 6,958	$ 5,058	$24,449	$ −57,082–77,764	
Non-whites	$ 967	$ −65	$34,951	$ −89,898–94,218	
Men	$ 7,409	$ 8,887	$24,818	$ −34,493–68,773	
Women	$ 3,619	$ 558	$30,529	$ −89,898–94,218	
Married	$ 8,514	$ 5,176	$36,178	$ −64,332–94,218	
Non-married	$ 1,792	$ 558	$24,266	$ −89,898–77,764	
Children < 5	$ −1,550	$ −974	$32,094	$ −89,897–60,508	
No children < 5	$ 6,826	$ 3,577	$28,122	$ −64,332–94,218	
Business still open in 1995	$ 9,005	$ 3,577	$24,373	$ −33,624–94,218	*
Business closed in 1995	$ −3,027	$ −161	$35,165	$ −89,898–77,764	

+1995 figure varies significantly from 1991

*p ≤ .10, **p ≤ .05, ***p ≤ .01

References

Abramovitz, M. (1996). *Regulating the Lives of Women: Social Welfare Policy from Colonial Times to the Present*, rev. ed. Boston: South End.

Aldrich, H. (1989). Networking among women entrepreneurs. In O. Hagan, C. Rivchun, & D. Sexton (Eds.), *Women-owned Businesses* (pp. 103–132). New York: Praeger.

Alisultanov, I., Klein, J., & Zandniapour, L. (2002, October). *Microenterprise as a Welfare to Work Strategy: One-Year Findings*. Washington, DC: Aspen Institute, Microenterprise Fund for Innovation, Effectiveness, Learning and Dissemination (FIELD), Research Report 2.

Allen, D. & Rahman, S. (1985). Small business incubators: A positive environment for entrepreneurship. *Journal of Small Business, 23* (3), 12–22.

Anderson, A. R. & Miller, C. J. (2003). "Class matters": Human and social capital in the entrepreneurial process. *Journal of Socio-Economics 32*, 17–36.

Ashe, J. (1985). The Pisces II Experience: Local Efforts in Micro-Enterprise Development. Washington, DC: Agency for International Development.

Association for Enterprise Opportunity (AEO) (2000). Access to Markets Institute. Chicago: Author.

————. (2002a, January–March). Public Funding for microenterprise development falls. *AEO Exchange 5*, 7.

————. (2002b, October). *National Microenterprise Strategy: Capturing the Promise of Microenterprise Development in the United States*. Arlington, VA: AEO. Retrieved from *http://www.microenterpriseworks.org*.

————. (2004). *Administration's FY2005 Budget Proposes to Eliminate the SBA Microloan and SBA Prime Programs*. Retrieved from *http://www.microenterpriseworks.org/news/PRhtml/PR05budget.htm*.

Bailey, S. (1993, Winter). Winners' Circles: Chicago's Experiment in Low-Income Enterprise. *Policy Review 63*, 82–85.

245

Balkin, S. (1989). *Self-Employment for Low-Income People*. New York: Praeger.

———. (1992). A Replication of the Grameen Bank in a United States Large City: A Description of, and Lessons from, the Full Circle Fund of the Women's Self-Employment Project of Chicago. (Working Paper, 92-1). Chicago: Roosevelt University, Department of Economics.

Bates, T. (1989). Small business viability in the urban ghetto. *Journal of Regional Science, 29* (4), 625–643.

———. (1993). *Banking on Black Enterprise: The Potential of Emerging Firms for Revitalizing Urban Economies*. Washington, DC: Joint Center for Political and Economics Studies.

———. (1996). The financial capital needs of black-owned businesses. *Journal of Developmental Entrepreneurship, 1* (1), 1–15.

———. (1997). *Race, Self-Employment, and Upward Mobility: An Illusive American Dream*. Washington, DC, Baltimore, & London: Woodrow Wilson Center Press, Johns Hopkins University Press.

Bates, T. & Bradford, W. (1979). *Financing Black Economic Development*. New York: Academic Press, Institute for Research on Poverty, Poverty Policy Analysis Series.

Bates, T. & Servon, L. (1996). Why loans won't save the poor. *Inc 18*, 27–28.

Becker, G. S. (1993). *Human capital: A theoretical and empirical analysis, with special reference to education* (3rd ed). Chicago: University of Chicago Press.

Bendick, M. Jr. & Egan, M. L. (1991, February). *Business Development in the Inner-City: Enterprise with Community Links*. New York: New School for Social Research.

Bendick, M. Jr. & Egan, M. L. (1987). Transfer payment diversion for small business development: British and French experience. *Industrial and Labor Relations Review 40* (4), 528–542.

Benus, J. M, Johnson, T. B., Wood, M., Grover, N., & Shen, T. (1995). *Self-Employment programs: A new reemployment strategy, Final Report of the UI Self-Employment Demonstration*. (Unemployment Insurance Occasional Paper, 95-4). Washington, DC: U.S. Department of Labor.

Benus, J. M., Wood, M., & Grover, N. (1994). A comparative analysis of the Washington and Massachusetts UI Self-Employment Demonstrations. Unemployment Insurance (Occasional Paper 94-3). Washington, DC: U.S. Department of Labor.

Bernstein, J. & Hartmann, H. (1999). Defining and characterizing the low-wage labor market. In *The Low-Wage Labor Market: Challenges and Opportunities for Economic Self-Sufficiency*. Prepared by the Urban Institute for Assistant Secretary for Planning and Evaluation. Washington, DC: U.S. Department of Health and Human Services. Retrieved from *http://aspe.hhs.gov/hsp/lwlm99/bernhart.htm*.

Beverly, S. G. & Sherraden, M. (1997). Investment in human development as a social development strategy. *Social Development Issues, 19* (1), 1–18.

Bhatt, N. (1997). Microenterprise development and the entrepreneurial poor: Including the excluded? *Public Administration and Development 17*, 371–386.

———. (2001). *Inner-City Entrepreneurship Development: The Viability of Microcredit Programs.* San Francisco: ICS Press.

Birch, D. (1987). *Job Creation in America: How Our Smallest Companies Put the Most People to Work.* New York: Free Press.

Birley, S. (1989). Female entrepreneurs: Are they really different? *Journal of Small Business Management 27* (1), 32–37.

Blank, R. (1989). Analyzing the length of welfare spells. *Journal of Public Economics 39*, 245–274.

Blau, F. D., Ferber, M. A. & Winkler, A. E. (1998). *The economics of women, men, and work.* (3rd ed.). Upper Saddle River, NJ: Prentice Hall.

Boden, R. J. Jr. (1999). Flexible working hours, family responsibilities, and female self-employment: Gender differences in self-employment selection. *American Journal of Economics and Sociology 58* (1), 71–83.

Bonavoglia, A. & Wadia A. (2001). Building businesses, rebuilding lives: Microenterprise and welfare reform. New York: MS. Foundation for Women.

Borjas, G. J. & Bronars, S. G. (1989, June). Consumer discrimination and self-employment. *Journal of Political Economy 97*, 581–605.

Boshara, R., Friedman, R. E., & Anderson, B. (1997). *Realizing the promise of micro-enterprise development in welfare reform.* Washington, DC: Corporation for Enterprise Development.

Briggs, X. de S. (1998). Brown kids in white suburbs: Housing mobility and the many faces of social capital. *Housing Policy Debate 9* (1), 177–221.

Brush, C. G. (1997). Women-owned businesses: Obstacles and opportunities. *Journal of Developmental Entrepreneurship 2* (1), 1–24.

———. (1990). Women and enterprise creation. In S. K. Gould & J. Parzen (Eds.), *Local Initiatives for Job Creation: Enterprising Women* (pp. 75–84). Paris: Organisation for Economic Co-operation and Development.

Buchignani, N. (1996). Using Folio Views for Qualitative Data Analysis. *Cultural Anthropology Methods 8* (2).

Buntin, J. (1997, March 3). Bad credit. *The New Republic*, 10–11.

Butler, J. S. (1991). *Entrepreneurship and Self-Help among Black Americans: A Reconsideration of Race and Economics.* Albany: State University of New York Press.

Carr, D. (1996). Two paths to self-employment? Women's and men's self-employment in the United States, 1980. *Work and Occupations 23* (1), 26–53.

Caskey, J. P. (1997). *Low Income American, Higher Cost Financial Services*. Madison, WI: Filene Research Institute.

Charmaz, K. (1988). The grounded theory method: An explanation and interpretation. In R. Emerson (Ed.), *Contemporary Field Research: A Collection of Readings* (pp. 109–126). Prospect Heights, IL: Waveland.

Chen, M. A., et al. (1996). Beyond Credit: A Subsector Approach to Promoting Women's Enterprises. Ottawa, Canada: Aga Khan Foundation.

Chen, M. A. & Dunn, E. (1996, June). Household economic portfolios. Microenterprise Impact Project (MIP), USAID Office of Microenterprise Development.

Clark, P., & Huston, T. (1993, August). Assisting the Smallest Businesses: Assessing Microenterprise Development as a Strategy for Boosting Poor Communities, An Interim Report. Washington, DC: Self-Employment Learning Project, Aspen Institute.

Clark, P. & Kays, A. J. (1995). *Enabling Entrepreneurship: Microenterprise Development in the United States*. Washington, DC: Self Employment Learning Project, Aspen Institute.

Clark, P., Kays, A. J. with Zandniapour, L., Soto, E. E., & Doyle, K. (1999). *Microenterprise and the Poor: Findings from the Self-Employment Learning Project Five Year Study of Microentrepreneurs*. Washington, DC: Economic Opportunities Program, Aspen Institute.

Clines, F. X. (1999, July 5). Nation's economic boom a faint echo in Appalachia. *New York Times*, A7.

CNN Money. (1998, August 10). Clothing for Us, By Us. Retrieved from *http://money. cnn.com/1998/08/10/busunu/fubu_pkg/*.

Cohen, M., Chen, M. A., & Dunn, E. (1996). *Household Economic Portfolios*. Washington, DC: Assessing the Impact of Microenterprise Services (AIMS). Household Economic Analysis/ Evaluation.

Coleman, J. S. (1988). Social capital in the creation of human capital: Organizations and institutions: sociological and economic approaches to the analysis of social structure. *American Journal of Sociology 94* (Supplement), 95–120.

Community Development Financial Institutions (CDFI) Fund. (2003). *FY 2003–FY 2008 Strategic Plan: Filling Financial Gaps across America*. Washington, DC: Treasury Department. Retrieved from *http://www.cdfifund.gov/docs/strategic_plans/03-08_plan.pdf*.

Conley, D. (1999). *Being Black, Living in the Red: Race, Wealth, and Social Policy in America*. Berkeley: University of California Press.

Consumer Federation of America Foundation (2002, May 13). *America Saves: One-Quarter of U.S. Households are Wealth Poor*. Retrieved from *http://www.america saves.org/back_page/savinginamerica_third.cfm*.

Cooper, A. C., Dunkelberg, W. C., Woo, C. Y., & Dennis Jr. W. J. (1990). *New Business in America: The Firms and Their Owners*. Washington, DC: NFIB Education Foundation.

Corporation for Enterprise Development (CFED). (1997). How can cities support microenterprise development? Amendment to *Rethinking Urban Economic Development*, chapter 4. Washington, DC: Author.

————. (n.d.). *Effective State Policy and Practice 1* (2). Washington, DC: Author.

Daniels, L. (2001). A guide to measuring microenterprise profits and net worth. *Small Enterprise Development 12* (4), 54–66.

Dean, W. J. (2001, March 5). Counseling Microentrepreneurs. *Pro Bono Digest*, 3.

Dennis, W. J. (1996). Self-employment: When nothing else is available? *Journal of Labor Research 17* (4), 645–661.

————. (1998). Business regulation as an impediment to the transition from welfare to self-employment. *Journal of Labor Research 19* (2), 263–277.

Devine, T. J. (1994, March). Characteristics of self-employed women in the United States. *Monthly Labor Review 117*, 20–34.

Doolittle, F., Guy, C. A., & Fink, B. L. (1991, August). *Self-Employment for Welfare Recipients: Implementation of the SEID Program*. Manpower Demonstration Research Corporation.

Drury, D., Walsh, S., & Strong, M. (1994). Evaluation of the EDWWA Job Creation Demonstration (Research and evaluation report series 94-G). Washington, DC: U.S. Department of Labor.

Dumas, C. (2001). Evaluating the outcomes of microenterprise training for low-income women: A case study. *Journal of Developmental Entrepreneurship 6* (2), 97–128.

Duncan, G. (1976). Earnings functions and nonpecuniary benefits. *Journal of Human Resources 11* (4), 462–483.

Dunn, E., Kalaitzandonakes, N., & Valdivia, C. (1996, June). Risk and the impacts of microenterprise services. Microenterprise Impact Project, US AID. Retrieved from *http://www.mip.org*.

Edgcomb, E.L. (2002). Improving microenterprise training and technical assistance: Findings for program managers. Washington, DC: Microenterprise FIELD, The Aspen Institute, February. Retrieved from *http://www.fieldus.org*.

Edgcomb, E. & Barton, L. (1998). Social intermediation and microfinance programs: A literature review. Washington, DC: Development Alternatives. Retrieved from *http://www.mip.org/pdfs/mbp/social.pdf*

Edgcomb, E. L. with Doub, M., Rosenthal, W., Rubens, D., Flint, C., Niebling, M., Rush, V., Williams, K., Losby, J. & Robinson J. (2002, February). *Improving Microenterprise Training and Technical Assistance Findings for Program Managers*.

Microenterprise Fund for Innovation, Effectiveness, Learning and Dissemination (FIELD). Washington, DC: Aspen Institute.

Edgcomb, E., Klein, J., & Clark, P. (1996). *The Practice of Microenterprise in the U.S.: Strategies, Costs, and effectiveness.* Washington, DC: Self Employment Learning Project: Aspen Institute.

Edgcomb, E. L., & Malm, E. (2002, August). *Keeping it Personalized: Consulting, Coaching and Mentoring for Microentrepreneurs.* Washington, DC: Aspen Institute, FIELD Best Practice Guide, volume 4.

Edin, K. (1993). *There's a Lot of Month Left at the End of the Money: How Welfare Recipients Make Ends Meet in Chicago.* New York: Garland.

Edin, K. & Lein, L. (1997). *Making Ends Meet: How Single Mothers Survive Welfare and Low-Wage Work.* New York: Russell Sage.

Ehlers, T. B. & Main, K. (1998). Women and the false promise of microenterprise. *Gender and Society 12* (4), 424–440.

Ehrenberg, R. G., & Smith, R. S. (1997). *Modern labor economics: Theory and public policy.* Reading, MA: Addison-Wesley.

Else, J. & Clay-Thompson, C. (1998, April). *Refugee microenterprise development: Achievements and lessons learned.* Iowa City: Institute for Social and Economic Development.

Else, J., Doyle, K., Servon, L. & Messenger, J. (2001, March). *The Role of Micro-enterprise Development in the United States.* Geneva: International Labour Organization and the Association for Enterprise Opportunity.

Else, J. with Gallagher, J. (2001, March). An overview of the microenterprise development field in the U.S. In J. Else, K. Doyle, L. Servon, & J. Messenger, *The Role of Microenterprise Development in the United States* (pp. 1–42). A Research Report. Geneva: International Labor Organization in cooperation with Arlington, VA: Association for Enterprise Opportunity.

Else, J., Krotz, D., & Budzilowicz, L. (2003, October 2nd ed.). *Refugee Microenterprise Development: Achievements and Lessons Learned.* Washington, DC: ISED Solutions, Report to U.S. Office of Refugee Resettlement (ORR), Administration for Children and Families, U.S. Department of Health and Human Services, Grant # 90RB00010.

Else, J. & Raheim, S. (1992, Fall). AFDC clients as entrepreneurs: Self-employment offers an important option. *Public Welfare 50*(4) 36–41.

Erickcek, G. A. (1997). The role of small business: A tale of two cities. *Upjohn Institute Employment Research 4* (2), 1–4. *http://www.upjohninst.org/publications/newsletter/ge-f97.pdf.*

Evans, D. S. & Jovanovic, B. (1989). Estimates of a model of entrepreneurial choice under liquidity constraints. *Journal of Political Economy 97* (4), 808–827.

Evans, D. S. & Leighton, L. (1989, September). Some Empirical Aspects of Entrepreneurship. *American Economic Review 79*, 519–535.

Everett, J. & Watson, J. (1998). Small business failures and external risk factors. *Small Business Economics 11* (4), 371–390.

Fairlie, R.W. (1999). The absence of the African-American owned business: An analysis of the dynamics of self-employment. *Journal of Labor Economics 17* (1), 80–108.

Federal Reserve of Chicago (2003). Glossary of Terms. Consumer and Economic Development Research and Information Center. Retrieved from *http://www.chicagofed.org/cedric/glossary.cfm*.

Federal Trade Commission (1998). Credit Scoring. Retrieved from *http://www.ftc.gov/bcp/conline/pubs/credit/scoring.htm*.

Fischer, E. M., Reuber, A. R., & Dyke, L. S. (1993). A theoretical overview and extension of research on sex, gender, and entrepreneurship. *Journal of Business Venturing 8*, 151–168.

Fisher, L., with Marton A. (contributor). (1997). *The Muffin Lady: Muffins, Cupcakes, and Quickbreads for the Happy Soul.* HarperCollins.

Fitzgerald, J. (1995). Local labor markets and local area effects on welfare duration. *Journal of Public Policy Analysis and Management 14* (1), 43–67.

Foderaro, L. W. (1997, November 12). Small grants help poor to start new business. *New York Times*, 6.

Fredland, J. E. & Little, R. D. (1985, Fall). Psychic income and self-employment. *Journal of Private Enterprise* 1 (1), 121–127.

Friedman, R. (1988). *The Safety Net as Ladder: Transfer Payments and Economic Development.* Washington, DC: Council of State Policy and Planning Agencies. Retrieved from *http://www.cfed.org*.

Friedman, R. Grossman, B., & Sahay, P. (1995). Building assets: Self-employment for welfare recipients. Washington, DC: Corporation for Enterprise Development.

Friedrich, A. & Rodriguez, E. (2001, August). National Council of La Raza, Financial Insecurity amid Growing Wealth: Why Healthier Saving Is Essential to Latino Prosperity. Available: *http://www.nclr.org/policy/briefs/Issue%20Brief%205.pdf*.

Gittell, R. & Vidal, A. (1998). *Community organizing: Building social capital as a development strategy.* Thousand Oaks, CA: Sage.

Grameen Bank (2004, March 14). Grameen Bank. Retrieved from *http://www.grameen-info.org/bank/GBGlance.html*.

Granovetter, M. (1973). The strength of weak ties. *American Journal of Sociology 78* (6), 1360–1380.

Greenberg, M. (1999, November). *Developing Policies to Support Microenterprise in the TANF Structure: A Guide to the Law.* Washington, DC: Center for Law and Social Policy and Field, Aspen Institute.

Grossman, K. D., Blair, A. K., & Thetford, T. (2002, July). *Connectors and Conduits: Reaching Competitive Markets from the Ground Up*. The Access to Markets Demonstration Final Report. Washington, DC: Aspen Institute, FIELD. Retrieved from *http://www.fieldus.org*.

Grossman, K. D. & Malm, E. with Francis, V. & Nelson C. (2003, August). Business First: Using Technology to Advance Microenterprise Development. Washington, DC: Aspen Institute, FIELD Best Practice Guild, volume 5.

Guarnizo, L. E. (1998). The Mexican ethnic economy in Los Angeles: Capitalist accumulation, class restructuring, and the transnationalization of migration. Davis: California Communities Program, University of California.

Hamilton, B. H. (2000). Does entrepreneurship pay? An empirical analysis of the returns of self-employment. *Journal of Political Economy 108* (3), 604–631.

Harris, K. M. (1993). Work and welfare among single mothers in poverty. *American Journal of Sociology 99* (2), 317–353.

Hashemi, S. M. (1997). Building up capacity for banking with the poor: The Grameen Bank in Bangladesh. In H. Schneider (Ed.), *Microfinance for the Poor?* (pp. 109–128). IFAD, OECD.

Haswell, S. & Holmes, S. (1989). Estimating the business failure rate: A reappraisal. *Journal of Small Business Management 27* (3), 68–74.

Hatch, C. R. (1988). *Flexible Manufacturing Networks: Cooperation for Competitiveness in a Global Economy*. Washington, DC: Corporation for Enterprise Development.

Hatch, R. (1991). The ties that bind: Networks and the making of Denmark's competitive edge. *Entrepreneurial Economy Review 9* (3), 13–18.

Himes, C. with Servon, L. J. (1998, April). *Measuring Client Success: An Evaluation of ACCIÓN's Impact on Microenterprises in the United States*. U.S. Issues Series 2. ACCIÓN International, Washington, DC.

Hirst, P. & Zeitlin, J. (1991). Flexible specialization versus post-Fordism: theory, evidence, and policy implications. *Economy and Society 20* (1), 1–56.

Hisrich, R. D. & Brush, C. G. (1987). Women entrepreneurs: A longitudinal study. In B. A. Kirchoff, N. C. Churchill, J. A. Hornaday, B. A. Kirchoff, O. J. Krasner, & K. H. Vesper (Eds.), *Frontiers in Entrepreneurship Research* (pp. 187–189). Wellesley, MA: Babson College.

Ho, R. (1998, March 9). Banking on plastic: To finance a dream, many entrepreneurs binge on credit cards. *Wall Street Journal*, A1, 10.

Holley, J. (1995). *Facilitating the Formation of Flexible Manufacturing Networks in Rural, Southeastern Ohio: Five Year Report*. Athens, OH: Appalachian Center for Economic Networks (ACEnet).

———. (1996). *A Model for Market and Product Development in Low-Income Communities*. Athens, OH: Appalachian Center for Economic Networks.

————. (1998, January). *Access to Markets: Making the Case for Market Development.* AEO Exchange. Photocopy.

Holley, J. & Wadia, A. (2001). Accessing lucrative markets: Growing women's businesses in low-income communities. New York: MS. Foundation for Women.

Holmquist, C. & Sundin, E. (1990). What's special about highly educated women.entrepreneurs? *Entrepreneurship and Regional Development, 2,* 181–193.

Holtz-Eakin, D., Joulfaian, D., & Rosen, H. S. (1994). Sticking it out: Entrepreneurial survival and liquidity constraints. *Journal of Political Economy 102* (1), 53–75.

Hossain, M. (1986). The impact of Grameen Bank on women's involvement in productive activities. Dhaka, Bangladesh: Institute for Development Studies.

Howard, C. (1997). *The Hidden Welfare State: Tax Expenditures and Social Policy in the United States.* Princeton: Princeton University Press.

Hudson, W.W. (1990). WALMYR Assessment Scale scoring manual. Tempe, AZ: WALMYR Publishing Co.

Hulme, D. (1997, August). Impact assessment methodologies for microfinance: A review. *AIMS Brief* No. 14. CGAP Working Group on Impact Assessment Methodologies, Consultative Group to Assist the Poorest (CGAP). *http://www. mip.org/pdfs/aims/brief16.pdf.*

Hung, C. R. (2002). From south to north: A comparative study of group-based microcredit programs in the developing countries and the United States. In J. H. Carr & Z. Y. Tong (Eds.), *Replicating Microfinance in the United States* (pp. 223–256). Washington, DC: Woodrow Wilson Center Press and distributed by Johns Hopkins University Press (Baltimore & London).

Johnson, E., J. Hinterlong, & M. Sherraden. (2001). Strategies for creating MIS technology to improve social work practice and research. *Journal of Technology in Human Services 18*(3/4), 5–22.

Johnson, M. A. (1998). An overview of basic issues facing microenterprise practices in the United States. *Journal of Developmental Entrepreneurship 3* (1), 5–21.

Kantor, P. (2000). *Promoting Women's Entrepreneurship Development Based on Good Practice Programmes: Some Experiences from the North to the South.* ILO SEED Program Series on Women's Entrepreneurship Development and Gender in Enterprises (WEDGE) (Working Paper 9). Geneva. Retrieved from *http:// www.ilo.org/public/english/employment/ent/sed/publ/pkantor.htm.*

Keeley, K. (1990). The role of intermediaries in strengthening women's business expansion activities. In S. K. Gould & J. Parzen (Eds.), *Local Initiatives for Job Creation: Enterprising Women* (pp. 75–94). Paris: Organisation for Economic Co-operation and Development.

Kibria, N., Lee, S. & Olvera, R. (2003). Peer lending groups and success: A case study of working capital. *Journal of Developmental Entrepreneurship 8* (1), 41–58.

Kirchoff, B. A. (1994). *Entrepreneurship and Dynamic Capitalism: The Economics of Business Firm Formation and Growth*. Westport, CN: Praeger.

Klein, J. (1994). *Small Steps toward Big Dreams*. Flint, MI: Charles Stewart Mott Foundation.

————. (2002, August). Entering the Relationship: Finding and Assessing Micro-enterprise Training Clients. Washington, DC: Aspen Institute, FIELD Best Practice Guide, volume 1.

Lang, R. E. & Hornburg, S. P. (1998). What is social capital and why is it important to public policy? *Housing Policy Debate 9* (1).

Langer, J. A., Orwick, J. A., & Kays, A. J. (1999). *1999 Directory of U.S. Microenterprise Programs*. Microenterprise Fund for Innovation, Effectiveness, Learning and Dissemination (FIELD), Aspen Institute.

Larance, L. Y. (2001). Fostering social capital through NGO design: Grameen Bank membership in Bangladesh. *International Social Work 44* (1), 7–18.

Lazear, E. (1981). Agency, earnings profiles, productivity, and hours restrictions. *American Economic Review 71* (4), 606–620.

Lewis, B. R. (1998). ATLAS/ti and NUD•IST: A comparative review of two leading qualitative data analysis packages. *Cultural Anthropology Methods 10* (3), 41–47.

Lieberson, S. (1980). *A Piece of the Pie: Black and White Immigrants since 1880*. Berkeley: University of California Press.

Light, I. H. (1972). *Ethnic Enterprise in America: Business and Welfare among Chinese, Japanese, and Blacks*. Berkeley: University of California Press.

Light, I. & Gold, S. J. (2000). *Ethnic Economies*. San Diego, CA: Academic Press.

Light, I. & Pham, M. (1998). Beyond creditworthy: Microcredit and informal credit in the United States. *Journal of Developmental Entrepreneurship, 3* (1), 35–51.

Light, I. & Rosenstein, C. (1995). *Race, Ethnicity, and Entrepreneurship in Urban America*. New York: Walter de Gruyter.

Li-Ron, Y. (1995, January). A database and then some. *PC Computing*.

Littlefield, E. Morduch, J., & Hashemi, S. (2003, January). Is microfinance an effective strategy to reach the millennium development goals? Washington, DC: Consultative Group to Assist the Poorest (CGAP), Focus Note 24. Retrieved from *http://www.cgap.org*.

Loscocco, K. A. & Robinson, J. (1991). Barriers to women's small-business success in the United States. *Gender & Society 5* (4), 511–532).

Loscocco, K. A., Robinson, J., Hall, R. H., & Allen, J. K. (1991). Gender and small business success: An inquiry into women's relative disadvantage. *Social Forces 70* (1), 65–85.

MacQueen, K. M., McLellan, E., Kay, K., & Milstein, B. (1998, June). Codebook development for team-based qualitative analysis. *Cultural Anthropology Methods*, 31–36.

Manser, M. & Picot, G. (1999, April). The role of self-employment in U.S. and Canadian job growth. *Monthly Labor Review 122*, 10–25.

Markowitz, H. (1952). Portfolio selection. *Journal of Finance 7*, 77–91.

Mars, G. & Ward, R. (1984). Ethnic business development in Britain: Opportunities and resources. In R. Ward and R. Jenkins (Eds.), *Ethnic Communities in Business* (pp. 1–19). Cambridge: Cambridge University Press.

Maxwell, J. A. 1992. Understanding and validity in qualitative research. *Harvard Educational Review 62* (3), 279–300.

McGuire, P. B. & Conroy, J. D. (1997). Bank-NGO linkages and the transaction costs of lending to the poor through groups: Evidence from India and the Philippines. In H. Schneider (Ed.), *Microfinance for the Poor?* (pp. 73–84) IFAD, OECD.

McKee, K., S. Gould, & Leonard, A. (1993). Self-employment as a means to women's economic self-sufficiency. Women Venture's Business Development Program. Seeds 15, Population Council. Retrieved from *http://www.popcouncil.org/publications/seeds/seeds15.html*.

Mellor, W. H. (1996, August 31). No jobs, no work: Local restrictions block the exits from welfare. *New York Times*, 19A.

Merton, R. K., Fiske, M, & Kendall P.L. (1990, 2d ed.). *The Focused Interview: A Manual of Problems and Procedures*. New York & London: Free Press.

Messenger, J. C. & Stettner, A. (2000). The Quality of Self-Employment Jobs in the United States. Geneva: International Labour Organisation, Enterprise Creation by the Unemployed, Microfinance in Industrialized Countries, The Social Finance Unit. Retrieved from *http://www.ilo.org/public/english/employment/finance/reports/us6.htm*.

Mester, L. J. (1997, September–October). What's the point of credit scoring? *Business Review* (Federal Reserve Bank of Philadelphia), volume 14, pp. 3–16. Retrieved from *http://www.phil.frb.org/files/br/brso97lm.pdf*.

Meyerhoff, D. (1997). Federal funding opportunities for microenterprise programs. *Journal of Developmental Entrepreneurship 2* (2), 99–109.

Microcredit Summit Secretariat (2001). Retrieved from *http://www.microcredit summit.org/*.

Microenterprise Fund for Innovation, Effectiveness, Learning, and Dissemination (FIELD) (1998). *An Introduction to FIELD: Mission, Goals and Policies*. Washington, DC: Aspen Institute. Retrieved from *http://www.fieldus.org*.

————. (2000a). Sources of Public Funding. Washington, DC: FIELD in collaboration with the Association for Enterprise Opportunity. Retrieved from *http://www.fieldus.org.*

————. (2000b, Fall). *Microenterprise Development in the United States: An Overview.* Washington, DC: Aspen Institute, FIELD, Microenterprise Fact Sheet Series, Issue 1. Retrieved from *http://www.fieldus.org.*

————. (2000c). Recruiting, Assessing and Screening TANF recipients. Washington, DC: FIELD in collaboration with the Association for Enterprise Opportunity, Issue 7. Retrieved from *http://www.fieldus.org.*

————. (2000d). Follow-up services: Post-loan and post training. Washington, DC: FIELD in collaboration with the Association for Enterprise Opportunity, Issue 4. Retrieved from *http://www.fieldus.org.*

————. (2003a). MicroMentor. Retrieved from: *http://www.micromentor.org/.*

————. (2003b). The Informal Economy and Microenterprise in the United States. Washington, DC: FIELD in collaboration with the Association for Enterprise Opportunity, Issue 7. Retrieved from *http://www.fieldus.org.*

Midgley, J. (1995). *Social Development: The Developmental Perspective in Social Welfare.* London & Thousand Oaks, CA: Sage.

————. (1999). Growth, redistribution, and welfare: Toward social investment. *Social Service Review 73* (1), 3–21.

Miles, M. B. & Huberman, M. A. 1994. *Qualitative Data Analysis: A Sourcebook of New Methods.* Beverly Hills, CA: Sage Publications.

Miller, D. C. (1990). *Women and social welfare: A feminist analysis.* New York: Praeger.

Mishel, L. R. & Bernstein, J. (1995). *The State of Working America 1995.* Armonk, NY: M.E. Sharpe.

Mokry, B. W. (1988). *Entrepreneurship and Public Policy: Can Government Stimulate Business Startups?* New York: Quorum Books.

Mondal, W. I. & Tune, R. A. (1993). Replicating the Grameen Bank in North America: The Good Faith Fund Experience. In A. N. M. Wahid (Ed.), *The Grameen Bank: Poverty Relief in Bangladesh* (pp. 225–234). Boulder: Westview.

Morales, A., Balkin, S., & Persky, J. (1995, November). The value of benefits of a public street market: The case of Maxwell Street. *Economic Development Quarterly,* 304–330.

Morris, L. A. (1999). Exits, employment, earnings, and recidivism among welfare recipients in North Carolina, 1995 to 1998. Doctoral dissertation, Public Policy Analysis. Chapel Hill, NC: University of North Carolina.

Mustafa, Z. (1998, January). Access to markets: Making the case for market development. *AEO Exchange* (Association for Enterprise Opportunity newsletter). Retrieved from *http://www.wwa.com/~aeo.*

National Business Incubation Association (2001, July 30). What is Business Incubation? Retrieved from *http://www.nbia.org/whatis.html*.

National Economic Development & Law Center (NEDLC) and the Coalition for Women's Economic Development (CWED). (1999, January). *The Challenge of Microenterprise: The CWED Story*. Oakland, CA: NEDLC and the CWED.

National Endowment for Financial Education (2001). Education Programs. Retrieved from *http://www.nefe.org/pages/educationalprograms.html*.

Nee, V., Sanders, J. M., & Sernau, S. (1994). Job transitions in an immigrant metropolis: Ethnic boundaries and the mixed economy. *American Sociological Review 59*, 849–872.

Neff, G. (1996, October). Microecredit, microresults. *Left Business Observer 74*. Retrieved from *http://www.panix.com/~dhenwood/Micro.html*.

Nelson, C. (2002, August). Building Skills for Self-Employment: Basic Training for Microentrepreneurs. Washington, DC: Aspen Institute, FIELD Best Practice Guide, volume 2.

Newman, K. S. (1999). *No Shame in My Game: The Working Poor in the Inner City*. New York: Knopf and Russell Sage Foundation.

Novogratz, J. (1992). Hopeful change: The potential of microenterprise programs as a community revitalization intervention. New York: Rockefeller Foundation.

Office of Refugee Resettlement (2002). Refugee *Microenterprise Development Projects*. *Retrieved from http://www.acf.dhhs.gov/programs/orr/policy/sl0217at.htm*.

Oliver, M. L. & Shapiro, T. M. (2001). Wealth and racial stratification. In N. J. Smelser, W. J. Wilson, & F. Mitchell (Eds.), *America Becoming: Racial Trends and Their Consequences*, vol. 2 (pp. 222–252). Washington, DC: National Academy Press.

Oliver, M. L. & Shapiro, T. M. (1995). *Black Wealth/White Wealth: A New Perspective on Racial Inequality*. New York: Routledge.

Openair-Market Net (2001, July 30). What is OPENAIR-Market Net? Retrieved from *http://www.openair.org/opair/faq.html*.

Orszag, P. R. (2001, April 13). Asset Tests and Low Savings Rates Among Lower-Income Families. Washington, DC: Center for Budget and Policy Priorities. Retrieved from *http://www.cbpp.org/4-13-01wel.htm*.

Otero, M. & Rhyne, E. (1994). *The New World of Microenterprise Finance: Building Healthy Financial Institutions for the Poor*. West Hartford, CT: Kumarian.

Page-Adams, D. & Sherraden, M. (1996). What We Know about Effects of Asset Holding: Implications for Research on Asset-Based Anti-Poverty Initiatives (Working Paper 96-1). St. Louis: Center for Social Development, Washington University.

Parker, J. & Pearce, D. (2001). Microfinance, grants, and non-financial responses to poverty reduction: Where does microcredit fit? CGAP Focus Note 20. Washington, DC: Consultative Group to Assist the Poorest (CGAP).

Parker, S. C. (1996). A time series model of self-employment under uncertainty. *Economica 63*, 459–275.

Pavetti, L. A. (1993). The dynamics of welfare and work: Exploring the process by which women work their way off welfare. Doctoral dissertation, Malcolm Wiener Center for Social Policy Working Papers: Dissertation Series, John F. Kennedy School of Government, Harvard University.

Peirce, N. R. & Steinbach, C. F. (1987). *Corrective Capitalism: The Rise of America's Community Development Corporations*. New York: Ford Foundation.

Piore, M. J. & Sabel, C. F. (1984). *The Second Industrial Divide: Possibilities for Prosperity*. New York: Basic.

Plimpton, L., & Greenberg, M. (2000, March). Key State TANF Policies Affecting Microenterprise. Washington, DC: Center for Law and Social Policy in collaboration with Microenterprise Fund for Innovation, Effectiveness, Learning and Dissemination (FIELD). Retrieved from *http://www.fieldus@aspeninst.org*.

Porter, K. H. & Dupree, A. (2001, August). Poverty trends for families headed by working single mothers (1993 to 1999). Washington, DC: Center for Budget and Policy Priorities.

Portes, A. & Sensenbrenner, J. (1993). Embeddedness and immigration: Notes on the social determinants of economic action. *American Journal of Sociology 98*(6): 1320–1350.

Putnam, R. D. (1993). *Making Democracy Work: Civic Traditions in Modern Italy*. Princeton, NJ: Princeton University Press.

Putnam, R. D. (1998). Foreward (Special issue on social capital). *Housing policy debate 9* (1), v–viii.

Raheim, S. (1996). Microenterprise as an approach for promoting economic development in social work: Lessons from the Self-Employment Investment Demonstration. *International Social Work 39*, 69–82.

———. (1997). Problems and prospects of self-employment as an economic independence option for welfare recipients. *Social Work 42* (1), 44–53.

Raheim, S. & Alter, C. F. (1995, April). Self-Employment Investment Demonstration Final Evaluation Report, Part One: Participant Survey, Iowa City: University of Iowa School of Social Work.

Raheim, S. & Alter, C. F. (1998). Self-employment as a social and economic development intervention for recipients of AFDC. *Journal of Community Practice 5* (1/2), 41–61.

Raheim, S., Alter, C. F., & Yarbrough, D. (1996). Evaluating microenterprise programs: Issues and lessons learned. *Journal of Developmental Entrepreneurship 1* (2), 87–103.

Raheim, S. & Bolden, J. (1995). Economic empowerment of low-income women through self-employment programs. *AFFILIA: Journal of Women and Social Work 10* (2), 138–154.

Raheim, S. & Friedman, J. J. (1999). Microenterprise development in the heartland: Self-employment as a self-sufficiency strategy for TANF recipients in Iowa 1993–1998. *Journal of Microfinance 1* (1), 67–90.

Raijman, R. (2001). Mexican immigrants and informal self-employment in Chicago. *Human Organization 60* (10), 47–55.

Robichaud, Y., McGraw, E., & Roger, A. (2001). Toward the development of a measuring instrument for entrepreneurial motivation. *Journal of Developmental Entrepreneurship 6* (2), 189–201.

Rodriguez, C.R. (1995). *Women, Microenterprise, and the Politics of Self Help.* New York: Garland.

Roy, A. D. (1951, June). Some Thoughts on the Distribution of Earnings. *Oxford Economic Papers 3*, 135–146.

Rubin, H. J. & Rubin, I. S. (1995). *Qualitative interviewing: The art of hearing data.* Thousand Oaks: Sage.

Rubin, B. M. & Zorn, C. K. (1985). Sensible state and local economic development. *Public Administration Review 45*, 333–339.

Rubin, H. J. & Sherraden, M. S. (forthcoming). Community economic and social development. In M. O. Weil (Ed.) and D. Gamble, M. Reisch, L. Gutierrez, R. Cnaan, & B. Mulroy (Sec. Eds.), *Handbook of Community Practice.* Sage.

Sanders, C. K. (2000). Microenterprise versus the Labor Market among Low-Income Workers. Doctoral dissertation. St. Louis, MO: Washington University.

———. (2002). The impact of Microenterprise Assistance Programs: A comparative study of program participants, nonparticipants, and other low-wage workers. *Social Service Review 76* (2), 321–340.

Sanders, C. K. & Scanlon, E. (2000). Mortgage lending and gender. *AFFILIA: Journal of Women and Social Work 15* (1), 9–30.

Schreiner, M. (1999a, December). Self-employment, microenterprise, and the poorest Americans. *Social Service Review*, 496–523.

———. (1999b). Lessons for microenterprise programs from a fresh look at the Unemployment Insurance Self-Employment Demonstration. *Evaluation Review 23* (5), 503–526.

———. (1999c). *A review of evaluations of microenterprise programs in the United States.* Manuscript. Center for Social Development, Washington University in St. Louis. Retrieved from *http://www.gwbweb.wustl.edu/users/csd*.

Schreiner, M. & Woller, G. (2003). Microenterprise development programs in the United States and in the developing world. *World Development 31* (9), 1567–1580.

————. (2002). Evaluation and microenterprise programs in the United States. *Journal of Microfinance 4* (2), 67–91.

————. (2003, January). Scoring: The next breakthrough in microcredit? (CGAP Occasional Paper 7). Washington, DC: Consultative Group to Assist the Poorest (CGAP). Retrieved from *cgap.org/assets/images/OP7_CreditScoring.pdf.*

Schreiner, M. & Morduch, J. (2002). Replicating microfinance in the United States: opportunities and challenges. In J. H. Carr & Z.Y. Tong (Eds.), *Replicating Microfinance in the United States.* Washington, DC: Woodrow Wilson Center Press and distributed by Johns Hopkins University Press (Baltimore & London).

Schreiner, M., Sherraden, M., Clancy, M., Johnson, E., Curley, J., Grinstein-Weiss, M., Zhan, M., & Beverly, S. (2001, February). Savings and Asset Accumulation in Individual Development Accounts. A Research Report. St. Louis: Center for Social Development, Washington University.

Schuler, S. R. & Hashemi, S. (1994). Credit Programs, Women's Empowerment, and Contraceptive Use in Rural Bangladesh. *Studies in Family Planning 25*(2), 65–76.

Seidman, L. C. (2001). Assets and the tax code. In T. M. Shapiro & E. N. Wolff (Eds.), *Assets for the Poor: the Benefits of Spreading Asset Ownership* (pp. 324–356). New York: Russell Sage.

Sen, A. K. (1999). *Development as freedom.* New York: Knopf Books.

Servon, L. J. (1996). Microenterprise Programs and Women: Entrepreneurship as Individual Empowerment. *Journal of Developmental Entrepreneurship 1* (1), 31–55.

————. (1997). Microenterprise programs in U.S. inner cities: Economic development or social welfare? *Economic Development Quarterly 11* (2), 166–180.

———— (1998). Credit and social capital: The community development potential of U.S. microenterprise programs. *Housing Policy Debate 9* (1), 115–149.

————. (1999). *Bootstrap Capital: Microenterprise and the American Poor.* Washington, DC: Brookings Institution Press.

Servon, L. J. & Bates, T. (1998). Microenterprise as an exit route from poverty: Recommendations for programs and policy makers. *Journal of Urban Affairs 20* (4), 419–441.

Servon, L. J., Doshna, J. P., & Bloustein, E.J. (2000). *Structuring and Sustaining the Relationships that Support U.S. Microenterprise Programs.* Geneva: International Labour Office (ILO). Retrieved from *http://www.ilo.org/public/english/emplyment/finance/reports/us3.htm.*

Severens, A. C. & Kays, A. (1997). *1996 Directory of U.S. Microenterprise Programs.* Washington, DC: Self-Employment Learning Project, Aspen Institute, in collaboration with the Association for Enterprise Opportunity.

Shaver, K. (1997, February 21). Rules batter woman rising from welfare via muffins. *St. Louis Post-Dispatch*, 14A.

Sherraden, M. (1989). Poverty and transaction costs. St. Louis: Washington University.

———. (1991). *Assets and the Poor: A New American Welfare Strategy*. Armonk: ME Sharpe.

———. (2001). Youth service as strong policy. St. Louis: Center for Social Development, Washington University (Working Paper 01-12).

Sherraden, M. S. & Barrera, R. E. (1995). Qualitative Research with an Understudied Population: In-Depth Interviews with Women of Mexican Descent. *Hispanic Journal of Behavioral Sciences 17*(4), 452–470.

Sherraden, M. S. & Ninacs, W. A. (1998). *Community Economic Development and Social Work*. New York: Haworth.

Sherraden, M. S. & Sanders, C. K. (1997, October 4). Social Work with Low-Income Microentrepreneurs: Micro, Mezzo, and Macro Innovations, National Association of Social Workers, Baltimore, MD.

Sherraden, M.S., Sanders, C. K., & Sherraden, M. (1998, January). From the Eyes of the Entrepreneurs: Microenterprise as an Anti-Poverty Strategy. St. Louis: Center for Social Development, Washington University. Report to the Self Employment Learning Project, Aspen Institute.

Solomon, L. D. (1992). Microenterprise: Human reconstruction in America's inner cities. *Harvard Journal of Law and Public Policy* 15 (1), 191–221.

Spalter-Roth, R. M., Hartmann, H. I. & Shaw, L.B. (1993). Exploring the characteristics of self-employment and part-time work among women. Washington, DC: Institute for Women's Policy Research.

Spalter-Roth, R., Soto, E., & Zandniapour L. (1994). *Micro-enterprise and Women: The Viability of Self-Employment as a Strategy for Alleviating Poverty.* Washington, DC: Institute for Women's Policy Research.

Ssewamala, F. M. (2003). Saving for Microenterprise in Individual Development Accounts: Factors Related to Performance. Doctoral dissertation. Washington University, St. Louis, Missouri.

Stack, C. B. (1974). *All Our Kin: Strategies for Survival in a Black Community*. New York: Harper.

Staley, S. R., Husock, H., Bobb, D. J., Burnett, H. S., Creasy, L., & Hudson, W. (2001). Giving a Leg Up to Bootstrap Entrepreneurship: Expanding Economic Opportunity in America's Urban Centers. Policy Study 277. Retrieved from *http://rppi.org/ps277.html*.

Stoesz, D. & Saunders, D. (1999, September). Welfare capitalism: A new approach to poverty policy? *Social Service Review*, 380–400.

Stone, B. (1997, April/May). Intercooperation and the co-op movement: A proposal. *GEO: Grassroots Economic Organizing 26.*

Stoner, C. R. Hartman, R. I., & Aurora, R. (1990). Work-home role conflict in female owners of small businesses: An exploratory study. *Journal of Small Business Management*, January, 30–38.

Straatmann, S. & Sherraden, M. S. (2001). Welfare to self-employment: A case study of the First Step Fund. *Journal of Community Practice 9* (3), 73–94.

Strauss, A. & Corbin, J. 1990. *Basics of Qualitative Research: Grounded Theory Procedures and Techniques.* Newbury Park, CA: Sage.

Surgeon, G. P. (1997). CDFIs and the future of microlending. *Perspectives: Federal Reserve Bank of Dallas*, 6–8.

Sutin, P. (2000, February 20). Merchants reject plan for upgrading Soulard Market. *St. Louis Post-Dispatch*, C1.

Taub, R. (1998). Making the Adaptation Across Cultures and Societies: A Report on an Attempt to Clone the Grameen Bank in Southern Arkansas. *Journal of Developmental Entrepreneurship 3*(1), 53–69.

Tomaskovic-Devey, D. (1993). *Gender and Racial Inequality at Work: The Sources and Consequences of Job Segregation.* Ithaca, NY: ILR Press.

U.S. Department of Labor (1994). Self-Employment as a Reemployment Option: Demonstration Results and National Legislation (Unemployment Insurance Occasional Paper 94-3).

———. (1995). *Self-Employment programs: A new reemployment strategy, Final Report of the UI Self-Employment Demonstration.* Unemployment Insurance (Occasional Paper 95-4).

U.S. Department of Treasury (2001). *Crossing the Bridge to Self Employment: A Federal Microenterprise Resource Guide.* Interagency Workgroup on Microenterprise Development.

U.S. Small Business Administration (SBA) (1999). *The Facts about Small Business 1999.* Washington, DC: U.S. Small Business Administration, Office of Advocacy.

———. (2000, August). Principles of Federal Government Support for Microenterprise Development. Washington, DC: Small Business Administration. Retrieved from *http://www.sba.gov/microenter/policypaperaugust2000.pdf.*

———. (2002). Glossary. Retrieved from *http://app1.sba.gov/glossary.*

———. (2003a, May 13). The Microloan Program: Moving Toward Performance Management. Retrieved from *http://www.sba.gov/ig/03-26.pdf.*

———. (2003b). Frequently Asked Questions: Small Business Statistics and Research. Retrieved from *http://app1.sba.gov/faqs/faqindex.cfm?areaID=2.*

Uzzi B. & Gillespie, J. J. (1999, March). What small firms get capital and what cost: Notes on the role of social capital and banking networks, *Proceedings* (Federal Reserve Bank of Chicago, Business Access to Credit Conference), 413–444. Retrieved from *http://www.chicagofed.org/cedric/publications/BusAcc/Content.pdf.*

Vélez-Ibañez, C. (1983). Bond of mutual trust: The cultural systems of rotating credit associations among urban Mexicans and Chicanos. New Brunswick, NJ: Rutgers University Press.

Vroman, W. (1997, December). *Self employment assistance: Revised report.* Washington, DC: Urban Institute (Report prepared for U.S. Department of Labor, Contract F-5532-5–00-8030).

Waldinger, R. D. (1986). *Through the Eye of the Needle: Immigrants and Enterprise in New York's Garment District.* New York: New York University Press.

————. (1995). The 'other side' of embeddedness: A case-study of the interplay of economy and ethnicity. *Ethnic and Racial Studies 18* (3), 555–580.

Waldinger, R. Aldrich, H., & Ward, R. (1990). *Ethnic entrepreneurs: Immigrant Business in Industrial Societies.* Newbury Park, CA: Sage.

Walker, B. A. & Blair, A.K. (2002). *2002 Directory of U.S. Microenterprise Programs.* Washington, DC: Microenterprise Fund for Innovation, Effectiveness, Learning and Dissemination (FIELD), The Aspen Institute and The Association for Enterprise Opportunity.

Warren, M. R., Thompson, J. P., & Saegert, S. (2001). The role of social capital in combating poverty. In S. Saegert, J. P. Thompson, & M. R. Warren (Eds.), *Social Capital and Poor Communities* (pp. 1–30). New York: Russell Sage.

Wilkens, R. & Holley, J. (1992). *Revitalizing Regional Economies by Providing a Telecommunications Infrastructure which Support Small Manufacturing Firms.* Athens, OH: Appalachian Center for Economic Networks (ACEnet).

Willis, R. J. (1986). *Wage determinants: A survey and reinterpretation of human capital functions, Handbook of Labor Economics,* vol 1. Elsevier, Amsterdam: North Holland.

Woller, G. M, Wheeler, G., & Checketts, N. (1999). Evaluation practices in microcredit institutions. *Journal of Development Entrepreneurship 4* (1), 59–80.

Woolcock, M. J. (1998). Social capital and economic development: Toward a theoretical synthesis and policy framework. *Theory and Society 27,* 151–208.

WSEP (1996). Women's Self-Employment Project 1986–1996: A Decade of Opportunity for the Women of Chicago. Chicago: Author.

Yunus, M. (1999, November). The Grameen Bank. *Scientific American,* 114–119.

Zinger, J. T., LeBrasseur, R. & Zanibbi, L. R. (2001). Factors influencing early state performance in Canadian microenterprises. *Journal of Developmental Entrepreneurship 6* (2), 129–150.

About the Authors

Margaret Sherrard Sherraden is a Professor of Social Work at the University of Missouri-St. Louis, and Research Professor at the Center for Social Development (CSD) at Washington University in St. Louis. She holds a doctorate in sociology from Washington University (1989), a master's degree from the School of Social Service Administration at the University of Chicago (1974), and a bachelor's degree in sociology and Spanish from Beloit College (1972). Her research, publishing, and teaching are in the areas of social and economic development, poverty, immigration and health, and international social welfare policy. Past research includes a Fulbright-funded dissertation study of health and poverty policy in Mexico (1987), research on birth outcomes among Mexican immigrants in Chicago, and community economic development in Missouri. Presently, she is leading an in-depth interview study of participants in a matched savings program of Individual Development Accounts (IDAs), part of large longitudinal national demonstration at CSD (1997–2003), leading research on a tri-national North American youth community service project, and conducting research on a children's saving account demonstration in St. Louis. She is recipient of the 2001 Teaching Excellence award at the University of Missouri-St. Louis.

Cynthia K. Sanders is Assistant Professor of Social Work at the University of Missouri-St. Louis, and Faculty Associate at the Center for Social Development at Washington University in St. Louis. She holds a doctorate in social work from the George Warren Brown School of Social Work at Washington University (2000), a master's in social work from the University of Utah (1994) and bachelor's in science degrees in economics and political science from the University of Utah (1987). Her research interests focus on social policy and poverty, economic development with low-income women, economic security in low-income households, and women's issues. Her recent research examined the economic outcomes for poor participants of microenterprise assistance programs in the

265

United States and whether or not such programs were having an effect on economic well being when compared to other low-income workers. Her current research explores economic education and planning with low-income women experiencing domestic violence, including evaluation of an IDA program targeted toward battered women. She teaches in the areas of social welfare policy, research methods, and social work generalist practice.

Michael Sherraden is Benjamin E. Youngdahl Professor of Social Development and founding director of the Center for Social Development (CSD), George Warren Brown School of Social Work, Washington University in St. Louis. Sherraden was educated at Harvard (AB, 1970) and the University of Michigan (MSW, 1976; PhD, 1979). He has been a Visiting Professor at the National University of Mexico (1987–88), and the National University of Singapore (1992–93), a Distinguished Visiting Professor at Ben Gurion University in Israel (2001), and Zellerbach Visiting Professor at University of California, Berkeley (2003–04). He is a recipient of a Fulbright Research Fellowship (1992–93), the Distinguished Faculty Award from Washington University (1994), the Excellence in Community Development Award from the Neighborhood Reinvestment Training Institutes (2001), and the Flynn Prize for innovation in social policy from the University of Southern California (2001). Sherraden has given a number of major academic lectures, including the O'Leary Lecture, Ohio State University (1996); the Roatch Lecture, Arizona State University (1998); the Sarnat Lecture, University of Southern California (2001); and the Fauri Lecture, University of Michigan (2002).

Index

Portes, Alejandro, 80
portfolio theory, 26–28
poverty: alleviation of, 184; in asset theory, 4; effects on, 101, 106–7, 177; and
Grameen Bank, 3, 7, 8; and income diversification, 26, 27, 28; and local
economy, 133, 150; microenterprise as
solution to, 2; and microentrepreneurs,
50; movement out of, 112; and self-
employment income gains, 38, 39; traditional approaches to, 2; women in,
23, 40
pricing, expertise in, 137, 138–39
product, 73, 125, 137, 138, 164
Program for Investment in Microentrepreneurs (PRIME) Act, 10
public assistance, 3, 43–44, 48, 49, 50,
194. *See also* social assistance; welfare
public policy: on microenterprise, 2, 3–7;
self-employment as, 51; support for
microenterprise in, 3–7; on welfare,
51; and welfare-to-work, 51
purchasing, expertise in, 137, 138–39

race/ethnicity: and business assets, 103;
and business growth, 130–31; and
business outcomes, 101, 102; discrimination by, 24, 29, 64, 70, 152, 178; and
financial outcomes, 110; and household assets, 107; and household net
worth, 108; and income-to-needs ratio,
106; and liability, 103; and net worth,
103, 108; research in, 197; and resource availability, 25; and resource
distribution, 25; in social networks, 25;
solidarity with, 130–31, 135, 150. *See
also* African Americans; Latino/as;
Whites
Raheim, Salome, 13, 42, 43, 44
religious groups, 62, 96, 97, 118, 123
research, directions for, 175–76, 196–98
resource availability, 24–25, 181. *See
also* capital; human capital; loans; networks; social capital; training

risk, 26–28, 27, 60, 161
Rivercities of Iowa/Illinois Self-
Employment Program (RISE), 43–44,
44
role model, 51, 52, 59, 62, 64, 74, 167,
179, 180
Rosenstein, Carolyn, 24, 25, 63, 64, 173
Rotary Club, 189
Rural Economic Development Center
(REDC), 15, 16, 17

Sanders, Cynthia, 39
savings, 5, 12, 71–72, 117, 120, 161–62,
186–87
Schreiner, Mark, 7, 187, 188, 193–94
sector development, 191
self-employment: agency model in, 22; in
asset theory, 28–29; assistance for, 9;
autonomy from, 44; basic resources
for, 185; combined with wage employment, 40, 98, 148, 182; and compensating differential theory, 23;
demographic characteristics of, 48–50;
and disadvantaged worker theory,
23–24; discrimination in, 24; in diversification theory, 26–28; empowerment from, 44, 45; and feminist theory,
23; financial rewards of, 21–22; flexibility in, 44; goal clarification for, 185;
hours worked in, 38, 40; and human
capital theory, 21–22, 25, 26; income
from, 22, 30; income gains from, 30,
38–41; informal, 50; as investment,
28; investment model in, 22; learning
model in, 22; matching model in, 22;
monetary rewards of, 21–22, 30,
38–41, 56, 57–59, 64; motivations for,
21–29, 47–65, 178–81; non-monetary
rewards of, 23, 29, 64, 172–73, 178,
179; preference for, 156, 177; psychological traits in, 21; as public policy,
51; as rational choice, 21, 22; risks of,
60; self-esteem from, 44–45; skills for,
197; in social network theory, 25–26;